The Future of Global Economic Governance

Marek Rewizorski • Karina Jędrzejowska •
Anna Wróbel

Editors

The Future of Global
Economic Governance

Challenges and Prospects in the Age
of Uncertainty

 Springer

Editors
Marek Rewizorski
University of Gdańsk
Gdańsk, Poland

Karina Jędrzejowska
University of Warsaw
Warsaw, Poland

Anna Wróbel
University of Warsaw
Warsaw, Poland

ISBN 978-3-030-35338-4   ISBN 978-3-030-35336-0   (eBook)
https://doi.org/10.1007/978-3-030-35336-0

Acknowledgments: This book is part of the "Global Economic Governance – Actors, Areas of Influence, Interactions" research project (OPUS, 2016/23/B/HS5/00118) funded by the National Science Centre, Poland.

Contents

Notes on Contributors

Karina Jędrzejowska is Assistant professor at the University of Warsaw. She is a graduate of the University of Manchester (MSc Globalisation and Development, 2008), Warsaw School of Economics (MA Finance and Banking, 2007) and the Institute of International Relations (MA International Relations, 2005), University of Warsaw. She has received PhD in political science from the University of Warsaw on the basis of dissertation 'Sovereign Default in International Relations' (2011). Since April 2017, she is Governing Board Member and Treasurer of the World International Studies Committee (WISC). Her expertise lies in reform of international monetary system, international financial architecture and governance, sovereign debt restructuring, economic and monetary nationalism and development finance and theory. Publications by Karina Jędrzejowska include over 40 papers and book chapters on international financial institutions and global financial and monetary governance. She is member of the Polish Association of International Studies (Polskie Towarzystwo Studiów Międzynarodowych, PTSM), International Studies Association (ISA), Central and East European International Studies Association (CEEISA), European International Studies Association (EISA) and Development Studies Association (DSA).

Artur Kluź is Founding Donor and Chairman of the Advisory Board of the Centre for Technology and Global Affairs at the University of Oxford. Mr. Kluź is a venture capital investor and lawyer with extensive international affairs experience. He is currently Managing Partner of Kluz Ventures, an investment firm focused on developing breakthrough technologies and global growth strategies.

Marina Larionova is Vice President for International Relations of the Russian Union of Industrialists and Entrepreneurs (RSPP) and Head of the Center for International Institutions Research (CIIR) of the Russian Presidential Academy of National Economy and Public Administration (RANEPA). She is also Russia B20 Sherpa. During the Russian 2013 G20 presidency, Dr. Larionova was Sherpa of the G20-B20 Dialogue Efficiency Task Force. She is author, co-author and editor of several books on global governance, G7/G8 and G20 system, BRICS and other international institutions. Dr. Larionova is the Editor-in-Chief of the *International Organisations Research Journal* (IORJ) (http://iorj.hse.ru/en/about). She holds a doctorate in political science and a doctorate in philology.

Jonathan Luckhurst is Associate Professor of International Relations at the Graduate School of International Peace Studies, Soka University of Japan. His research focuses on Group of Twenty (G20), global economic governance, global policy and governance networks, international negotiations, IPE and international relations. He is the author of *The Shifting Global Economic Architecture: Decentralizing Authority in Contemporary Global Governance* (Palgrave Macmillan, 2017) and *G20 Since the Global Crisis* (Palgrave Macmillan, 2016).

Iryna Nesterenko is a PhD candidate in political science at the University of Siegen, Germany, and a lecturer at the Adult Education Center in Bochum. She obtained her MA in 'European Culture and Economy' from the Ruhr University of Bochum and a BA from the Adam Mickiewicz University, Poland. She also received advanced training in energy economics and law at the Institute for Mining and Energy Law in Bochum.

Bartłomiej E. Nowak is political scientist; he holds a PhD in economics (Warsaw School of Economics). He is former Chair of International Relations at the Vistula University (2014–2017) and Executive Director at the Center for International Relations in Warsaw (2010–2013). He is also Research Associate at the Centre for Technology and Global Affairs at the University of Oxford. He was a fellow at the European University Institute in Florence (2018), Transatlantic Academy in Washington D.C. (2013–2014) and the Carnegie Council for Ethics in International Affairs (2014–2017, non-resident). Previously, Dr. Nowak has held a number of executive and advisory policy-making positions, including the European Parliament (2004–2009), the Convention on the Future of Europe (2002–2003), the National Council of European Integration (2002–2004) and the Initiative YES in Referendum (2002–2003).

Sang-Chul Park is political scientist. He has received PhD degrees in political science in August 1993 in Germany and economics in February 1997 in Sweden. His dissertations discussed 'Technopolises in Japan'. He also passed a habilitation examination (full professorship) in political science in November 2002 in Germany as well as a docent evaluation (Swedish habilitation) in economics in September 2004 in Sweden. He is currently a Full Professor at Graduate School of Knowledge-based Technology and Energy, Korea Polytechnic University. He was an Adjunct Professor at the Center for Science-based Entrepreneurship, Korea Advanced Institute of Science and Technology (KAIST), and a Visiting Professor at Seoul National University, South Korea. He was also a Private Docent at Justus Liebig University in Giessen, Germany, and Visiting Professor at Gothenburg University, Sweden. He served as Associate

Professor at Gothenburg University, Sweden, from 2001 to 2003 and as Associate Professor at Okayama University, Japan, from 2003 to 2006. He also stayed as Visiting Professor at Fudan University, China, in September 2014 and as Visiting Scholar at the Asian Development Bank Institute, Japan, in October 2014. His research interests concern industrial policy and regional development and studies on innovation systems and on science parks and innovative clusters in particular. Currently, his research areas are expanded towards energy policy, sustainable development strategy, high technology ventures and international business and trade. In addition, he was a member of editorial advisory board for *Korea Observer* (SSCI Journal) as well as a member of editorial review board for *Journal of Small Business Management* (JSBM) (SSCI Journal). In 2013, he became the editor of *Asia Pacific Journal of EU Studies* (APJEUS). In 2014, he also became a member of editorial board in *International Journal of Innovation and Regional Development* (IJIRD). In 2016, he serves as associate editor for *International Journal of Management and Enterprise Development* (IMED) (SCOPUS Journal) and a member of Managing Editorial Board in *Australian and New Zealand Journal of European Studies.*

Marek Rewizorski is political scientist and lawyer; Associate Professor at the Institute of Political Science, University of Gdańsk; principal investigator of research grants SONATA (2011–2014) and OPUS (2017–2020) awarded by the National Science Centre in Poland; member of EISA and ISA; expert of the Polish National Agency for Academic Exchange (NAWA); visiting researcher at the European University Institute in Florence (June 2018); and author of over 100 publications in international relations and political science. His research interests include international political economy, global governance, G7/G20, BRICS and emerging markets. He is the editor of *The European Union and the BRICS. Complex Relations in the Era of Global Governance.* London/New York: Springer 2015. His recent publication is the article 'A Rising Tide that Lifts no Boats'. The European Union and the Development of the Transnational Economy of Crimigration. *World Political Science,* 15(1), 2019.

Stefan A. Schirm is Professor of Political Science at the Ruhr University of Bochum, Germany, where he holds the Chair of International Politics. He taught at the Universities of Munich and Stuttgart and served as J.F. Kennedy Fellow at the Center for European Studies, Harvard University, and as Robert Schuman Fellow at the European University Institute. His research focuses on global economic governance and the societal approach to IPE. His articles appeared in journals such as *Cambridge Review of International Affairs, Journal of Contemporary European Studies, European Politics and Society, Review of International Studies, International Political Science Review, Global Affairs* and *European Journal of International Relations.*

Aukje van Loon is Postdoctoral Research Associate and Lecturer at the Chair of International Politics, Ruhr University of Bochum, Germany. She studied at the Robert Gordon University, Scotland, and Ruhr University of Bochum, Germany, and obtained her PhD in social science from the latter in 2017. She is author of the forthcoming book *Domestic Politics in European Trade Policy: Ideas, Interests and Variation in Governmental Trade Positions* (Routledge) and co-editor of the two-volumed *Global Europe* books (Springer). Her main research interests are EU trade policy and post-crisis European economic governance, topics on which she published amongst others in *The European Union and the BRICS* (Springer), *the Journal of Contemporary European Studies* and *European Politics and Society.*

Anna Wróbel is Assistant Professor at the University of Warsaw and PhD in political science (2007). Her doctoral dissertation is on the policy of liberalization of international trade in services and postgraduate studies in foreign trade at the Warsaw School of Economics (2004). She is a graduate of the Institute of International Relations, University of Warsaw (2003); founder member of the Polish International Studies Association (Polskie Towarzystwo Studiów Międzynarodowych, PTSM); and Governing Board Member and Treasurer of Polish International Studies Association—Warsaw Branch. Her research interests include global trade governance, World Trade Organization, international trade in services, food security, international trade in agri-food commodities, economic dimension of globalization, EU trade policy and economic integration in Asia Pacific.

Introduction: Beyond Gridlock? Challenges and Prospects for Global Economic Governance

Marek Rewizorski, Karina Jędrzejowska, and Anna Wróbel

> *When I pronounce the word Future, the first syllable already belongs to the past. When I pronounce the word Silence, I destroy it. When I pronounce the word Nothing, I make something no non-being can hold.*
> *(Wisława, Szymborska, 'Three Oddest Words', Poems, new and collected, 1957–1997. Transl. by Stanislaw Baranczak and Clare Cavanagh. New York: Harcourt Brace, 1998).*

Global governance, both in its political and economic dimensions, resembles a normative framework set up by state and non-state actors to "[p]romote cross-border co-ordination and co-operation in the provision or exchange of goods, money, services and technical expertise in defined issue areas of the world economy" (Moschella and Weaver 2014: 4; Barnett and Duvall 2005: 39–75). However, this framework is considered highly insufficient and unreliable in the context of the "messy" (Haas 2010) or "cosmopolitan" (Held 2003) multilateralism of the postcrisis era and the related uncertainty as to the direction, speed, intensity, and nature of changes, which leave decision-makers helpless. This book looks at the economic dimension of global governance. In particular, it adds to the literature on global economic governance by looking at:

This chapter is part of the "Global Economic Governance—Actors, Areas of Influence, Interactions" research project (OPUS, 2016/23/B/HS5/00118) funded by the National Science Centre, Poland.

M. Rewizorski (✉)
Institute of Political Science, University of Gdańsk, Gdańsk, Poland
e-mail: marek.rewizorski@ug.edu.pl

K. Jędrzejowska · A. Wróbel
University of Warsaw, Warsaw, Poland
e-mail: k.jedrzejowska@uw.edu.pl; awrobel@uw.edu.pl

- Challenges facing global economic governance (GEG)
- Consequences of the mechanisms that trigger changes to the established international order
- Prospects for the future of multilateralism, which is in a state of flux

The global economic governance framework is widely perceived as an imperfect ideational construct. This is due to the fact that it is affected by chaotic multilateralism, fragmentation, uncertainty, and the competing narratives of East versus West, North versus South, where the end of history was denied by recurring crises, the relative decline of established powers, emerging of the new hubs of economic radiance, and multiplication of challenges which have not been properly addressed by policy- and decision-makers. Even naming them all is a hopeless task, as new ones continually enter the stage. There is no doubt, however, that the future of GEG and its architecture seems to be shaped by the need to address such challenges, both old and new, as the stalled Doha negotiations, the surge of populism and renouncing of "unfair" macroeconomic policies by the public, new policies affecting the operation of Global Value Chains (GVCs), digital trade, e-commerce, environmental issues, the global infrastructure gap, volatility in global commodity prices, and, finally, disenchantment with Western models of development and aid, which called into question many of the solutions worked out during the era of the Washington Consensus, and neoliberal prescriptions for growth based on the "TINA-Principle."[1] The difficulties in finding effective solutions have been extensively depicted by Thomas Hale, David Held, and Kevin Young (2013) in a rather gloomy and disheartening account on the state of contemporary global politics. In their vision of "gridlock," complex interdependence is a far cry from the initial findings of Keohane and Nye (1977, 2011), characterized by three distinctive features: (1) the existence of different channels of interaction (interstate, transnational, transgovernmental) that occur between actors of international relations (Keohane and Nye 2011: 20); (2) the lack of hierarchical positioning of problems in world politics, thus blurring the distinction between "low" and "high," as well as "internal" and "external" policy (Ibid.: 20), and (3) the decline in importance of the issues of military security, which are no longer seen as the only priority in foreign policy, giving way to socioeconomic problems (Ibid.: 21). It is also important to acknowledge the changing roles of international organizations, which from agents of relatively minor importance after World War II have been transformed into control centers or catalysts of interdependence based on normative principles, standards, procedures, shared values, and collectively achieved goals.

---

[1]TINA—there is no alternative—is a political slogan usually attributed to the former British PM Margaret Thatcher. She thought there was no alternative to neoliberal reform. As an admirer of the Austrian economist Friedrich Hayek, the Prime Minister of the UK believed in the capacity of maximally liberalized markets in safeguarding the stability and prosperity of the national and international economy. At the same time, she wildly rejected any attempts at government regulation, in the conviction that functionalist attempts at government regulation are bound to fail and lead to authoritarianism, if not totalitarianism. See Neuhäuser (2018). TINA. *Crisis. Journal of Contemporary Philosophy*. Issue 2: Marx from the Margins: A Collective Project, from A to Z, p. 15.

Hale, Held, and Young are far less optimistic when referring to global economic governance as "gridlocked," or enmeshed in so-called self-reinforcing interdependence, where "existing institutions solve some problems they were initially designed to address, but also fail to address problems which have emerged from the very global economic system they have enabled" (Hale et al. 2013: 10). While recognizing the distinctive dynamics of each unique area of global policy, they argue that it is possible to identify the underlying structural drivers of the gridlock that cut across various policy fields. They distinguish a quartet of intersecting obstacles described as "growing multipolarity, institutional inertia, harder problems and fragmentation" (Hale et al. 2013: 35). Indeed, there is no denying that international institutions (international standards, international regimes, and international organizations), consumed in particular by the institutional inertia and "harder problems" have become insufficient mechanisms to ensure the effectiveness of global economic governance. But why? In our book we propose four explanations.

1. The Diffusion of Power In the ongoing phase of globalization, dubbed by Klaus Schwab as the "fourth industrial revolution" (4IR) or "Globalization 4.0" (Schwab 2016) new technological breakthroughs coincide with the rapid emergence of ecological constraints, the advent of an increasingly multipolar international order, and rising inequality (see Cerny 2005; Held 2003; Kahler and Lake 2009; Acemoglu and Robinson 2012; Deaton 2013). More evident than in the last quarter of the twentieth century is the transfer of power from developed countries to emerging economies, accompanied by rapid expansion (mushrooming) of non-state actors, such as global corporations (Dicken 2015), civil society and NGOs (Kaldor 2003; Keck and Sikkink 1998; Scholte 2011), or credit rating agencies (Sinclair 2005), to name but a few. This process leads to the emergence of several issues: (1) a proliferation of non-territorial entities that may increase barriers to international cooperation, which can further contribute to increasing the transaction costs of negotiated agreements; (2) focusing of cost reduction driven governments on increasing participation in these institutions and pushing for changing the model of governance, which casts doubt on matters of fairness (the fair distribution of benefits); (3) an increasing number of states that are considered prominent in various fields of international cooperation, which may reduce chances of a reconciliation of interests and the achievement of compromise and cooperation.

2. Unplugged Institutions Here we refer to certain actors of global governance, among which a special role is played by international organizations, arranged in a pattern resembling the type of network equilibrium points set under certain conditions in order to meet the emerging needs of the time, and reflecting the balance of power and interests. Over time, changes in the conditions in which international institutions operate cause a mismatch between their resources and declared objectives, and the new environment in which they operate (Rewizorski 2016). As a result, they are becoming less effective (unplugged). The emergence of crisis leads to a weakening of them (as the example of the G7 shows) or the disappearance of old mechanisms and replacing them with new ones (e.g., G20, BRICS) better adapted to the new operating conditions, but without guaranteeing their long-term utility (c.f. Cooper 2016; Cooper and Thakur 2013, 2018; Kirton 2013; Stuenkel 2015).

3. Intermestication Compared to the traditional model of cooperation, developed after World War II and dressed in the golden straitjacket of multilateralism, "complex interdependence" in the era of global governance goes beyond what is interstate and enters the "minefield" of transnationalism (Held 2018: 63–76). The increasing complexity and widening scale of divergent problems make it difficult to find a satisfactory political solution. For example, climate change is more difficult to overcome than the problems of the past decades, such as air pollution and greenhouse gas emissions. Intellectual property is harder to secure globally than it is to set a timetable for the reduction of trade tariffs, etc. New problems go beyond the logic defined by national boundaries and appear in areas where the level of confusion as to the knowledge of the political objectives, resources, capabilities, and interests of the actors of global governance leads to anxiety and often paralyzes effective action. This uncertainty is accompanied by the overlap of old and new problems, increasingly penetrating society, and requiring costly adjustment policy and an increasing amount of resources (Hale et al. 2013: 44). Blurring boundaries between what is "internal" and "external" is reflected in the consequences of decisions that seemingly fit into the logic of intra-regulation. The Turkish government's decisions affect the increasing or decreasing migration pressures in Europe, and at the same time raise questions about the sense of security of Europeans; increasing subsidies for Polish or French farmers under the Common Agricultural Policy (CAP) may deeply affect the cultivation of clementines in Algeria or barley in Morocco; regulation of mortgages in Florida could destabilize the banking sector in Iceland, etc. All this grand mismatch of unresolved issues was once described as "intermestication" (see Rosenau 1997).

4. Fragmentation According to the *Yearbook of International Organizations*, in 1951 there were 123 intergovernmental organizations and 832 NGOs. In 2018, their number amounted to 7726 and 62,621 respectively (UIA 2018: xxxii). The proliferation of various non-state actors (some of which are private actors) has brought both benefits and losses (Biersteker and Hall 2002; Cutler et al. 1999). On the one hand, the more intensive competition between divergent actors allows for effective addressing of major cross-border problems (see Boot et al. 2006). On the other hand, incessantly extended regulatory mechanisms have led to a "race to the bottom." To put it simply, policy coordination has become a slave to a "shredded" jurisdictional authority held by non-state actors (Mattli 2001; Mattli and Büethe 1993). What is more, many actors of global governance are acting often in the same areas, therefore duplicating their activity and wasting resources, which de facto leads to rising transaction costs of drafted agreements. And here is a paradox of global governance. In a world transformed by globalization and the technological revolution in communication, as well as the diffusion of very diverse "groups of relay" widely inhabiting the transnational transmission belt, it is harder than ever to reach the recipient.

1 Analytical Approach

Witnessing the mass of obstacles to the multilayered, multisectoral, and multi-actor system of global governance, characterized as a "multi-actor system in which institutions and politics matter in important ways to the determination of global policy outcomes, that is, to who gets what, when, and why" (Held 2018: 68), this book can be seen as an effort to continue the discussion on reshaping liberal institutions for a pluralist global order beyond the prescriptions of the so called "First World" (the established powers in the existing international order) toward more equal cooperation on global and regional levels (see Xing 2014), and moving beyond the already mentioned "gridlock." When discussing the challenges and prospects for the future of global economic governance, the contributors of this book decided to: (1) analyze the substance of GEG in trade, finance, and development; (2) elaborate on the drivers of fundamental shifts in global economic steering toward arguably a "Post-Western World" (Stuenkel 2015); and (3) discuss observations related to its dynamics. In particular, the authors of the chapters examining how authority shifts in the global governance architecture have been influenced by contestation of particular legitimizing discourses since the global financial crisis. They have also critically assessed the technological challenge to global economic governance, discussed the opportunities and risks faced by the major informal groupings—G20 and BRICS—in reshaping global economic governance, looked at "old" challenges such as protectionism in the new context of trade conflicts, global value chains and the spread of new technologies; deepened theorization of regional financial governance using case studies; looked into the puzzle of discordant governmental positions in euro crisis management politics in-depth, proposed answers to questions about EU–WTO relations in the context of the functionality or dysfunctionality of global trade governance, contributed to studies into development—external energy policy and domestic preferences in the EU and its member states.

This book has a mainly analytical character with elements of a descriptive approach. It can be used as a compass to navigate the turbulent seas of "global polyarchy." The analysis is primarily locked within a finance–trade–development global governance epistemological triangle, offering an overview of changes within the GEG landscape (challenges, risks, normative, and institutional patterns of behavior) (Fig. 1).

The book combines various perspectives in the field of Political Science and constructivist International Relations (IR) to explain fundamental challenges for the future of global economic governance. The choice of societal approach as an ideational core supplemented by liberal accounts (the three stands of new institutionalism, the comparative international political economy) allows not only to analyze contextual, external factors influencing the design of GEG, but also facilitates exploration of domestic factors for government policies, the preferences of local interest groups, and even tracing the patterns of anti-establishment activism which, as shown by the election of Donald Trump, the Brexit vote, and the electoral

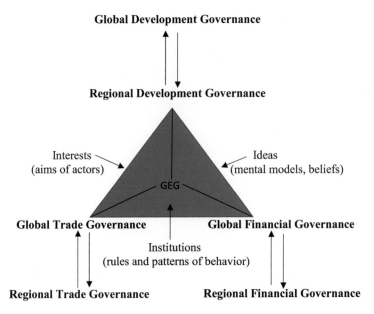

Fig. 1 Analytical approach used in the book (levels of analysis and areas of interest). Source: Editors' own elaboration

successes of anti-establishment parties in some member states of the European Union, may contribute to the delegitimization of the "Western" mode of global economic steering.

Furthermore, the choice of specific analytical "tool-box" was dictated by the need for a departure from the limitations and rigidness of neoclassical economics. This perspective reduces social outcomes to individuals which are perfectly rational, utility-maximizing, and where even collective outcomes are efficient. Consequently the book questions Hegemonic Stability Theory (HST), as dominated by researchers focused more on foreign policy than International Political Economy (IPE), and treating powerful states (i.e., the USA, China) as rational, calculating, individual entities, using their political and economic clout to gain their hegemonic position in the global economic system. Instead of witnessing "unipolar moments" in global economic governance, we experience the uplifting of a global city where "the center of command" is more dispersed than concentrated in someone's hands. GEG can be metaphorically depicted as a global city, bustling with institutional life and activity beyond the perimeters of the regulatory scope of governments, and with a high street designed and built, until recently, solely by established Western brands with their formal and informal institutions, formal and informal sets of principles, norms, and practices (including self-governance agreements) that comprise a general consensus among defined groups of actors about appropriate behavior in key issue areas. However, since the Asian Crisis a power shift in global economic governance has been in progress, with more and more Global South actors affecting it, and centers of global trade and financial power moving toward the emerging economies. As in the past, this "flexing of muscles" between high street city dwellers is observed with scrutiny by individuals, private regulators, non-corporate, informal groups of society (see Keck and Sikkink 1998; Scholte 2011) and at the same time the current state of play in GEG is violently contested by the poor countries, impoverished locals, hidden in the shanty towns, somewhere in the suburbs of the global city.

Having noted this diversity, the contributors to this book questioned purely realistic or neorealistic "Hobbesian" reading of International Relations. Global economic governance is beyond the reach of traditional equilibrium-seeking approaches because of the constant flux and difficult to predict emergence of actor networks, authority shifts, legitimizing and delegitimizing discourses which have been shaping global economic governance since the "Asian" crisis. It erupted in the second half of the 1990s and dealt a critical blow to the "Western" institutions of integrational economic governance, accustomed to prescribing supplements, instead of medicines.

2 Chapter Contributions

Chapter "Parallel Orders? Emerging Powers, Western Discontent, and the Future of Global Economic Governance", by Stefan A. Schirm, develops a fresh look at traditional modes of global economic governance which are increasingly challenged by two rather novel drivers of international relations: emerging powers and anti-establishment voters in Western countries. He observes that the election of Donald Trump and the Brexit vote, on the one hand, as well as the growing assertiveness and new institutions of the BRICS emerging powers, on the other hand, exemplify the new developments. Since both challenges share a preference for nation-centered politics and demand a higher share in international power and resources, an order seems nascent which shows distinct features compared to traditional global governance shaped by universal rules, supranational and international organizations. The chapter looks at the development of parallel orders which can be countered by better including the demands of challengers in the reformed conduct of global economic governance, which aims at stronger legitimacy through improved accountability and inclusiveness.

Chapter "Networks Decentralizing Authority in Global Economic Governance", by Jonathan Luckhurst, analyzes how governance networks contributed to decentralizing global economic governance since the 2008 financial crisis. He argues that the growing international influence of networks of private, public, intergovernmental, and civil society actors has important effects on authority, especially due to their policy contestation, advocacy, and capacity to shift the global governance agenda. This was augmented by increasing engagement and integration as interlocutors and policy actors, particularly in informal global governance settings such as the G20. Global governance networks interact through transnational professional "ecologies." This chapter also analyzes the links between governance networks and broader practice communities. The research includes evidence from participant observation, semi-structured interviews, public statements, and document analysis. It deploys analytical tools, especially from social constructivism, discourse analysis, and the sociology of professions.

Chapter "Global Economic Governance and the Challenge of Technological Revolution" by Bartłomiej E. Nowak and Artur Kluź aims to explore how new technologies influence transformations in global economic governance. The chapter aims to grasp various dimensions of this impact, one that poses a big challenge to global economic governance. In identifying the ways out of "gridlock" it looks at three widely debated trends. First, the authors show how new technologies dramatically change the nature of global economic problems, which current institutions must follow and find up-to-date responses to. Second, they indicate that the technological revolution offers many opportunities, but is contributing to stronger competition and inequality in the world. Third, they look at innovative forms of governance for managing the delivery of global public goods that becomes even more difficult than in the past.

Chapter "In Pursuit of Better Economic Governance: The Contribution of the G20 and BRICS" by Marina Larionova looks into the history of attempts to reform the international monetary and trading systems, and examines G20 and BRICS engagement with international organizations for better economic governance, focusing on the IMF, the MDBs, and the WTO. She argues that the G20 and BRICS must increase efforts to create a global governance system that reflects the new economic and technological realities, responds to persistent challenges, and creates the conditions for balanced and inclusive growth.

Chapter "Multilateralism in Peril? Murky Protectionism and the Populist Backlash Against Globalisation" by Marek Rewizorski focuses on two phenomena that may impact upon the faith of members of the global trade system in the value of maintaining this system. The phenomena concerned are postcrisis, murky protectionism on the one hand, and populism on the other, both of which undermine and subvert the tenets of multilateralism. The first part of this chapter analyzes murky protectionism as a challenge to trade multilateralism. The second part is dedicated to populism and provides an opportunity to seek answers to the questions of why international trade is becoming such a sensitive and important political matter, and why populists have made free trade the main reason for political opposition to globalization.

Chapter "Protectionism as Challenges for the Global Trade Governance" by Sang-Chul Park, which finishes the first part of the book, is devoted to protectionism as a set of challenges to global trade governance. The author of this chapter addresses the serious condition of global economics affected by protectionism and offers a summary of possible outcomes of protectionism. The chapter draws attention to the development of the global trade system and the WTO as the new global trade governance. Park also investigates and analyzes various challenges for the WTO in how to restore and strengthen global governance, although its powers are rather limited due to the rapid spread of protectionism. Additionally, the author explores the reasons behind and impacts of protectionism that affect global trade governance.

Chapter "From Global to Regional Financial Governance? The Case of Asia-Pacific" by Karina Jędrzejowska aims at providing an overview of the shift between global and regional institutions of financial governance. The chapter examines the Asia-Pacific area from the global financial governance perspective and argues that as a result of the East Asian crisis in 1997 and global financial crisis of 2007–2008, a multilayered financial governance has developed. Parallel to the further development and reform of global financial institutions, several regional financial arrangements developed. The author analyzes the shift toward regional governance of financial affairs, which has been visible within the broad Asia-Pacific region, where most attention has been given to the new providers of financial stability, such as the Chiang Mai Initiative Multilateralization or the ASEAN+3 Macroeconomic Research Office. Yet, as she notes, there were also several changes in financing of regional development, including the establishment of the New Development Bank and the Asian Infrastructure Investment Bank.

Chapter "Societal Dynamics in European Economic Governance: A Comparative Analysis of Variation in British and German Governmental Stances" by Aukje van Loon explores societal dynamics in European economic governance. The author examines conflicting governmental stances surrounding two reform proposals in postcrisis European Union (EU) economic governance, namely the setup of the European Supervisory Authorities (ESAs) and the introduction of a European Financial Transaction Tax (FTT). Both issues were fiercely debated, with discordant stances in revamping Economic and Monetary Union (EMU), specifically coming from the UK and Germany. Following the societal approach to preference formation, this chapter provides a comprehensive overview of national preferences, and illustrates that governmental stances toward ESAs and the FTT were strongly shaped by two societal dynamics, sectoral interests and value-based ideas.

Chapter "European Energy Governance: The Pursuit of a Common External Energy Policy and the Domestic Politics of EU Member States Preferences" by Iryna Nesterenko extends the societal approach in studies on European economic governance to the common external energy policy in the EU which emerges from rapid changes in the international system. The author argues that rising competition for available resources, increasing demand for fossil fuels in China and India, alongside the structural changes in gas markets from regional to global, means high security risks to the supply of existing energy imports to EU member states. Considering these international shifts, it is therefore puzzling why, until now, no meaningful common external energy policy has emerged in the EU. The author argues that the preferences of member states' governments are being influenced by domestic economic interest groups and geopolitical relations with the suppliers.

Finally, chapter "The Functionality and Dysfunctionality of Global Trade Governance: The European Union Perspective" by Anna Wróbel provides the European Union's perspective on issues of the functionality and dysfunctionality of global trade governance. The chapter aims at answering the question of whether the World Trade Organization is still an effective instrument for the realization of the trade interests of members, in particular the European Union. The following sections of the chapter are devoted to finding answers to several questions, namely: Does the

WTO remain the main source of international trade rules for the European Union? What are the consequences of bilateral free trade agreements for the EU's involvement in the Doha Round negotiations? What is the EU's response to US attempts to destabilize the dispute settlement mechanism? What action has the European Union taken to counteract the marginalization of the WTO?

References

Acemoglu, D., & Robinson, J. (2012). *Why nations fail: The origins of power, prosperity and poverty.* London: Profile Books.

Barnett, M., & Duvall, R. (2005). Power in global governance. In M. Barnett & R. Duvall (Eds.), *Power in global governance.* Cambridge: Cambridge University Press.

Biersteker, T. J., & Hall, R. B. (Eds.). (2002). *The emergence of private authority in global governance.* Cambridge: Cambridge University Press.

Boot, A. W. A., Tood, T. M., & Schmeits, A. (2006). Credit ratings as coordination mechanisms. *Review of Financial Studies, 19*(1), 81–118.

Cerny, P. (2005). Power, markets and authority: The development of multi-level governance in international finance. In A. Baker, A. Hudson, & R. Woodward (Eds.), *Governing financial globalization.* New York: Routledge.

Cooper, A. F. (2016). *The BRICS – A very short introduction.* Oxford: Oxford University Press.

Cooper, A. F., & Thakur, R. (2013). *The group of twenty (G20).* London: Routledge.

Cooper, A. F., & Thakur, R. (2018). The BRICS in the evolving architecture of global governance. In T. G. Weiss & R. Wilkinson (Eds.), *International organization and global governance* (2nd ed.). New York: Routledge.

Cutler, C., Haufler, V., & Porter, T. (Eds.). (1999). *Private authority and international affairs.* New York: SUNY Press.

Deaton, A. (2013). *The great escape: Health, wealth and the origins of inequality.* Princeton, NJ: Princeton University Press.

Dicken, P. (2015). *Global shift: Mapping the changing contours of the world economy.* London: Sage.

Haas, R. (2010, January 6). The case for messy multilateralism. *Financial Times.*

Hale, T., Held, D., & Young, K. (2013). *Gridlock. Why global cooperation is failing when we need it most.* Cambridge-Malden: Polity Press.

Held, D. (2003). From executive to cosmopolitan multilateralism. In D. Held & M. Koenig-Archibugi (Eds.), *Taming globalization: Frontiers of governance.* Cambridge: Polity Press.

Held, D. (2018). The diffusion of authority. In T. G. Weiss & R. Wilkinson (Eds.), *International organization and global governance* (2nd ed.). New York: Routledge.

Kahler, M., & Lake, D. (2009). Economic integration and global governance – Why so little supranationalism? In W. Mattli & N. Woods (Eds.), *The politics of global regulation.* Princeton University Press: Princeton, NJ.

Kaldor, M. (2003). *Global civil society: An answer to war.* Cambridge: Polity Press.

Keck, M. E., & Sikkink, K. (1998). *Activists beyond borders: Advocacy networks in international politics.* Ithaca, NY: Cornell University Press.

Keohane, R. O., & Nye, J. S. (1977). *Power and interdependence: World politics in transition.* Boston: Little Brown.

Keohane, R. O., & Nye, J. S. (2011). *Power and interdependence. World politics in transition* (4th ed.). New York: Longman.

Kirton, J. J. (2013). *G20 governance for a globalized world.* Farnham: Ashgate.

Mattli, W. (2001). Private justice in a global economy: From litigation to arbitration. *International Organization, 55*(4), 919–947.

Mattli, W., & Büethe, T. (1993). Setting international standards: Technological rationality or the primacy of power? *World Politics, 56,* 1–42.

Moschella, M., & Weaver, C. (2014). *Handbook of global economic governance. Players, power and paradigms.* London: Routledge.

Neuhäuser, Ch. (2018). TINA. *Krisis. Journal of Contemporary Philosophy.* Issue 2: Marx from the Margins: A Collective Project, from A to Z.

Rewizorski, M. (2016). *The partnership of convenience: The OECD and the G20 in global governance.* Commentary No 4/2016, Institute of East-Central Europe, Lublin. Accessed May 25, 2019, from http://www.g20.utoronto.ca/biblio/rewizorski-g20-oecd-2016.pdf

Rosenau, J. N. (1997). *Along the domestic-foreign frontier: Exploring governance in a turbulent world.* Cambridge: Cambridge University Press.

Scholte, J. A. (Ed.). (2011). *Building global democracy? Civil society and accountable global governance.* Cambridge: Cambridge University Press.

Schwab, K. (2016). *The fourth industrial revolution.* Geneva: World Economic Forum.

Sinclair, T. J. (2005). *The new masters of capital: American bond rating agencies and the politics of creditworthiness.* Ithaca, NY: Cornell University Press.

Stuenkel, O. (2015). *The BRICS and the future of global order.* Lanham: Lexington.

UIA. (2018). *Yearbook of international organizations 2018-2019. Guide to global civil society networks* (Vol. 4, 55th ed.). Brussels: Union of International Associations.

Xing, L. (Ed.). (2014). *The BRICS and beyond. The international political economy of the emergence of a new world order.* Farnham: Ashgate.

Part I
Development, Trade, and Finance: Global Challenges

Parallel Orders? Emerging Powers, Western Discontent, and the Future of Global Economic Governance

Stefan A. Schirm

1 Domestic and International Challenges for Global Economic Governance

The future of global economic governance will probably be determined less by the Western countries and their traditional political and economic elites than the past and present. This assessment rests predominantly on the analysis of two recent developments, specifically on the rise of two groups of actors whose goals differ from the aims of the former drivers of global economic governance (GEG): emerging powers and anti-establishment voters in the USA and Europe.

On the one hand, emerging powers such as Brazil, Russia, India and especially China (the BRICS) considerably gained economic clout as well as political influence in the last two decades. The *economic* dimension of this rise includes an impressive growth of Gross Domestic Product (GDP), per capita incomes, industrial base and share in world trade. The big emerging economies' GDP is supposed to surpass established industrialised countries' GDP in the near future. The *political* dimension of the rise of emerging powers can be seen in their increasing demands for more influence in traditional International Organisations (IOs) such as the United Nations

This chapter is a revised and shortened version of a paper presented at the 12th Pan-European Conference of the European International Studies Association (EISA) in Prague, September 2018. A substantially revised and expanded version was published as Stefan A. Schirm (2019b), In pursuit of self-determination and redistribution: emerging powers and Western anti-establishment voters in international politics. *Global Affairs* (7 April, doi.org/10.1080/23340460.2019.1603079).

S. A. Schirm (✉)
Ruhr University Bochum, Bochum, Germany
e-mail: stefan.schirm@ruhr-uni-bochum.de

© Springer Nature Switzerland AG 2020
M. Rewizorski et al. (eds.), *The Future of Global Economic Governance*,
https://doi.org/10.1007/978-3-030-35336-0_2

(especially in the UN Security Council), the World Bank and the International Monetary Fund (IMF). In addition, the BRICS countries (meanwhile also including South Africa) created several new IOs which follow the BRICS' priorities and are not controlled by the Western countries. The most important BRICS' IOs include the Asian Infrastructure and Investment Bank (AIIB), the New Development Bank (NDB) and the Shanghai Cooperation Organisation (SCO). Thus, the emerging powers most probably will co-determine the future of global economic governance inside the established IOs *and* in parallel through the new IOs created by them as well as in the G20 which includes both established and emerging countries. The rise of emerging powers implies that the domestic interest groups, the national institutions as well as the value-based ideas of emerging powers' societies which shape governmental preferences (Schirm 2013) will have a stronger influence on GEG than in past decades.

On the other hand, the future of global economic governance will probably also be influenced more than before by the domestic politics of Western countries as well, since most of the North American and West European countries show a considerable discontent among voters regarding the current international economic order. The electoral success of the Brexit campaign to leave the European Union (EU) and the election of Donald Trump to President of the USA are the most visible symptoms of a growing dissatisfaction among Western voters with the established elites and with the national and international distribution of power and wealth. Brexit, Trump and the anti-establishment movements in Italy (Lega, Cinque Stelle), France (Giletes Jaunes), Greece (Syriza), Germany (AfD) as well as in many other Western countries express scepticism regarding established elites and demand more national autonomy vis-à-vis IOs such as the EU, the IMF and the UN as well as more political influence and a reallocation of economic resources in their favour. This implies that the traditional political and economic elites, big business and well as established NGOs are challenged in their predominance over global economic governance by new actors in the domestic politics of Western countries whose clout is stemming from persistent societal discontent.

Thus, both the rise of emerging powers and the rise of anti-establishment movements in Western countries seem to change international politics in a similar direction, since both aim at more national autonomy and at increasing their respective share of political power and economic wealth following domestic concerns. This argument will be explored and evidenced in this chapter. First, the rise of emerging powers and Western anti-establishment movements will be examined shortly regarding their foundations and characteristics. Second, the aims of both novel features of international politics will be assessed regarding their similarities and their impact on global economic governance. Third, the conclusion will discuss possibilities for improving the legitimacy and adequacy of global economic governance through a better inclusion of the demands from domestic politics and emerging powers in reformed IOs and in an enhanced role of the G20.

2 How Emerging Powers Change Global Economic Governance

Emerging powers can be defined as countries whose economic resources increased considerably and as countries aspiring for more self-determination and influence in their regions and in global politics (Armijo and Roberts 2014; Brawley 2007; Destradi 2010; Kahler 2014; Schirm 2010). China, India and Brazil are the most important emerging powers since they have strongly expanded their economies, their share in world trade and their industrial output in the last two decades. They also succeeded in lifting a large part of their populations from poverty to national middle class income levels. Russia's economic re-emergence since 2000 made it join the original BRIC group of emerging powers, a term coined by two Goldman Sachs economists pointing at these four countries' predicted ability to surpass Western countries' GDP in the decades to follow. Besides these big emerging powers, several countries qualify as middle-sized emerging countries such as Turkey, Mexico, Indonesia, South Korea and Malaysia. Established industrialised countries partly also acted as emerging powers regarding their aspirations for a greater role in world politics. Germany's and Japan's (ultimately failed) diplomatic campaign together with Brazil and India for a permanent seat in the UN Security Council is one of the most prominent examples of established Western countries pursuing an anti-status quo strategy regarding their place in the international order (Schirm 2010). This chapter, however, will focus on the non-Western emerging powers. The term 'West' is used for the 'G7 plus' countries of Western Europe, North America and Japan. Supposedly 'Western' values and policies such as democracy and multilateralism are also pursued in many other countries which are commonly not considered 'Western' such as Brazil and India.

The BRIC countries became the most influential and respected group of emerging powers. A decade ago, the leaders of the four countries started meeting on a regular basis. The activities of BRICS in the last 10 years qualify the group as one of the two most influential novel institutionalised regimes in world politics in the twenty-first century—the other is the G20 (see below). The BRICS' increasing autonomy can be seen in many political positions which considerably diverge from Western, US-led policies such as

- Criticising the Western regime change intervention in Libya 2011 as contrary to national sovereignty and to the UNSC resolution
- Abstaining from supporting Western criticism of Russia's annexation of the Crimea
- Opposing Western sanctions against Iran
- Criticising Western reluctance to substantially increase emerging powers' voting shares in the IMF and the World Bank
- Rejecting Western 'intrusion' in the domestic politics of other countries through good governance and universalist standards.

In addition to these exemplary policy positions, the BRICS also proved autonomy regarding the institutional dimension of world politics. South Africa was admitted to the now BRICS group in order to include Africa, and leaders' summits were complemented by regular consultations on the ministerial level (such as finance).

In addition, several new international organisations were founded such as the Contingent Reserve Arrangement (CRA) and the New Development Bank (NDB) which are supposed to complement and partly substitute the IMF and the World Bank. Both new organisations are dominated by the BRICS and not by Western countries. Furthermore, some of the BRICS joined in founding and steering regional organisations such as the Asian Investment and Infrastructure Bank (AIIB), the Shanghai Cooperation Organisation (SCO), the India–Brazil–South Africa alliance (IBSA), etc. The BRICS' diverging policy positions and their newly created institutions increasingly constitute a 'parallel order' to the traditional international order dominated by Western countries and elites (Stuenkel 2016: 120–180).

In addition to these divergences from Western policies and institutions, the BRICS refuse Western style market liberalisation and especially resent financial market liberalisation pointing at liberalised financial markets as having decisively caused both the global financial crisis 2008 and economic inequality within Western countries. Indeed, the global financial crisis did not affect the highly regulated BRICS' financial markets directly and only had temporary negative repercussions on the BRICS through losses in exports to crisis-ridden Western countries. Research has shown that the BRICS economic systems show variation from more to less free market and qualify as 'state permeated', 'patrimonial' or 'corporatist' economies as opposed to Western 'liberal' or 'coordinated market economies' (Hall and Soskice 2001; Nölke et al. 2015; Vasileva-Dienes and Schmidt 2018).

These differences vis-á-vis Western IOs, policies and economic systems, however, should not be overstated since emerging powers show ambiguities in their international economic relations and their domestic economic policies. While striving for national autonomy and increased influence, they integrated into the established system in order to benefit from its advantages. All BRICS used the Bretton Woods institutions such as the WTO, the IMF and the World Bank in order to increase their exports to Western countries, attract foreign direct investment (FDI) and to obtain loans from Western banks. Thus, the BRICS demand autonomy and criticise Western dominance on the one hand and perform as responsible stakeholders in the World Trade Organisation (WTO), the G20 and the IMF, etc. on the other hand.

Emerging powers differ considerably regarding their domestic political and economic systems and regarding their international relations. For instance, China qualifies politically as an authoritarian system with strong governmental (party) control of the economy. Brazil, in comparison, is a democracy with courts and media being rather independent from the government. Traditionally, Brazilian governments are economically interventionist but do not systematically control the economy. In international trade negotiations, Brazil prioritises a liberalisation of trade in agriculture due to its competitive agricultural sector, while China prioritises a liberalisation of trade in manufactured goods and India is cautious regarding both agriculture and industry due to its rather weak competitiveness in both sectors and instead shows more openness than the other two emerging powers vis-à-vis a liberalisation in services.

Internationally, emerging powers were not conceded permanent seats in the UNSC (in the case of India and Brazil), nor were they empowered to the degree desired in the IMF and the World Bank. They were, however, included as equals in the major novelty in global economic governance in the new millennium, the G20. The Group of the 20 largest economies is the first and only international body to include established as well as emerging powers whose leaders meet annually since 2008 (Kirton 2013; Luckhurst 2012). The G20 is not a formal international organisation, but rather an institutionalised regime, which considers itself as the 'the premier forum for its members international economic cooperation and decision-making' (G20 2011). The G20 managed to agree on a modest redistribution of voting rights in the IMF (still unsatisfactory for the BRICS), to prevent major protectionist measures after the eruption of the global financial crisis in 2008 and to monitor global trade imbalances. On most issues, emerging and established powers did not align among their own peer group (G7 vs. BRICS), but rather followed domestic material interests and value-based ideas in aligning with those countries which shared their preferences (Schirm 2013). For instance, the major export countries China and Germany followed their domestic export lobbies in rejecting the demands for a cap on exports raised, among others, by the USA which in turn followed domestic sectors threatened by imports. Thus, the G20 seems to constitute a model for future global economic governance in several respects: First, it integrates established and emerging powers in intergovernmental cooperation; second, the agenda is not only dominated by Western interpretations; and third, both emerging and Western powers perform as responsible stakeholders following domestic political influences.

The current challenge to the established modes of global economic governance is not that emerging powers will leave the system altogether. The danger to the *established* system is that emerging powers increasingly become politically distant from it, create alternative organisations and grow economically independent from that system. Thus, the challenge is to avoid a split which obstructs common positions possibly needed for global governance (of trade, security, terrorism, poverty, health, environment, etc.). The rise of trade among emerging countries and between emerging countries and developing countries, the rise of international trade conducted in BRICS currencies (especially in Renminbi) or as barter trade are expected to continue. The same holds true regarding the BRICS' policy positions' divergence from those Western positions which are driven by Western domestic sectoral interests and societal groups demanding specific interpretations of free market and universal rules often without acknowledging the possible legitimacy of alternative interpretations of political and economic models brought forward by emerging powers and equally based on (their) domestic politics (Etzioni 2017).

3   How Western Countries' Domestic Politics Influence Global Economic Governance

The second challenge to current global economic governance derives from domestic political developments in those Western industrialised countries which initiated and steered the process of globalisation in the last decades. It was foremost the USA,

Canada, the UK and other Western European countries as well as Japan which decided to liberalise their own economies and to promote the cross-border liberalisation of trade in goods and services, of capital and (in parts) labour. This liberalisation was supported, governed and legally anchored by international economic treaties and by the organisations of the Bretton Woods System such as the WTO (formerly GATT) and the IMF, which were (and still are) largely dominated by the Western countries. The aim of economic liberalisation was to stimulate growth by enhancing the efficient allocation of resources through competition, specialisation and economies of scale. This aim was widely achieved and world GDP considerably grew in the core decades of globalisation since the 1970s. World trade increased faster than world GDP, cross-border liberalisation was the key driver of the growth of world GDP. For the last decades, more than two-thirds of world trade, capital flows and investment occur in and among the group of established and emerging economies indicating that these countries were the main beneficiaries of globalisation.

Therefore, it seems puzzling why economic liberalisation and the established international economic order are increasingly opposed in Western countries. The answer to this question leads directly to the domestic politics and economy of these countries and to the core question of International Political Economy (IPE) on the *distribution* of gains. In order to understand Western discontent, the analysis has to reach beyond the simplifying notion of 'countries' and 'states' and examine the distribution of the gains of globalisation among different actors and groups *within* the countries at stake. Regarding actorness, government politicians play a central role because they ultimately decide on international treaties which have distributional effects internationally and nationally. Government politicians in democratic political systems are responsive to the demands of powerful domestic groups due to their interest to remain in office (Moravcsik 1997). While voters' value-based ideas and material interests might shape governmental preferences in a more general way, ideas and interests of well organised, articulate and funded lobby groups influence governmental politicians in a specifically targeted way in promoting special interests (Schirm 2013). Helen Milner writes on domestic actors' economic interests: '(. . .) cooperation among nations is affected less by fears of other countries' relative gains or cheating than it is by the domestic distributional consequences of cooperative endeavours. Cooperative agreements create winners and losers domestically; therefore they generate supporters and opponents' (Milner 1997: 9). Hence, the analysis of the IPE and of global economic governance has to examine the domestic material, institutional and ideational foundations of governmental preferences with domestic politics theories such as the Societal Approach (Schirm 2016, 2018, 2019a).

In sum, globalisation and global economic governance have distributional effects domestically and offer a wide field for activities of well-organised lobby groups. These lobby groups have increasingly captured the benefits of globalisation in industrialised countries, while the governments have not substantially compensated those parts of the electorate which lost or did not benefit much from globalisation. Hence, the process of economic liberalisation did contribute to increasing GDP and incomes *on average*, but the gains were distributed in a very unequal way. While the financial sector, the consulting and media business, transnational corporations and foundations massively profited from liberalised financial markets and trade, many blue-collar workers and the public service as well as large parts of the middle class did either suffer a loss, not reap any benefits or only participate only in a modest way. This picture is especially accentuated in the USA (Bremmer 2018: 27), but even in the social market economy of Germany with its large welfare transfer system, the household income (purchase power) of the bottom 30% did not increase since 1991 (Bofinger 2016). At the same time, Germany's export industry has reached record levels of profits and export volume—often with the help of governmental politicians who promote the companies' interests in state visits, international negotiations and shield manufacturers from cost-inflicting technical and environmental standards. On the other side of the Atlantic, US car manufacturing workers often lost their jobs as a result of (a) the transfer of automotive production to cheaper production sites in countries such as Mexico, of (b) competition from East Asia, and of (c) automation which became necessary due to tougher international competition. US consumers in general benefitted from cheaper car prices and the owners of successful car manufacturers profited from cheaper production and higher sales.

Unequal gains from open borders for finance and trade were exacerbated by the global financial crisis which erupted in 2008. Financial industry institutions such as Goldman Sachs, American International Group, Royal Bank of Scotland, Hypo Real Estate (Deutsche Bank) and Commerzbank were rescued by national governments; that is, by the tax payer in the form of financial aid or guarantees with the argument, these financial institutions would be 'systemically relevant' for the stability of the international economy. Thus, private financial companies which had paid their owners and executives huge compensations convinced the governments to infuse large amounts of public money to keep them in business and dramatically reduce their losses. The basic rules of the market economy were eliminated in a scheme which allowed profits to stay private while potential and actual losses were socialised. The management of the Eurozone crisis showed similarities since the rescue packages to countries with severe solvency problems such as Greece primarily bailed-out the private US, British, French and German banks which were heavily exposed in the crisis countries and would have had to write off loans without the help of tax payer funded financial transfers (and guarantees) to the Greek, Spanish, Portuguese governments, etc. Again, private financial institutions which had profited from lending money were now shielded from losses through governmental intervention.

This huge success of the banking lobby can be attributed to the very close relationship between political decision makers and the financial industry, a phenomenon coined as 'Wall Street–US Treasury Complex' and 'the revolving door between Wall Street and US government'. This tight link is also apparent in other Western countries such as Germany whose Christian-Democratic chancellor Merkel chose the then CEO of Deutsche Bank, Josef Ackermann, as her chief advisor in the global financial crisis and whose current Social-Democratic finance minister Scholz chose the Co-President of Goldman Sachs Germany as his deputy in charge of financial market regulation. Higgott (2018: 5) concludes on the (mal-) functioning of financial markets and the relationship between government/elite ('states') and society: 'Dysfunctional markets under conditions of an asymmetrical reward system continue to exacerbate dysfunctional relations between states and markets that have for some time now been eroding the social bond between states and their societies'.

In sum, open borders for finance and trade led to an unequal distribution of political influence and economic wealth. Anti-establishment movements have typically addressed these distributional issues as core elements of their electoral campaigns (Fukuyama 2018; King 2017: 100–115; Streeck 2018). For instance, Donald Trump argued that the liberalisation of trade has led to a loss of jobs in traditional US industries and that globalisation has benefitted countries such as China, Mexico and Germany while hurting US workers. The Brexit campaign insinuated that the membership in the EU would have brought more damage than benefits to the UK in form of job losses, financial transfers to Brussels and a surge in migration to the UK. The Alternative for Germany (AfD) first focused on the costs of saving the financial industry and crisis-ridden countries for the German taxpayer in the Eurocrisis and turned to oppose unlimited migration after Chancellor Merkel opened German borders for migrants and refugees in 2015. The left-wing anti-establishment parties of Syriza (Greece), Cinque Stelle (Italy) and Podemos (Spain) criticise national elites for an unequal distribution of wealth and emphasise national self-determination regarding foreign conditions for financial aid imposed by the IMF and the Euro-Group as core issues. The new left- and right-wing movements share an anti-globalist and anti-establishment orientation in arguing that the national political establishments and international organisations have privileged elite interests, especially transnational financial and corporate interests to the detriment of large parts of the population. In addition, right-wing and some left-wing movements (Cinque Stelle, Aufstehen) also share the opposition to unrestricted migration fearing a loss of cultural community, new distributional conflicts, and a reduction of public resources to be spent on national citizens (Gardels 2017; Bröning 2018).

4   How Will the Challenges Alter Global Economic Governance?

The rise of emerging powers will probably shape the future of global economic governance by two trends. First, in addition to the persistence of traditional institutions of globalisation (such as the IMF, the UN and the WTO), recent formal and informal institutions (such as the G20 and the BRICS' organisations) may gain power. The latter are characterised by national self-determination and seek global governance as issue-related inter-governmental cooperation rather than as the implementation of universal rules by international organisations and transnational experts. According to Amitai Etzioni, such a 'nation-centred system' is 'based on nation-states, high respect for their sovereignty, and agreements among nations rather than liberal concepts of individual rights, liberalising regime change, and global governance' (Etzioni 2017: 1, 2018).

Second, as a consequence of a stronger role of nation-states, future global economic governance will possibly be less determined by material interests and values of transnational elites, but rather more by the interests and ideas dominant in the domestic politics of the member states of international cooperative agreements because of governments' accountability towards their citizens. Clearly, national elites can also capture the political process to the detriment of large parts of the population as is evident regarding the unequal distribution of wealth in China and regarding the private profits and socialised losses of the financial industry in Western countries. A stronger role of the democratic nation-state in international negotiations, however, structurally enhances the accountability of governments vis-a-vis their societies. In other words, the weaker non-accountable transnational networks and international organisations become in steering global governance, the stronger the role of the 'two-level game' (Putnam 1988), which national governments have to play in order to reach a 'win-set' which attracts both domestic and international support.

How will Western domestic discontent shape the future of global economic governance? Anti-establishment movements in Western countries differ considerably regarding their localisation on the right or left sides of the political spectrum, regarding the role of the government in steering the economy, regarding welfare state provisions, health policy, migration, etc. They do, however, by and large share the criticism of the perceived unjust distribution of power and wealth in their countries, the opposition towards liberalising globalisation and the mistrust towards national as well as transnational elites. The common ground of left and right anti-establishment movements became apparent in Greece where the socialist Syriza governs with a right-wing party and 2018 in Italy where the leftist Cinque Stelle formed a coalition government with the right-wing Lega party. In the USA, while differing very much on many issues, both Donald Trump and Bernie Sanders shared the criticism of free trade and globalisation as having hurt American workers and as having contributed to a very unequal distribution of wealth (King 2017: 109; Bremmer 2018: 18).

Thus, besides the programmatic differences between the anti-establishment movements, their common ground is considerable and leads to clear trends for global economic governance, since they aim at increasing national self-determination through a reduction of the international commitments. Strengthening national autonomy ('take back control') was one of the most important motivations for Brexit voters in the UK to favour leaving the European Union and is frequently found in President Trump's arguments for leaving international commitments such as the Trans Pacific Partnership (TPP) and the Paris Agreement. Italy's Cinque Stelle and Lega have both at times articulated (and then moderated) their desire to leave the EU, while the AfD wishes Germany to leave the European Monetary Union (EMU). Therefore, if these movements continue to influence politics, the trend regarding the future of global economic governance points to a weakening of binding international rules and institutions and to a strengthening of national autonomy as well as influence.

Hence, the impact of both emerging powers and Western anti-establishment voters will most probably strengthen a 'nation-centered system' and weaken trans- and supranational institutions and elites. If the latter resist a redistribution of power, the world might watch an even further division and split in international politics between the established and the new nation-centred order.

5 Strategies for a More Inclusive and Legitimate Global Economic Governance

While challenging the established international order and distribution of power and wealth, both emerging powers and Western anti-establishment movements can function as triggers for a reform of international cooperation which would increase its legitimacy and efficiency. First, if emerging powers would participate more in the gains of the international economic order and have a stronger influence on it, the system would have more worldwide legitimacy because it would rest on higher acceptance by the community of states. Western countries and especially the USA might lose some influence on, for instance, IMF conditionality, UNSC decisions and on the global projection of economic liberalism. The then stronger nation-centred system would be based on the support of more countries and could especially count on an enhanced participation of emerging powers. The support of the latter might also make international cooperation more efficient due to emerging powers' stronger commitment of resources to the management of common problems. In addition, broader support by member states in a reformed system might also lead to a more efficient domestic implementation of international agreements, especially if domestic material interests and value-based ideas of member states' societies are included more in cooperative endeavours and international leadership (Schirm 2010: 198).

Anti-establishment movements in Western countries might contribute to a higher domestic legitimacy of international cooperation if their rise triggers a better inclusion of voters which are dissatisfied with globalisation and thereby leads to a change in the distribution of power and wealth within Western countries. Hence, if established elites are made to understand through elections that the sustainability of international economic policies in democracies also depends on domestic support, they might indeed reconsider established policy patterns and opt for a more inclusive approach to the distribution of power and wealth. International politics needs domestic support to reach legitimacy and efficiency and this support depends on a non-elitist sense of community which more broadly includes the material interests and value-based ideas of the respective societies. Thus, a reformed international order and nation-centred system requires the established elites to cede some of their ideational power and material benefits, but it could ensure a more legitimate international system because it would rest on broader support both domestically within Western countries and from emerging powers.

The probable costs in economic efficiency of a lighter version of open-border liberalisation might seem justified considering the then possible stronger public support of the international economic order within the affected societies. In other words: 'a society is more than just an economy, and the benefits of social cohesion would justify a modest economic cost' (Colgan and Keohane 2017: 43). Also from the perspective of those favouring economic globalisation, a lighter version of globalisation should be preferable to an end of globalisation and defined borders preferable to closed borders. One of the strongest supporters of liberalisation and globalisation, the weekly *The Economist*, concludes in a survey on the retreat of global business: 'The result will be a more fragmented and parochial kind of capitalism, and quite possibly a less efficient one—but also, perhaps, one with wider public support' (Jan. 28, 2017: 17).

Regarding global economic governance, the G20 can serve as an example for some features of an internationally cooperative nation-centred system with a thinner layer of rules: The G20 bears a very low degree of institutionalisation, does not possess an own bureaucracy and budget. It operates on a purely inter-governmental basis, thus having to coordinate the plurality of interests and ideas important to its member countries and their societies and elites. The G20 does not attempt at supra-nationalising the plurality of goals of its member states, but rather rests on the agreement of heads of states on issue-specific compromises. The national governments steering the G20 can be captured by elites as well, but are structurally more accountable to their citizens than any international organisation and transnational network. The G20 could enhance societal ownership in international cooperation by acknowledging the diversity of economic and political systems, of protectionism and liberalisation. The crisis of globalisation, global governance and of the Eurozone has shown that one size does not fit all, since the neoliberal Washington consensus, EMU rules and other global norms did not lead to overall convergence, but instead often to new friction. Thus, the intergovernmental coordination of the G20 might be better suited than traditional IOs in dealing with plurality of cultures as well as economic and political models.

A reformed and inclusive G20 could, for instance, establish understandings on a broader economic participation of the populace, on higher corporate and individual taxation of winners of globalisation (financial industry, TNCs, private foundations) and on a compensation of those who lose or do not benefit much from globalisation. Another strategy to acknowledge plurality and self-determination can consist in the G20's coordination of different degrees of national openness to globalisation as a flexible process. Countries may temporarily and selectively withdraw from economic openness and international organisations and later join again according to their specific levels of societal acceptance and economic hardship induced by open borders. Along this line of thought, Rodrik (2011: 253) argues regarding the WTO: '(. . .) countries may wish to restrict trade or suspend WTO obligations—exercise 'opt outs'—for reasons other than a competitive threat to their industries. Distributional concerns, conflicts with domestic norms and social arrangements, prevention of the erosion of domestic regulations, or developmental priorities would be among such legitimate grounds'.

The main obstacle for a reform of IOs and global economic governance consists in the huge benefits which the established order offers for private and public elites especially (but not only) in Western countries. Bremmer (2018: 166) argues: 'The sense of crisis isn't yet strong enough, because so many globalists continue to profit from the system as it is, and walls of various kinds will protect them, temporarily, from real danger'. Private special interests are not only lobbying national governments, but also on the international level, for instance at the WTO, the EU and at G20 summits. Both big business and single-issue NGO lobby groups have legitimate interests, but do not represent a broad spectrum of societal interests and values, are not democratically accountable to the populace, cannot (and do not intend) to reconcile or balance differing interests within and among societies. Therefore, a stronger role of nation states in global governance might well be a blessing, since governments, especially democratically elected governments, are in principle more accountable to the populace than private groups and have to balance and reconcile the plurality material interests and value-based ideational expectations which characterise any society.

In sum, the rise of both emerging powers and Western anti-establishment movements was enabled by economic globalisation, created elements of a parallel order, but can also trigger an adjustment of the traditional international economic order to their demands. The economic rise of emerging powers and their political aspiration for changing global economic governance would not have been feasible without the huge economic benefits these countries obtained through the participation in global trade and investment managed by the traditional IOs of the Bretton Woods system and enabled by the openness of Western markets. Rising production and growing exports of emerging powers correlated to a large extend with a reduction of manufacturing in Western countries and with a transfer of production from Western countries to emerging economies. This development caused substantial hardship in Western countries and liberalisation led to a very unequal distribution of the gains of globalisation within these countries. The latter, in turn, were core reasons for the rise of anti-establishment movements in Western countries which now challenge the national and international distribution of power and wealth. Thus, both challenges to the established economic order and traditional global economic governance are consequences of this order and mode of governance. Following the demands of both challenges for a more inclusive distribution of power and wealth on national and international levels with the strategies outlined above might increase the acceptance and support of national and international political order. Making economic governance more accountable towards the societies and countries concerned by strengthening the role of democratic nation-states through intergovernmental cooperation could enhance the legitimacy of global economic governance and avoid parallel or conflicting world orders.

References

Armijo, L. E., & Roberts, C. (2014). The emerging powers and global governance: Why the BRICS matter. In R. Looney (Ed.), *Handbook of emerging economies* (pp. 503–524). New York: Routledge.

Bofinger, P. (2016, Dezember 9). Entschädigt die Verlierer der Globalisierung! Die Brexit-Befürworter und die Trump-Wähler sind zurecht unzufrieden. Viele Länder tun zu wenig für den sozialen Ausgleich. *Die Zeit.*

Brawley, M. R. (2007). Building blocks or a BRIC wall? Fitting U.S. foreign policy to the shifting distribution of power. *Asian Perspective, 31*(4), 151–175.

Bremmer, I. (2018). *Us vs. them. The failure of globalism*. New York: Portfolio/Penguin.

Bröning, M. (2018). Lob der Nation. Weshalb wir den Nationalstaat nicht den Rechtspopulisten überlassen dürfen. In *Internationale Politik und Gesellschaft*. Friedrich-Ebert-Stiftung.

Colgan, J. D., & Keohane, R. O. (2017). The liberal order is rigged. Fix it now or watch it wither. *Foreign Affairs, 96*, 36–44.

Destradi, S. (2010). Regional powers and their strategies: Empire, hegemony, and leadership. *Review of International Studies, 36*(4), 903–930.

Etzioni, A. (2017, September 11). *An international order without globalism*. Available at SSRN. Retrieved from https://ssrn.com/abstract=3035438 or https://doi.org/10.2139/ssrn.3035438

Etzioni, A. (2018). The rising (more) nation-centered system. *The Fletcher Forum of World Affairs, 42*(2), 29–53.

Fukuyama, F. (2018). The populist surge. *The National Interest, 13*(4). Retrieved from https://www.the-american-interest.com/2018/02/09/the-populist-surge/

G20. (2011). *Official web-site G20*. Retrieved from https://www.g20.org/about_g20

Gardels, N. (2017, December 22). Open societies need defined borders. *The Washington Post*.

Hall, P. A., & Soskice, D. (2001). An introduction to varieties of capitalism. In P. A. Hall & D. Soskice (Eds.), *Varieties of capitalism* (pp. 1–68). Oxford: Oxford University Press.

Higgott, R. (2018). Globalism, populism and the limits of global economic governance. *Journal of Inter-Regional Studies, 1*(1), 2–23.

Kahler, M. (2014). Rising powers and global governance: Negotiating change in a resilient status quo. *International Affairs, 89*(3), 711–729.

King, S. D. (2017). *Grave new world. The end of globalization, the return of history*. New Haven: Yale University Press.

Kirton, J. J. (2013). *G20 governance for a globalized world*. Farnham: Ashgate.

Luckhurst, J. (2012). The G20 and ad hoc embedded liberalism: Economic governance amid crisis and dissensus. *Politics & Policy, 40*(5), 740–782.

Milner, H. V. (1997). *Interests, institutions, and information. Domestic politics and international relations*. Princeton, NJ: Princeton University Press.

Moravcsik, A. (1997). Taking preferences seriously. A liberal theory of international politics. *International Organization, 51*(4), 515–555.

Nölke, A., ten Brink, T., Claar, S., & May, C. (2015). Domestic structures, foreign economic policies and global economic order: Implications from the rise of large emerging economies. *European Journal of International Relations, 21*(3), 538–567.

Putnam, R. D. (1988). Diplomacy and domestic politics: The logic of two level games. *International Organization, 42*(3), 427–460.

Rodrik, D. (2011). *The globalization paradox. Democracy and the future of the world economy*. New York: Norton.

Schirm, S. A. (2010). Leaders in need of followers. Emerging powers in global governance. *European Journal of International Relations, 16*(2), 197–222.

Schirm, S. A. (2013). Global politics are domestic politics. A societal approach to divergence in the G20. *Review of International Studies, 39*(3), 685–706.

Schirm, S. A. (2016). Domestic ideas, institutions or interests? Explaining governmental preferences towards global economic governance. *International Political Science Review, 37*(1), 66–80.

Schirm, S. A. (2018). The domestic politics of European preferences towards global economic governance. *New Global Studies, 12*(3), 303–324.

Schirm, S. A. (2019a). Domestic politics and the societal approach. In T. Shaw, L. Mahrenbach, R. Modi, & X. Yi-Chong (Eds.), *The Palgrave handbook of contemporary international political economy* (pp. 103–117). London: Palgrave.

Schirm, S. A. (2019b). In pursuit of self-determination and redistribution: Emerging powers and western anti-establishment voters in international politics. *Global Affairs, 5*(2), 115–130.

Streeck, W. (2018). Europe under Merkel IV. *American Affairs, 2*(1), 162–192.

Stuenkel, O. (2016). *Post western world. How emerging powers are remaking global order.* Cambridge: Polity Press.

The Economist. (2017, January 28). The retreat of the global company. *The Economist,* 14–17.

Vasileva-Dienes, A., & Schmidt, V. A. (2018). Conceptualising capitalism in the twenty-first century: The BRICs and the European periphery. *Contemporary Politics.* https://doi.org/10.1080/13569775.2018.1555746

Networks Decentralizing Authority in Global Economic Governance

Jonathan Luckhurst

1 Introduction

This chapter analyzes how global governance networks of state and non-state actors contributed to decentralizing authority in global economic governance since the global financial crisis (GFC). It fits well with the heterogeneous-actor and societal approaches deployed by contributors to the present volume, contrary to unitary, state-centric analytical frameworks.

The first section introduces the analytical approach, which deploys tools particularly from social constructivism, discourse analysis, and the sociology of professions. The second focuses on explicating the significance of global governance networks. The third section indicates governance networks' role in decentralizing global governance authority, before and since the GFC. The fourth links this to the significance of legitimizing discourses for political contestation among global governance networks, particularly on global macroeconomic, financial, development, and trade governance. These sections indicate both the constitutive and instrumental effects of politico-discursive contestation between global governance networks.

This study indicates how the GFC influenced authority shifts and undermined conventional wisdom in global economic governance. The focus on the role of networks emphasizes the significance of *relationality* and agency, not just of individuals but also collectively through networks. This points to the importance of analytical contextualization, by focusing on the relations, processes, and practices of global governance.

J. Luckhurst (✉)
Soka University, Tokyo, Japan
e-mail: luckhurst@soka.ac.jp

© Springer Nature Switzerland AG 2020
M. Rewizorski et al. (eds.), *The Future of Global Economic Governance*,
https://doi.org/10.1007/978-3-030-35336-0_3

2 Analytical Approach

The first key topic is how the analytical framework contributes to understanding the influence of global economic governance networks. There is also an important focus on "legitimizing" discourses, deploying a qualitative discourse-analytic approach to assessing the effects of such discourses on global economic governance.

Global economic governance networks consist of private, intergovernmental, supranational, state, quasi-state, and/or non-state actors. They contest and contribute to the production of global economic governance, as sometimes complex and heterogeneous networks of actors and interlocutors (cf. Sørensen and Torfing 2007: 3). This chapter indicates the significance of global governance networks for *decentralizing authority* in global economic governance, since the 1990s and, increasingly, after the GFC.

Several recent scholarly studies have focused on "authority" in global governance (see Broome and Seabrooke 2015; Eccleston et al. 2015; Luckhurst 2016a, 2017, 2019; Zürn 2018). The present author's own research emphasizes the significance of three key forms of authority, namely its *strategic*, *political*, and *cognitive* dimensions (see Luckhurst 2016a, 2017, 2019). This constitutes a useful analytical framework for understanding authority effects in international relations and global governance. The argument in the present chapter is that global governance networks contribute significantly to decentralizing authority in global economic governance in these three aspects: the *strategic* dimension, by influencing international perceptions of the strategic capacities of state and other actors; the *political*, by influencing understandings of actors' political rights and responsibilities (cf. Ruggie 1982: 380); and in *cognitive* terms, by influencing perceptions of the professional competencies of actors (cf. Broome and Seabrooke 2015).

This analytical approach to "authority" indicates the increasing diversification of international relations and global governance, in terms of actors, organization, and policy issues. It thus shares Amitav Acharya's (2014: 1–11) emphasis on the growing heterogeneity of international relations, what he refers to as the "multiplex world." The latter conceptualization indicates the diversity of contemporary international relations, implicitly with reference to authority and normative heterogeneity. Other scholars have also emphasized this diversification, particularly among the actors and networks involved in global governance (Dingwerth and Pattberg 2006; Luckhurst 2017; Rosenau 1995).

The focus here on global governance networks' support for specific policy *practices*, while deploying legitimizing discourses to contest or advocate those practices, helps ground the analysis in particular contexts of social interaction. This is because, as noted by Emanuel Adler and Vincent Pouliot (2011: 6), "practices" indicate "socially meaningful patterns of action which, in being performed more or less competently, simultaneously embody, act out and possibly reify background knowledge and discourse in and on the material world."

Similar to John Karlsrud's (2016) research on linked ecologies involved in United Nations (UN) peacekeeping, this chapter combines analytical insights from constructivism and the sociology of professions. It further integrates the "practice" approach noted above, in addition to a discourse-analytic focus on political contestation (see Glynos et al. 2009; Howarth 2000), complementing constructivist arguments about how crises weaken the influence of conventional policy wisdom (Widmaier et al. 2007). This constitutes a middle-range and eclectic analytical approach, focused on explicating how global governance networks influence global economic governance through linked "ecologies" of diverse professional actors, without positing universal claims about the general significance of global governance networks. This complements the constructivist dimension of the analysis, which includes a focus on "relationality" (Qin 2016), hence emphasizing the significance of *relations*, rather than structures or individual agents, for understanding how global governance authority is constituted. This is indicative of the social construction of *authority*, which is based on others' perceptions and recognition of an actor's authoritativeness (Hopf 1998: 179–179; Reus-Smit 2007: 44).

The other key component of the analytical approach is its focus on *legitimizing discourses*, especially how global governance networks and practice "communities" politically instrumentalize them. This notion of "legitimizing discourses" has been deployed by international relations scholars of critical discourse analysis (De Ville and Orbie 2014), plus in the author's own research on global economic governance and the Group of Twenty (G20) (Luckhurst 2016a, b, 2017). Legitimizing discourses provide ideational resources that are instrumentalized for asserting legitimacy claims. This has authority effects *to the extent* that others are persuaded, since actors' authority is constituted through socially constructed perceptions. Global governance networks and actors instrumentally deploy rhetorical tools or narrative constructions in processes of political contestation, in attempting to sway global governance and policy practices and norms.

3 The Significance of Global Governance Networks

This section examines the significance of global governance networks for global economic governance, particularly in the case of the G20. This emphasis on global governance networks has similarities with International Relations research on transnational networks and advocacy coalitions (cf. Keck and Sikkink 1999; Slaughter 2015), plus Emanuel Adler's (2008) focus on "communities of practice." These conceptualizations point to the growing heterogeneity of international relations and global governance since the 1990s.

"Global governance" comprises "the formal and informal management of cross-border issues with worldwide, or 'global', repercussions, involving complex interlinkages between diverse actors and organizational contexts" (Luckhurst 2017: 2). James Rosenau (1992: 2) notes "in a world where authority is undergoing continuous relocation—both outward toward supranational entities and inward toward subnational groups—it becomes increasingly imperative to probe how governance can occur in the absence of government." The present chapter focuses on how global governance networks contribute to this "governance without government," with the effect of further decentralizing authority in global economic governance. It argues that global governance networks are crucial, particularly in *transnational* contexts of network relations, in which relatively thin socialization processes increase the scope for new forms of political engagement and contestation (Seabrooke 2014: 54–56).

Global economic governance is constituted through complex and heterogeneous contexts, practices, networks, and actors, beyond just formal or even informal intergovernmental settings. Transnational global governance networks involve state, non-state, and intergovernmental actors. In the case of the G20, for example, this often indicates cooperation between G20 member officials and international organization officials (see Baker and Carey 2014; Eccleston et al. 2015; Luckhurst 2016a), as well as non-state actors involved in G20 working groups and its official engagement forums. The author of this chapter has spent the past few years conducting semi-structured interviews and participant observation research on the G20 engagement groups, finding evidence of networked engagement *between* these forums and their respective participants on some shared policy goals. These G20 outreach processes have significantly expanded since 2008, contributing to decentralizing global governance authority, especially by increasing the influence of heterogeneous global governance networks, particularly on issues such as sustainable development and gender and wealth inequalities (Luckhurst 2016a, 2017).

The G20 has become an important "hub" of global economic governance (see Luckhurst 2019); hence global governance networks that contest and influence its policy agenda, also influence the broader politico-discursive context of global economic governance. The increased contestation of global economic governance norms and practices since the GFC indicates a significant "crisis effect" (see Widmaier et al. 2007). This undermined the influence of conventional wisdom, increasing opportunities for what some poststructuralists would call "repoliticization" (De Goede 2004; Edkins 1999: 125–143), or greater political contestation due to crisis contingencies, authority shifts, policy contestation, and the agency of governance networks and broader communities of practice. There is also a rationalist argument that when the future becomes unpredictable, ". . .actors' preferences about future outcomes will not dictate their choices of alternatives in the present" (Keohane 2002: 265). This further indicates how uncertainty increases the prospects for effective political contestation of existing policy norms and practices during crises, by decreasing perceived strategic, rational constraints on decision-making.

The significance of global economic governance networks is further indicated by important policy shifts since the GFC. There is substantial evidence, for example, of how global governance networks influenced the shift to macroprudential financial regulation and sustainable development in global governance circles since the GFC. This further indicates the significance of their political contestation in times of crisis, when conventional legitimizing discourses become more contestable. Political contestation often has slower or more incremental effects at other times, but remains a key aspect of the political significance of global governance networks, especially for decentralizing authority in global economic governance.

4 Governance Networks' Role in Decentralizing Global Governance Authority

The end of the Cold War had significant consequences for global economic governance and domestic policymaking. There were diverse political and economic effects, including the growing trend for transnational, non-state actors to influence global policy debates. The claim that the USA had become a "unipolar" power by the 1990s (Krauthammer 1990), though always a simplification, was superseded by a growing perception that leading developing states were catching up with wealthy states, economically, by the early 2000s (Luckhurst 2017: 44–45).

This shifting context of international relations and global economic governance contributed to decentralizing authority among state actors, while also changing the balance between state and non-state actors. The integration of more heterogeneous actors in global governance, including those in transnational governance networks, has been a growing trend since the 1990s. It was partly facilitated by new technologies, especially the Internet (Keck and Sikkink 1999: 95–99; Scholte 2004), which enabled civil society organizations (CSOs) to increase their influence on international policy debates. In the 1990s, the UN led the way in this expansion of civil society engagement from international organizations, granting consultative status to hundreds of CSOs and also engaging with them in a series of high-profile conferences, especially the crucial 1992 Rio Earth Summit (Clark et al. 1998: 6). This indicated the importance attached by the UN to its civil society interlocutors, but also their new status as global governance "stakeholders."

There were significant examples of the growing influence of CSOs on global *economic* governance in the 1990s. One was the successful CSO campaign against the implementation of the OECD's proposed Multilateral Agreement on Investment, which effectively mobilized public opposition through a global advocacy campaign (Smythe 2000). Another interesting instance was the role of CSO advocacy in preventing the IMF's then managing director, Michel Camdessus, from changing its rules to prohibit members' use of capital controls (Rodrik 2012: 90–95). In both cases, CSOs were able to use the Internet to disseminate their arguments and increase public awareness of the issues, in order to reduce the capacity of policymakers and officials to implement policies that were opposed by significant segments of civil society.

Partly due to this effective advocacy, plus the growing significance of the "anti-globalization" movement at the turn of the millennium, international organizations such as the UN and the Bretton Woods institutions increasingly began to engage with civil society actors as global governance "stakeholders." This indicated the broader inclusion of such actors in global policy debates, including those linked to global economic governance. This augmented the capacity of actor networks, beyond the confines of the most influential western states or IFIs, to influence policy agendas in the new post-Cold War context. Some traditional International Relations scholars, including several defined as liberals and realists, have been slow to adjust their analytical frameworks to account for this diversification of actors and networks.

Global governance scholars such as Rosenau (1992) were much more responsive to contemporary developments, by analyzing this trend in international relations and global governance circles.

The post-Cold War period constituted a significant transition for global governance, in particular, increasing the prospects for multilateral cooperation across diverse policy fields. The role of governance networks was crucial on issues of global climate governance, involving scientists, CSOs, intergovernmental and national policymakers; and in reassessing international humanitarian norms, again with significant contributions from CSOs, as well as international human rights lawyers (see Keck and Sikkink 1999: 95–99). Scholars such as Margaret Keck and Kathryn Sikkink (1999) indicated the significant normative shift in global governance circles, to the broad acceptance that CSOs should be engaged as stakeholders on key policy issues such as climate change and economic development. This sometimes had reciprocal benefits; for example, Arturo Santa-Cruz (2005) notes how CSOs contributed to enhancing perceptions of state legitimacy in the post-Cold War period, by increasing transparency and sometimes public trust in political processes of democratization (Santa-Cruz 2005: 680–686). Richard Price (2003: 584) emphasizes the growing professionalization of CSO actors involved in global governance networks, in terms of their expertise and resources; this further enhanced their abilities to constitute and integrate within global governance networks that sometimes included intergovernmental and state actors.

The seismic effects of the GFC subsequently brought further changes to global governance authority. This accelerated some of the global authority shifts that began to take shape in the 1990s. A series of financial crises in Asia and Latin America, in the first post-Cold War decade, significantly undermined confidence in global economic leadership from the USA and its Group of Eight (G8) allies, especially among policymakers and citizens of developing states. There was also widespread criticism of the Bretton Woods institutions, particularly due to the IMF's imposition of damaging structural-adjustment programs in return for emergency loans (Cooper 2008: 254; Rodrik 2012: 90–95; Sohn 2005). This prompted greater policy contestation on core economic governance norms and practices, also dividing IMF and World Bank staff by the early 2000s, along broadly opposing institutional positions on the merits of the so-called Washington Consensus on economic development. The cognitive authority of erstwhile advocates of the 1990s Washington Consensus was undermined by the growing perception of its significant policy flaws.

The GFC further weakened support in global governance circles for the Washington Consensus. The latter had included market liberalization and deregulation policies commonly considered "neoliberal," but did not sufficiently suit the needs of many developing states. The GFC increased the willingness of developing state policymakers to criticize the former Washington Consensus and question the cognitive authority of leading IFIs and wealthy state officials. This weakening of erstwhile conventional policy wisdom in global economic governance, particularly on core macroeconomic policy issues such as market efficiency and deregulation, indicated that the GFC was a key moment or "critical juncture" that further decentralized strategic, political, *and* cognitive authority.

The GFC, then, undermined confidence in and adherence to the economic policy prescriptions of G8 governments and officials. Due to the strategic exigencies of the global crisis, especially following the collapse of Lehman Brothers investment bank in September 2008, G8 leaders accepted an augmented role for the G20 as a summit-level crisis committee, recognizing the economic and political benefits of including leading developing states in a global economic rescue strategy. The global economic governance authority effects were important, especially in terms of diversifying the actors involved, with key policy consequences. On issues such as macroprudential financial regulation and sustainable development, the post-2008 emphasis in global governance shifted to more of the priorities and preferences of leading developing states, particularly in Asia (Luckhurst 2017: 163–174). In both policy contexts, there was a refocusing from deregulation and market imperatives to a growing prioritization of the state's strategic economic role (Luckhurst 2016a: 26–30). Importantly for the present analysis, there is substantial evidence that global governance networks involving non-state, as well as state and intergovernmental actors, were key to these shifts in global economic governance. This is indicated by the analysis, below, of how legitimizing discourses influence political contestation in these contexts.

The G20's significant influence in decentralizing global governance authority was indicated by its policy agenda expansion from 2010 onward, when the Korean G20 Presidency introduced topics beyond the crisis-period emphasis on financial regulation and boosting economic growth, by including development policy issues. This was significant because effectively it meant non-G8 states and civil society actors were able, through their agency, to expand the G20 policy agenda beyond the core economic growth and financial reform priorities and agenda of the leading wealthy states. Global governance networks, through their engagement and advocacy efforts within the G20, have contributed to the subsequent agenda expansion (see Luckhurst 2016a, 2019).

5 Legitimizing Discourses and Contested Global Economic Governance

Constructivists introduced the notion of *cognitive* authority, as noted earlier, which is useful to indicate how legitimizing discourses influence the "authoritativeness" of global governance actors (see Eccleston et al. 2015). This is because actors derive cognitive authority from legitimizing discourses, when the latter increase perceptions of their intellectual gravitas and professional credibility.

The decade following the GFC has been a significant period of political contestation, in domestic as well as global economic governance. Global governance networks have been important for this contestation, either through their advocacy or opposition to particular policy approaches. Legitimizing discourses provide ideational resources, as well as constituting the bounds of actor rationality or beliefs (cf. Clegg 2006; Hopf 2010; Kahneman 2003; Sen 1977; Simon 1955), for political contestation between competing policy advocates, including global governance networks.

Three significant legitimizing discourses in global economic governance since the GFC undermined the pre-crisis conventional wisdom on markets and economic efficiency. One was the revival of scholarly, popular, political, and policymaking interest in the economic thought of John Maynard Keynes, during the GFC. Keynes' analysis recognized the social embeddedness of the economy, emphasizing the benefits of reducing negative societal effects from potentially dysfunctional market economies. Renewed interest in his ideas and their policy application, especially during 2008–2009, indicated greater acceptance of the need to take seriously the social costs of economic policies, compared with the pre-GFC neoclassical conventional wisdom that detached economic analysis from its social context. A second legitimizing discourse that has grown in popularity comes from behavioral economics, gaining prominence through the work of Nobel laureates Daniel Kahneman and Robert Shiller. This is another indicator of growing interest in the social embeddedness of economic relations, in this case how social psychology influences the behavior of market actors. A third ideational shift since the GFC has been the increased scholarly, public, and policymaking focus on societal *inequality*; this was indicated by the mass popularity of Thomas Piketty's (2014) *Capital in the Twenty-First Century*. This constituted another legitimizing discourse for questioning market efficiency, while emphasizing the need to reduce inequality both in wealthy and developing nations, a topic on which new classical economics and public choice scholars of market efficiency contribute little.

A key consequence of such important ideational shifts was their influence on cognitive authority markers. This constituted two new normative principles of global economic governance, specifically the rejection of the rational expectations model of economic actors, in favor of more socially embedded accounts; and the second was increased *inclusivity* of global economic governance, initially through the augmented role for leading developing states in its most important multilateral fora and institutions, but also, importantly, an expansion of the actors involved that also increased the salience of a wider range of policy issues. This indicated a political rejection of the pre-GFC dominance of an élite group of wealthy states, especially the G7/G8. It also brought an important shift in the policy norms and practices of global economic governance. The G20 was a crucial forum for the diffusion of these new normative principles, constituting new global governance norms and practices.

There is substantial evidence to indicate how global economic governance networks constitute, deploy, or instrumentalize legitimizing discourses, also for the constitutive effects of the latter on global governance. As noted earlier, the GFC augmented opportunities for global governance networks to contest existing legitimizing discourses, often in the form of conventional policy wisdom, due to the crisis effect in undermining the cognitive authority of these conventional policy approaches and their advocates and policy claims. The G20, in particular, was a crucial forum for augmenting the influence of more heterogeneous global governance networks. However, the BRICS forum,[1] as well as the Basel Committee for

---

[1] BRICS = Brazil, Russia, India, China, South Africa.

Banking Supervision and the Financial Stability Board, also contributed to this increasingly diverse context of global economic governance, by augmenting the influence of members from non-G7 states in core global economic policymaking processes during the GFC.

It is useful briefly to assess four cases of global governance networks deploying legitimizing discourses, to contest global fiscal, financial, development, and trade governance norms and practices. There is substantial evidence of networks deploying legitimizing discourses to contest the norms and practices of global macroeconomic governance since the GFC. There were several politically contested legitimizing discourses during the GFC, built on competing narratives about the causes and consequences of the GFC. This was also influenced by pre-GFC political–economic developments and debates, as noted earlier, particularly on the significance of the Washington Consensus and its flaws (Rodrik 2006; World Bank 2005). One core underlying principle at stake concerned the economic functions of the state and markets, a key focus for political contestation in international policymaking since the 1930s (see Luckhurst 2017: 85–88).

There was also significant growth in usage of the signifier "sustainable" during and since the GFC, sometimes implicitly referencing the embedded liberalism argument that some market flaws should be resolved through public policymaking and, increasingly, multilateral cooperation (cf. Ruggie 1982). Influential intellectuals advanced these claims (see Stiglitz 2012; Piketty 2014), as did multilateral policy networks and actors (G20 Framework Working Group and OECD 2015). This constituted another key legitimizing discourse, deployed by a global economic governance network that favored socially and environmentally sustainable economic growth policies, rather than austerity or free-market-focused policies.

Advocates of a Keynesian fiscal stimulus strategy became highly influential in global economic governance during the GFC, for about 12 months, following the September 2008 bankruptcy of Lehman Brothers investment bank. This led to what some called the "Keynesian revival," but even though its prevalence would not endure, it lasted long enough to make possible the substantial fiscal stimulus strategy agreed at the London G20 Summit of April 2009 (G20 2009). Claims articulated with this legitimizing discourse were contested, especially by advocates of fiscal austerity, following the Greek debt crisis and the start of the Eurozone crisis in 2010. These proponents of austerity included members of Angela Merkel's government in Germany, but also Republicans in the USA and Conservatives in the UK. Their political contestation of the Keynesian-style fiscal stimulus policies integrated arguments presented by academic and expert critics, who constructed an alternative legitimizing discourse on the merits of what they argued to be the debt- and deficit-reducing effects of austerity policies (see Alesina and Ardagna 2009; Reinhart and Rogoff 2010). This indicated how legitimizing discourses could be instrumentalized to influence global economic governance norms and practices.

The second case to consider is financial regulation. The global governance network on macroprudential financial regulation successfully shifted global economic governance to incorporate the macroprudential policy agenda. This occurred during the GFC, as the effects of the crisis increased the openness to policy experimentation in global governance circles, due to the evident failures of pre-GFC microprudential policymaking approaches. It led to the G20 endorsement of macroprudential financial governance, in particular the Basel III Accords in 2010 (G20 2010; BCBS 2010). The policy shift was the result of a highly successful campaign from advocates of the macroprudential financial regulatory approach, a global governance network led by staff from the Bank for International Settlements (see Baker 2013: 129; Borio 2009: 39). It effectively normalized or legitimized macroprudential financial regulation, constituting an enduring shift in financial governance norms and practices.

There is substantial evidence that a global governance network on sustainable development, the third case to consider, influenced the increasing emphasis on sustainable economic development in global economic governance since the GFC. This is not so much a case of political contestation, as the success of this sustainable economic development governance network has been so comprehensive that it has constituted something close to a dominant consensus in post-GFC global development governance. It does point to the importance of legitimizing discourses, though, as civil society activists and organizations, backed by leading scholars such as Dani Rodrik, Jeffrey Sachs, and Joseph Stiglitz, supported efforts from developing states and newly industrialized Republic of Korea to bury the former Washington Consensus under a new sustainable development consensus. The Korean G20 Presidency of 2010, reinforced by these other advocates, managed to initiate this shift with their "Seoul Development Consensus" (G20 2010). The UN's Sustainable Development Goals advanced this notion of sustainability still further. This political shift in global development governance indicated how the global governance network on sustainable development effectively deployed a legitimizing discourse of *sustainable* development, to marginalize the more free-market-oriented and universally prescriptive Washington Consensus on development.

More recently, with the election of Donald Trump as US president, there has been increasing contestation of global trade governance. Perhaps surprisingly, this has constituted a form of decentralizing authority in this context, by challenging and undermining the authority of the World Trade Organization and of leading trade experts, who until recently have generally treated protectionist policy measures as unacceptable trade practices. The willingness of the Trump Administration to adopt protectionist practices on trade also, arguably, diminishes the cognitive and political authority of the US government, by indicating the willingness of the Trump Administration to undermine multilateral cooperation and ignore global trade norms and practices. This further indicates how the recent decentralizing authority shifts in global economic governance have been influenced by state, as well as non-state, actors and networks.

6   Conclusion

This chapter indicates how networks of state, non-state, and intergovernmental actors contributed to decentralizing authority in global economic governance since the end of the Cold War. This decentralizing authority constituted a context of greater actor heterogeneity in international relations and global governance, due to technological, social, economic, and political shifts.

The GFC was particularly significant for further decentralizing authority and, thus, increasing the diversity of global economic governance actors and networks. The G20, in particular, has become a hub of decentralizing global governance authority since the GFC. The inclusion of diverse global governance networks in its policy processes has augmented the diversity of global economic governance. This constituted important policy shifts, especially on macroprudential financial regulation and sustainable economic development. The section on legitimizing discourses indicates how networks influenced politico-discursive contestation in global economic governance, particularly on fiscal policies, financial regulation, economic development, and increasingly on trade in recent years. In a context of crisis and heightened uncertainty, global economic governance networks contested and, in some cases, shifted global governance norms and practices. Legitimizing discourses were deployed to increase their potential for success.

The effective agency of global economic governance networks indicates the analytical flaws of state-centric approaches to international relations and global governance. Many scholars of global governance have adjusted their analytical lens to account for this actor diversity, while "mainstream" North American International Relations scholars often have not, particularly those from the realist school. The present chapter further indicates that materialist and rationalist accounts also are insufficient, that it is necessary to consider how cognitive authority and normative contestation influence global economic governance.

References

Acharya, A. (2014). *The end of American world order*. Cambridge: Polity Press.

Adler, E. (2008). The spread of security communities: Communities of practice, self-restraint, and NATO's post-cold war transformation. *European Journal of International Relations, 14*(2), 195–230.

Adler, E., & Pouliot, V. (2011). International practices. *International Theory, 3*(1), 1–36.

Alesina, A., & Ardagna, S. (2009). *Large changes in fiscal policy: Taxes versus spending* (National Bureau of Economic Research (NBER), Working paper no. 15438).

Baker, A. (2013). The new political economy of the macroprudential ideational shift. *New Political Economy, 18*(1), 112–139.

Baker, A., & Carey, B. (2014). Flexible 'G Groups' and network governance in an era of uncertainty and experimentation. In T. Payne & N. Phillips (Eds.), *Handbook of international political economy of governance*. Cheltenham: Edward Elgar.

BCBS. (2010). *Basel III: A global regulatory framework for more resilient banks and banking systems*. Basel: Bank for International Settlements. Accessed September 19, 2015, from http://www.bis.org/publ/bcbs189.htm

Borio, C. (2009). Implementing the macroprudential approach to financial regulation and supervision. *Financial Stability Review*, No. 13, September. Paris: Banque de France.

Broome, A., & Seabrooke, L. (2015). Shaping policy curves: Cognitive authority in transnational capacity building. *Public Administration, 93*(4), 956–972.

Clark, A. M., Friedman, E. J., & Hochstetler, K. (1998). The sovereign limits of global civil society: A comparison of NGO participation in UN world conferences on the environment, human rights, and women. *World Politics, 51*(1), 1–35.

Clegg, S. (2006). The bounds of rationality: Power/history/imagination. *Critical Perspectives on Accounting, 17*, 847–863.

Cooper, A. F. (2008). Executive but expansive: The L20 as a project of 'new' multilateralism and 'new' regionalism. In A. F. Cooper, C. W. Hughes, & P. de Lombaerde (Eds.), *Regionalisation and global governance: The taming of globalisation?* (pp. 249–264). Routledge: Abingdon.

De Goede, M. (2004). Repoliticizing financial risk. *Economy and Society, 33*(2), 197–217.

De Ville, F., & Orbie, J. (2014). The European commission's neoliberal trade discourse since the crisis: Legitimizing continuity through subtle discursive change. *The British Journal of Politics and International Relations, 16*(1), 149–167.

Dingwerth, K., & Pattberg, P. (2006). Global governance as a perspective on world politics. *Global Governance, 12*, 185–206.

Eccleston, R., Kellow, A., & Carroll, P. (2015). G20 endorsement in post crisis global governance: More than a toothless talking shop? *British Journal of Politics and International Relations, 17*, 298–317.

Edkins, J. (1999). *Poststructuralism and international relations*. Boulder, CO: Lynne Rienner.

G20. (2009, April 2). London summit – Leaders' statement 2 April 2009. *G20 Leader Forum*. Accessed October 5, 2018, from http://www.g20.utoronto.ca/summits/2009london.html

G20. (2010). *The G20 Seoul summit leaders' declaration*, November 11. Accessed October 5, 2018, from http://www.g20.utoronto.ca/2010/g20seoul-doc.html

G20 Framework Working Group and OECD. (2015). *Inequality and inclusive growth: Policy tools to achieve balanced growth in G20 economies*. Antalya, Turkey, October. Accessed June 27, 2017, from https://www.oecd.org/g20/topics/framework-strong-sustainable-balanced-growth/Inequality-and-Inclusive-Growth-Policy-Tools-to-Achieve-Balanced-Growth-in-g20-Economies.pdf

Glynos, J., Howarth, D., Norval, A., & Speed, E. (2009, August). *Discourse analysis: Varieties and methods*. ESRC National Centre for Research Methods Review paper.

Hopf, T. (1998). The promise of constructivism in international relations theory. *International Security, 23*(1), 171–200.

Hopf, T. (2010). The logic of habit in international relations. *European Journal of International Relations, 16*(4), 539–561.

Howarth, D. (2000). *Discourse*. Buckingham/Philadelphia: Open University Press.

Kahneman, D. (2003). Maps of bounded rationality: Psychology for behavioral economics. *The American Economic Review, 93*(5), 1449–1475.

Karlsrud, J. (2016). *Norm change in international relations: Linked ecologies in UN peacekeeping operations*. New York: Routledge.

Keck, M. E., & Sikkink, K. (1999). Transnational advocacy networks in international and regional politics. *International Social Science Journal, 51*(159), 89–101.

Keohane, R. O. (2002). *Power and governance in a partially globalized world*. New York: Routledge.

Krauthammer, C. (1990). The unipolar moment. *Foreign Affairs: America and the World, 70*(1), 23–33.

Luckhurst, J. (2016a). *G20 since the global crisis*. New York: Palgrave Macmillan.

Luckhurst, J. (2016b). The G20's growing political and economic challenges. *Global Summitry: Politics, Economics, and Law in International Governance, 2*(2), 161–179.

Luckhurst, J. (2017). *The shifting global economic architecture: Decentralizing authority in contemporary global governance*. New York: Palgrave Macmillan.

Luckhurst, J. (2019). The G20 hub of decentralizing global governance authority. *International Organisations Research Journal, 14*(2), 7–30.

Piketty, T. (2014). *Capital in the twenty-first century*. Cambridge, MA: Harvard University Press.

Price, R. (2003). Transnational civil society and advocacy in world politics. *World Politics, 55*, 579–606.

Qin, Y. (2016). A relational theory of world politics. *International Studies Review, 18*(1), 33–47.

Reinhart, C., & Rogoff, K. (2010). Growth in a time of debt. *American Economic Review: Papers & Proceedings, 100*, 573–578.

Reus-Smit, C. (2007). International crises of legitimacy. *International Politics, 44*(2/3), 157–174.

Rodrik, D. (2006). Goodbye Washington consensus, hello Washington confusion? A review of the World Bank's. *Journal of Economic Literature, 44*(4), 973–987.

Rodrik, D. (2012). *The globalization paradox: Why global markets, states, and democracy can't coexist*. Oxford: Oxford University Press.

Rosenau, J. N. (1992). Governance, order, and change in world politics. In J. N. Rosenau & O.-E. Czempiel (Eds.), *Governance without government: Order and change in world politics* (pp. 1–29). Cambridge: Cambridge University Press.

Rosenau, J. N. (1995). Governance in the twenty-first century. *Global Governance, 1*, 13–43.

Ruggie, J. G. (1982). International regimes, transactions, and change: Embedded liberalism in the postwar economic order. *International Organization, 36*(2), 379–415.

Santa-Cruz, A. (2005). Constitutional structures, sovereignty, and the emergence of norms: The case of international election monitoring. *International Organization, 59*, 663–693.

Scholte, J. A. (2004). Civil society and democratically accountable global governance. *Government and Opposition, 39*(2), 211–233.

Seabrooke, L. (2014). Epistemic arbitrage: Transnational professional knowledge in action. *Journal of Professions and Organization, 1*(1), 49–64.

Sen, A. (1977). Rational fools: A critique of the behavioral foundations of economic theory. *Philosophy and Public Affairs, 6*(4), 317–344.

Simon, H. (1955). A behavioral model of rational choice. *Quarterly Journal of Economics, 69*(1), 99–118.

Slaughter, S. (2015). Building G20 Outreach: The role of transnational policy networks in sustaining effective and legitimate summitry. *Global Summitry, 1*(2), 171–186.

Smythe, E. (2000). State authority and investment security: Non-state actors and the negotiation of the multilateral agreement on investment at the OECD. In R. A. Higgott, G. R. D. Underhill, & A. Bieler (Eds.), *Non-state actors and authority in the global system* (pp. 74–90). New York: Routledge.

Sohn, I. (2005). Asian financial cooperation: The problem of legitimacy in global financial governance. *Global Governance, 11*(4), 487–504.

Sørensen, E., & Torfing, J. (2007). Introduction: Governance network research: Toward a second generation. In E. Sørensen & J. Torfing (Eds.), *Theories of democratic network governance* (pp. 1–24). Basingstoke: Palgrave Macmillan.

Stiglitz, J. E. (2012). *The price of inequality*. London: Allen Lane.

Widmaier, W., Blyth, M., & Seabrooke, L. (2007). Exogenous shocks or endogenous constructions? The meanings of wars and crises. *International Studies Quarterly, 51*(4), 747–759.

World Bank. (2005). *Economic growth in the 1990s: Learning from a decade of reform*. Washington, DC: World Bank. Accessed October 5, 2018 from http://www1.worldbank.org/prem/le ssons1990s/chaps/frontmatter.pdf

Zürn, M. (2018). *A theory of global governance: Authority, legitimacy, and contestation*. Oxford: Oxford University Press.

Global Economic Governance and the Challenge of Technological Revolution

Bartłomiej E. Nowak and Artur Kluź

1 Introduction

In his "World Order," Henry Kissinger argued that new technologies have profound transformative effect on global politics. They can outdo both strategy and doctrine of foreign policy in a way that will dramatically change the nature of leadership and capacity to solve problems by humans. It will have both negative and positive consequences of which we are not even aware (Kissinger 2015). By comparison, at the down of new millennium Buzan and Little shared the view that transformative effect of technologies is visible mostly in area of human interaction, which may challenge territorial organization of politics and culture (Buzan and Little 2000). Understatement, to say the least. Kissinger later seemed to be horrified by the potential of Artificial Intelligence (AI) and human's unpreparedness to deal with it (Kissinger 2018). All in all, he was right. The technological shift is already visible in all areas of global politics. It changes the logic of power, competition, collective action, and many more.

This chapter will focus on one specific area of technological influence: namely, global economic governance. Next to security domain, here the impact is the most observable. It starts with question what influence new technologies have over the nature of global economic problems. Second, it analyzes the opportunities and risks coming from this. Third, it argues for a new more innovative approaches in global economic governance.

B. E. Nowak (✉)
Vistula University, Warsaw, Poland
e-mail: info@barteknowak.eu

A. Kluź
Centre for Technology and Global Affairs at the University of Oxford, Oxford, UK
e-mail: akluz@kluzventures.com

© Springer Nature Switzerland AG 2020   43
M. Rewizorski et al. (eds.), *The Future of Global Economic Governance*,
https://doi.org/10.1007/978-3-030-35336-0_4

2   New Technologies and Changing Global Economy

The global value chain revolution, which started at the end of twentieth century, had visibly reshaped the division of power in the world. Richard Baldwin called it "second unbundling" as the ICT allowed for offshore of know-how at almost no cost from the most developed countries of G7 toward some developing countries (Baldwin 2016) Moving ideas, data, words, or images costs almost nothing. Technology flow had become defined rather by international production networks than simply national borders. Countries who combined cheap labor force with cheap access to know-how have benefited the most. This new globalization was transformative, revolutionary, and disruptive in many areas, and within a short period of time produced "the great convergence." In his book Baldwin mentions four implications (Baldwin 2016: 144–145):

- Denationalization of comparative advantage.
- Services become a new value.
- The axis winners/losers moves deep inside the nations.
- Globalization is getting more unpredictable, uncontrollable and sudden.

This chapter argues that the next wave of technological revolution may transform the global economic order in even more complex way. Digitalization, Artificial Intelligence, and Blockchain technology together can profoundly change the old business models. International trade and finance could look very differently in decades to come. Credit Suisse research shows that due to automation an average lifespan of company listed on S&D 500 dropped from 60 years in 1950 to less than 20 years today (Sheetz 2017). Innovation becomes the key to competitiveness instead of building on low cost advantage. It will reshape strategies of both companies and nations. Organizations of global economic governance used to have problems with adjustment of their actions to fast changing reality. This problem will be even more explicit. In order to tackle it we need more, not less global cooperation.

To begin with, connectivity becomes defining factor for successful economic performance. It is both a source of wealth and disempowerment. Networks of global flows are broader and deeper than ever in the past. It follows Castells' vision of a "network society," in which he argued for an end of vertical inquiry of human activity and suggested to look at reality through the prism of horizontal setting (Castells 2010). According to McKinsey Global Institute, economies which are more connected can achieve 40% more benefits than those of less connection (McKinsey 2014). For countries, firms, and individuals it is getting more and more costly to stay aside. Knowledge-intensive flows, which include high R&D value or highly skilled labor force, are becoming increasingly dominant. They constitute half of total flows, and have gained prominence over capital and labor-intensive flows (McKinsey 2014). Delivery of data in real time drives marketing and sales decisions today. The use of Big Data and algorithms for faster and better decision-making could allow for more real-time decision-making. It will save cost, may reduce complexity of traditional process, but also result in job losses, privacy concerns, and democratic accountability problems. The issue of trust to a systems based on new technologies will be absolutely essential.

New technological breakthroughs involve artificial intelligence (AI), robotics, Internet of Things, nanotechnology, biotechnology, blockchain technology, energy storage, 3D printing, quantum computing, and more. Schwab calls it the "fourth industrial revolution" because of its speed, breadth and depth, and systemic impact (Schwab 2016: 8–9). It is shaped by fusion and interaction of different technologies that cross and overlap the physical, digital, and biological borders.

Global flows are already under extensive influence of new technologies. There are three main impacts coming from this: reduction of transaction costs, alteration of economics of production, and creation of new products or transformation of those already existing (Table 1).

Different types of new technologies will have differential impact on the nature of global economic problems. According to UNCTAD, the value of e-commerce transactions has risen from US\$16 trillion in 2013 to US\$25 trillion in 2015, i.e. 56% (UNCTAD 2017). Over the last 20 years trade in information technology products has tripled and reached US\$1.6 trillion in 2016 (WTO 2018: 5). The Internet of Things, AI, 3D printing, blockchain transform the nature of international trade: who trades, what is traded, and how it is traded. It will affect both trade in goods and services, and will have an impact on Intellectual Property Rights (IPR). They will change also traditional patterns of trade and comparative advantage in trade. Quality of digital infrastructure, regulation of IPR, data flows and privacy can become a new competitive edge. We will also observe growing importance of skills and possibly decline of labor, which is discussed later in this chapter.

Thanks to new technologies global trade could grow additional 2% annually in comparison to baseline scenario. Over the next 15 years it could amount between 31% and 34% of cumulated growth. The developing countries' share in world trade can grow from 46% today to 57% by 2030, assuming that they catch up with technological divide (WTO 2018: 11).

Artificial Intelligence can radically change our understanding of politics, economics, and social life. AI might be capable to execute any cognitive or operational task for which human intelligence is currently necessary. It can have an impact over decision-making process on economic policy: modeling complex negotiations, compliance and improving efficiency of complex international instruments, position and tactics of different actors. The AI progress within the last years was possible mainly due to three areas: step up change improvements in computing power and capacity, explosion of data, and progress in algorithms (Bughin et al. 2018: 5–6).

As regard economy, the AI will have implications mainly in three areas: productivity and output, employment, international trade and development (Cukier 2018: 29). The assessments of impact however vary extensively, up to methodology. The recent study on modeling AI effects by McKinsey estimates that in comparison to the next 5 years, AI contribution to growth may be even three/four times higher by 2030. It could contribute to economic output—approximately—US\$13 trillion and boost global GDP by 1.2% a year. It is also expected that by 2030 70% of companies will be using at least one type of AI technology, while almost half of big companies will be using full spectrum of AI (Bughin et al. 2018). In general, different studies show important potential both in terms of GDP rise, productivity, or employment cost

Table 1 Impact of new technologies on global flows

	Technology		Example	Impact of flows			
				Primary resources	Manufactured goods	Services	Data
Reducing transaction costs	Digital platforms	E-commerce	US consumer buys shoes from UK e-commerce site	–	◄	◄	◄
	Logistics technologies	Automated document processing	Paperless customs documentation	◄	◄	◄	◄
		Internet of things	IoT sensors track shipments from Brazil to Angola	◄	◄	◄	◄
		Next-gen transportation	New material enables shipping through Arctic route	◄	◄	–	–
		Autonomous vehicles	Autonomous vehicles move cargo in ports, airports, and warehouses	◄	◄	–	◄
	Data processing technologies	Blockchain	Blockchain enables automated cross-border insurance claims	–	–	◄	◄
		Cloud	An Australian company utilizes Google Cloud	–	–	◄	◄
Altering economics of production	Additive manufacturing	3D printing	3D printing of toys at home	–	►	◄	◄
			3D printing of hearing aids in Vietnam for global distribution	–	◄	–	–
	Automation	Advanced robotics	A company equips a new UK factory with robots to make appliance manufacturing viable	–	►	–	–
			Bangladesh automates textiles production, boosting productivity to gain global market share	–	◄	–	–
	Artificial Intelligence	Virtual assistants	A British retailer deploys virtual assistants for customer service calls,	–	–	►	►

		Example					
		substituting for offshore labor in a call center	–	–	–	◄	◄
Digital goods	Robotic process automation (RPA)	A Philippine company employs RPA in back office processing, reducing cost and increasing volume	–	–	▶	◄	◄
New goods	Streaming movies/music	Drake's new album is streamed a billion times globally in 1 week	▶	▶	▶	◄	◄
	Renewable energy	China increases electricity generation from renewable, reducing coal and LNG imports	–	–	–	–	–
	Electric vehicles	European consumers buy more EVs, requiring fewer imported parts and lower oil imports	▶	▶	▶	–	–
	Telemedicine	A German doctor relies on 5G to perform remote robotic surgery on a patient in Turkey	–	–	–	◄	◄

Transformation of existing products and creation of new products

Source: S. Lund, J. Manyika, J. Woetzel, J. Bughin, M. Krishnan, J. Seong, M. Muir (2019). *Globalization in Transition: The Future of Trade and Value Chains.* McKinsey Global Institute, p. 73

savings. On the other side, there is rather general agreement that AI can be very disruptive for the labor market and social stability (see Nahal and Tran 2015; Manyika et al. 2013, 2017; PwC 2017). Before it creates new jobs, the potential to destroy another is even faster.

Other interesting example is offered by the Blockchain technology, that can be applied in number of global economic governance areas: monetary policy of central banks, taxation, and tracking the corruption. Blockchain is sometimes called "trust machine" (The Economist 2015). Most of all, it allows to trace product and transactions and is highly resilient to cyberattacks. It has a great potential to become future trade infrastructure assuming that all trade procedures and finance are digitalized. Here digitalization can transform flows and reduce the marginal costs of production and distribution (The Economist 2015: 10–11) in three ways: (a) digital goods and services are created and change the nature of physical flows of goods. It allows to lower the cost of transport, access and marginal production; (b) enhancing the management and value of physical flows through "digital wrappers"; and (c) facilitation of cross-border production and exchange via digital platforms. Ganne argues that Blockchain technology can be employed in many ways to improve international trade: to substantially reduce different trade costs; make trade paperless; facilitate business-to-government and government-to-government processes at the national level and thus open new opportunities in number of WTO areas; allow to rise new generation of services; impact insurance and e-commerce areas; help administer intellectual property rights and help fighting with counterfeits; track the origin of products; enhance government procurement process; build trust and enhance the transparency of supply chains; open up new opportunities for micro-, small-, and medium-sized enterprises and small producers from developing countries (Ganne 2018).

Thanks to blockchain technology cost reduction in the financial sector and the shipping industry range between 15% and 30% while the removal of barriers is estimated on more than US$1 trillion of new trade in the next decade (Ganne 2018: xi–xii). These opportunities may only be realized if important technical issues like scalability, interoperability, and legal challenges are addressed. Additionally, International Finance Cooperation sees Blockchain role in promoting financial inclusion, which create opportunities for developing countries to leapfrog older technologies (IFC 2017). However, as with every other new technology, job losses and disruption to labor market may also be substantive.

The dominating narrative is that of a jobless world due to technological revolution. However, available studies do not confirm this very gloomy picture. For example, the OECD estimates that only 14% of jobs is under the risk of automation, which is much smaller number than those introduced by other researchers (OECD 2019). However, the situation is fast changing as there is increasingly less jobs that cannot be done by robots thanks to AI. Further 32% of jobs may look very differently than it is today. Acemoglu and Restrepo have found out that for every robot per 1000 employees in the US local communities 6.2 workers lost their jobs between 1990 and 2007 while their wages dropped by 0.7%. In the meantime other jobs were created in many other areas (Acemoglu and Restrepo 2017). In their other works they find the influence of automation and new tasks very ambiguous for the labor. Neither they support the claim for an end of human work, nor that technological change and occurrence of new tasks is favorable for labor (Acemoglu and Restrepo 2019a). The so-called "displacement effect," where automation replaces labor in tasks that it had previously performed, is counterbalanced on the other side by the reduction in the costs of production. It creates productivity effect and induces capital accumulation, new production tasks and, in consequence, new demand for labor (Acemoglu and Restrepo 2019b). The key is to find appropriate balance. It will not be easy, also due to a fact that transition to new tasks can be very disruptive and usually takes more time. No doubt, jobs will be different. Learning new skills demand also innovative institutional setting, which should be enabled by states. The contemporary states need reinvention in this mood (Micklethwait and Wooldridge 2013).

The analysis of technological impact on jobs however creates some problems as the data gathered marks yet an early stage of development in robotics. Forecasting is also very difficult as the entire impact will depend on supply of different skills, evolution of labor market institutions, demography, governmental R&D and tax policies, companies' strategies and larger economic system. Nonetheless, there are no doubts that international organizations and national authorities must take active steps in order to secure equal access to technology.

3   Technological Revolution, Competition, and Global Economic Governance

Institutions of global economic governance are clearly facing an adaptive challenge today. It demands on them to learn new ways, rethink values and attitudes, and clarify "what matters most, in what balance, with what trade-offs" (Heifetz 1999: 22). In global economy traditional boundaries between industries have completely changed. New technologies allowed to combine products and services. The digital revolution is dramatically changing the ways of collaboration between individuals, public institutions, and the private sector. It creates both important opportunities and risks. Erosion of traditional patterns of governance and power are among the most important. Fukuyama argued that the decay of political institutions is proceeded by the change of circumstances within which they exist. If they fail to adapt, the transition period to a new order could be very disturbing (Fukuyama 2014: 8).

Though institutions of global economic governance are trying to face up to this challenge, they are still at the beginning of road. Relatively the best fitted is the WTO framework, which is flexible enough to capture trade based on new technologies. The countries have also undertaken number of initiatives. For example, their *Aid for Trade* initiative is directed now to alleviate the digital divide. WTO countries decided not to impose custom duties on electronic transmissions until 2019, reduced tariffs on ICT products if a country concerned is a member of the WTO Information Technology Agreement, and within the framework of WTO Trade Facilitation Agreement inserted provisions on digital technologies. Most of the work of new technologies in trade is however done at the level of regional trade agreements. They are very different in their scope of regulation.

The United Nations convened the High Level meeting of the General Assembly on the implementation of outcomes of the World Summit on the Information Society (Geneva 2003, Tunis 2005). It called for establishment of Commission on Science and Technology for Development. It has also established Inter-agency Task Team on Science, Technology and Innovation for the Sustainable Development Goals and launched Technology Facilitation Mechanism which was the result of the Addis Ababa Action Agenda for the 2015 Third International Conference on Financing for Development. Science, Technology and Innovation also became important component of the Paris Agreement on Climate Change regarding mitigation and adaptation efforts.

Digital economy also became the subject of every G20 presidency, including separate ministerial conference (G20 2017), Digital Economy Development and Cooperation Initiative, and New Industrial Revolution Action Plan, among others. The data flows and their standardization has recently become one of the priorities of G20 Japanese presidency. Former NATO Secretary General, Anders Fogh Rasmussen is currently promoting the idea to launch the World Data Organization based on the example of the WTO (Rasmussen 2019).

The OECD member countries plus number of others have signed Ministerial Declaration on the Digital Economy, Innovation, Growth and Social Prosperity. Among others it commits them to: reduction of barriers to investment and adoption of digital technology in all sectors, development of global technical standards that enable interoperability and a secure, stable, open and accessible Internet, adoption of technologically neutral frameworks that promote competition, use of open, transparent and inclusive processes to shape global Internet governance, reduction impediments to e-commerce within and across borders (OECD 2016).

The UN Economic and Social Council underlines that "without appropriate science, technology and innovation policies, technologies, be they old or new, are unlikely to deliver progress regarding global development" (UNESC 2019). It may derail achievement of Agenda 2030 Sustainable Development Goals. The Council stresses the potential contribution of new technologies, including Big Data and machine learning to measure, monitor, and evaluate effectiveness of delivery in development policy. New technologies can improve food security, nutrition and agricultural development, promote energy access and efficiency, social inclusion, enable economic diversification, and transformation, productivity and competitiveness, confront diseases and improve health, improve access to educational learning and resources. Some of the examples of new technologies contribution to the SDG are presented in Table 2.

Table 2 Possible contribution to sustainable development goals by technology clusters

Technology cluster	Frontier technologies for the sustainable development goals until 2030	Opportunities in sustainable development goals areas
Biotech	Integrated disciplines in biotechnology of synthetic biology, systems biology and functional geonomics for applications in health (e.g., integration of "omics" applications, customized DNA sequences), industry (e.g., bio catalysis) and agriculture	Maintenance of genetic diversity of seeds, cultivated plants through utilization of genetic research (Sustainable Development Goal 2), research and development of vaccines and medicines for the treatment of communicable and noncommunicable disease (Goal 3) and cleaner energy services (Goal 7)
Digital Technologies	Internet of Things, 5G mobile phones, 3D printing, massive open online courses, data sharing technologies, emerging models for financial transactions (e.g., mobile money, digital currency exchanges, digital wallets), open science, smart agriculture and electricity grids	Manufacturing (Goal 9), resource efficiency (Goal 6 and 7), countries' extension of financial inclusion in developing countries (Goal 10) and resilient agriculture practices (Goal 2)
Nano-tech	Solar energy (nonmaterial solar cells) and organic and inorganic nanomaterials (e.g., graphene and carbon nanotubes)	Energy efficiency, increase of renewables in global energy mix (Goal 7), improvement of water quality and safe drinking water (Goal 6), medical and pharmaceutical industries (Goal 3)
Green technologies	Energy: modern cooking stoves, advances in battery technology, smart grids, solar desalination, third-generation photovoltaic (PV) (cooper, zinc, tin, sulfide, perovskite solar cells, nanomaterials such as organic solar PVs, and quantum dot solar cells), and ICT and water management	Environment, climate, biodiversity, sustainable production and consumption (Goal 7), clean air and water (Goal 6), sustainable agriculture (Goal 2)

Source: UNCTAD (2018), *Technology and Innovation Report 2018. Harnessing Frontier Technologies for Sustainable Development*, United Nations Conference on Trade and Development, Geneva, p. 4

4 Way Ahead: Adaptation of Global Governance

Nonetheless, the larger picture of global economic governance does not look so optimistic. Hale, Held and Young explain it as "gridlocked." They describe it through the so-called self-reinforcing interdependence: "existing institutions solve some problems they were initially designed to address, but also fail to address problems which have emerged from the very global economic system they have enabled" (Hale et al. 2013: 10). They mention four main factors that contributed to gridlock: growing multipolarity, institutional inertia, harder problems, and fragmentation (Hale et al. 2013: 35). Governance of new technological revolution is both a result and a cause of this situation. It was a product of globalization success and one of the factors that have also contributed to gridlock.

In an era of high-tech, government's regulation was always at least some steps behind the learning curve. Neither governments nor international governmental organizations could comprehend the rising problems. Technology went out of control before even governments attempted appropriate regulation. It would definitely need strong coordination on the global scale. However, more anarchical model, or "Balkanization"—as some call it—is becoming the global *modus operandi* for high-tech. For example, internet governance is increasingly characterized by regionalism, fragmentation. and multistakeholderism (Cogburn 2016: 252–271). There is no single institution that would manage it and the resources are mainly under private, not state control.

Governance of global economic problems in areas where new technologies have profound impact is getting even more difficult than in the past. As Slaughter has argued, policy makers have a big problem with seeing and understanding today reality. She proposes to combine the chessboard and the web perspectives into our mind-set. The first is classical embodiment of the world where states are predominant players of global politics. The web perspective is "a map not of separation, marking boundaries of sovereign power, but of connection, of the density and intensity of ties across boundaries" (Slaughter 2017: 7). In this sense international system is composed of overlapping networks, different networks to different extent, that are in constant interaction. Combination at strategic level demands that activities of both states, people, nations, and networks are taken into account in the same time. It changes the calculus of traditional strategic games. If connectivity is the key problem, then the playbook for strategies and the tools devised to implement them must also be different.

Multistakeholder approach goes beyond the traditional conception of international regimes. Transnational cooperation could potentially become more robust and solve dilemmas of global public goods delivery if it is organized by a connecting networks of coalitions and clubs. As shown by the example of climate change policy, "an interacting ecosystems of agreements, coalitions and initiatives across multiple levels of governance" may "substantially deepen international cooperation" and be more effective than a "single comprehensive regime with universal participation" (Hannam et al. 2015: 5). It may resemble the concept of polycentric governance, developed extensively by Ostrom, that is characterized by: different decision-making centers and different organizational levels of centers of power; relationship that takes place within the system of agreed rules and is persistent over time; rule of law; decentralized and legitimate systems of rules enforcement; participatory design of rules (including connection between them, transparent consequences, and order to change the rules); creation of rules should be based on incentives; openness of the system in terms of entry and exit (Aligica and Tarko 2012: 253). Polycentric governance can also be applied to larger systems, including global technological governance (Nowak 2017; Scholte 2017).

Finding new avenues for approaching new technologies is absolutely necessary. Technology speeds up transnational interdependence and thus the need for collective action (Peinhardt and Sandler 2015: 7). Thanks to new technologies international organizations could more robustly contain the effect of natural disasters, understand migration patterns, and facilitate access of vulnerable populations to development aid and financial services. In climate change policy AI may track spread of deserts, pollutants, pests, or deforestation. In global health policy it may help containing infectious diseases through tracking their spread and the transfer of know-how.

Thanks to AI delivery of global public goods has the potential to be improved, starting with appropriate analysis. The game theory can be widely applied here. It comes from the fact that different public goods demand different type of collective action. The so-called aggregation technology can trigger an important effect. It indicates the ways of how individual inputs contribute to provision of public goods thus making forecast more reliable (Peinhardt and Sandler 2015: 59–70). For example, curbing global warming needs "summation technology," i.e., the sum of individual contributions equals public good level while strategic implications are classical "prisoner's dilemma" or "chicken game." The "weakest link" technology refers only to the smallest effort that determine public good level, like in case of limiting terrorist funding or tracking the diffusion of disease. Here the strategic game would be "assurance." In case of "best shot" technology, the largest effort determines the public good level, like in case of discovering cures for disease. Here the strategic game is "coordination." Finally, in case of "threshold technology" certain good, like peacekeeping, must surpass the threshold to be effective (Barrett 2007).

Technology however poses many legal, cultural, and ethical questions. It can create both transnational public goods and bads. There are many fears of developments in AI. The most popular assumes that it will escape human control with unknown consequences or it may replace humans in many areas of their activity, which will be extremely disruptive for an entire social organization. Their risk of "digital authoritarianism—the use of AI to control society by authoritarian regimes, is growing and may result in both strengthening of authoritarian systems and in democratic retreat" (Wright 2018). China has already introduced a "Social Credit System" that intends to gather and use data from all aspects of life in order to influence and incentivize daily behavior: to reward the good ones and punish the wrong. To a lesser degree some countries may soon follow.

The AI can also cause a new tech divide between nations who have it and those who do not. Countries who are front-runners in adopting AI may easily capture new opportunities, attract new talents and technological clusters. PwC estimates that the biggest gains from AI will be in China (26% of GDP by 2030) and North America (14% respectively) (PwC 2017). China made a huge step forward in all major areas of innovation: global R&D companies, high-tech imports, quality of publications, or tertiary enrolment. It is now first or second in global rankings on R&D expenditures, number of researchers, patents and publications, and a great example for other middle-income economies (Dutta et al. 2018: XXXIII). In the world, most top-science technology clusters are placed in the USA, China, and Germany (Dutta et al. 2018: XII).

China has already pushed the race for leadership in the next industrial revolution to a new frontier. To become global leader it adopted national strategy, which identifies 10 priorities: next-generation information technology (including integrated circuits and specialized equipment, telecommunications equipment, operation systems, and industrial software), high-end numerical control tools and robotics, aerospace equipment, ocean-engineering equipment and high-tech ships, advanced railway equipment, energy savings and new energy vehicles, power equipment, agricultural machinery, new materials, biomedicine and high-performance medical devices (State Council 2015). Chinese 5G technology can also be a game changer that has potential to make currently existing technologies and fiber connections obsolete. 5G had already set the threshold for geopolitical competition between China and the USA. There is a risk that "global technology ecosystem gives way to two separate, politically divided and potentially noninteroperable technology spheres of influence" (Euroasia Group 2018), one lead by the USA, another by China. Third countries will have to choose their ally, especially taking into account that 5G becomes part of Chinese Belt and Road projects.

AI may change global economic power structures. Therefore, some already call for the access to AI to be treated as a new human right. Benioff argues that "today only a few countries and companies have access to the best AI in the world. And those who have it will be smarter, healthier, richer and of course their warfare will be significantly more advanced. (...) Those without AI will be less educated, weaker, poorer and sicker" (Butcher 2019). The digital divide both between developed and developing countries, and even within societies, is already one of the biggest obstacles for digital economy to flourish. It concerns both access to general services, e-commerce platforms, and legal frameworks. Even the most developed countries experience huge gaps in data collection. Robotics, which is well on the rise, is highly concentrated in just few countries (OECD 2017).

Inequality in the world can be speeded up by technological revolution in many policy areas: economic, financial, and environmental. For developing countries a big challenge would create re-shoring production back to advanced economies in consequence of use of new technologies. Cheap labor force, which is their key comparative advantage, would lose its competitive edge. There are big gaps between high-income economies and those less developed in all measures of innovation input and output, which will likely not diminish in the future. The lines of division clearly mark imbalances between different regions. According to *Global Innovation Index*, countries who are richer are more likely to have higher scores of innovation than the rest (Dutta et al. 2018: XXXV).

The winner-takes-all dynamic, or "the best vs. the rest," is evidently on the rise. The IMF has already found out that in most of the countries only the most dynamic, productive, and innovative firms could have risen their markups while the others did not (IMF 2019: 55–76). The OECD noted productivity boom among the top best firms, while the others have stagnated (Andrews et al. 2016). It will have profound consequences for the global system and may cause more conflicts and a sense of injustice.

5   Conclusion

Technological revolution can work for human progress. In the same time it can be very disruptive. While the old problems are solved, the new ones are created. A much more diffused global order, both in material and ideational terms, and much more competitive, can make global economic governance even harder than it is today. This is in era when we need strong international cooperation and collective action. Technology for globalization is what steroids are for a sportsman. The paradox is that politics becomes much more domestic or even local. We observe recurrence of identity and sovereignty politics.

Studying the impact of technological revolution on global governance is still in its infancy. In seeking ways beyond "gridlock" we must be very innovative and possibly fast. We should start with knowledge gaps.

References

Acemoglu, D., & Restrepo, P. (2017). *Robots and jobs: Evidence from US labor markets* (National Bureau of Economic Research Working Paper, no. 23285).

Acemoglu, D., & Restrepo, P. (2019a). *Automation and new tasks: How technology displaces and reinstates labor* (Working Paper 25684, National Bureau of Economic Research).

Acemoglu, D., & Restrepo, P. (2019b). Artificial intelligence, automation and work. In A. Agarwal, A. Goldfarb, & J. Gans (Eds.), *Economics of artificial intelligence. An agenda*. National Bureau of Economic Research 2019 (pp. 197–236).

Aligica, P. D., & Tarko, V. (2012). Polycentricity: From Polanyi to Ostrom and beyond. *Governance, 25*(2), 237–262.

Andrews, D., Criscuolo, C., & Gal, P. N. (2016). *The best versus the rest: The global productivity slowdown, divergence across firms and the role of public policy* (OECD Productivity Working Paper, No. 5).

Baldwin, R. (2016). *The great convergence. Information technology and the new globalization.* Cambridge: Belknap Press of Harvard University Press.

Barrett, S. (2007). *Why cooperate? The incentive to supply global public goods.* New York: Oxford University Press.

Bughin, J., Seong, J., Manyika, J., Chiu, M., & Joshi, R. (2018, September). *Notes from the AI frontier. Modeling the impact of AI on the world economy.* Discussion Paper, Mckinsey Global Institute.

Butcher, M. (2019). *World economic forum warns of AI's potential to worsen global inequality.* https://techcrunch.com/2019/01/23/world-economic-forum-warns-of-ais-potential-to-worsen-global-inequality/?guccounter=1&guce_referrer_us=aHR0cHM6Ly93d3cuZ29vZ2xlLnBsLw&guce_referrer_cs=QTHhjt9POWrZ61ZnhqbdyQ

Buzan, B., & Little, R. (2000). *International systems in world history. Remaking the study of international relations.* New York: Oxford University Press.

Castells, M. (2010). *The rise of the network society.* Oxford: Blackwell.

Cogburn, D. C. (2016). Cyberspace and social media. In A. Acharya (Ed.), *Why govern? Rethinking demand and progress in global governance* (pp. 252–271). Cambridge: Cambridge University Press.

Cukier, K. (2018). The economic implications of artificial intelligence. In M. L. Cummings, H. M. Roff, K. Cukier, J. Parakilas, & H. Bryce (Eds.), *Artificial intelligence and international affairs. Disruption anticipated* (pp. 29–42). London: The Royal Institute of International Affairs.

Dutta, S., Lanvin, B., & Wunsch-Vincent, S. (Eds.). (2018). *Global innovation index 2018. Energizing the world with innovation.* Geneva: Cornell SC Johnson College of Business, INSEAD, World Intellectual Property Organization.

Eurasia Group. (2018). *The geopolitics of 5G* (Eurasia Group White Paper).

Fukuyama, F. (2014). America in decay. The sources of political dysfunction. *Foreign Affairs, 93* (5), 5–26.

G20. (2017). *Shaping digitalization for an interconnected world.* G20 Digital Economy Ministerial Declaration, 6-7.04.2017.

Ganne, E. (2018). *Can blockchain revolutionize international trade?* Geneva: World Trade Organization.

Hale, T., Held, D., & Young, K. (2013). *Gridlock. Why global cooperation is failing when we need it most.* Cambridge: Polity Press.

Hannam, P. M., Vasconcelos, V. V., Levin, S. A., & Pacheco, J. M. (2015). Incomplete cooperation and co-benefits: Deepening climate cooperation with a proliferation of small agreements. *Climatic Change*, 1–15.

Heifetz, R. A. (1999). *Leadership without easy answers.* Cambridge: Harvard University Press.

IFC. (2017). *Blockchain opportunities for private enterprises in emerging markets.* Washington, DC: International Finance Corporation.

IMF. (2019). *World economic outlook.* Washington, DC: International Monetary Fund.

Kissinger, H. A. (2015). *World order.* New York: Penguin Books.

Kissinger, H. A. (2018, June). How the enlightenment ends. *The Atlantic.*

Lund, S., Manyika, J., Woetzel, J., Bughin, J., Krishnan, M., Seong, J., et al. (2019). *Globalization in transition: The future of trade and value chains.* New York: McKinsey Global Institute.

Manyika, J., Chui, M., Bughin, J., Dobbs, R., Bisson, P., & Marrs, A. (2013). *Disruptive technologies: Advances that will transform life, business, and the global economy.* New York: McKinsey Global Institute.

Manyika, J., Chui, M., Miremadi, M., Bughin, J., George, K., Willmott, P., et al. (2017). *A future that works: Automation, employment, and productivity.* New York: McKinsey Global Institute.

McKinsey Global Institute. (2014). *Global flows in a digital age: How trade, finance, people, and data connect the world economy.* San Francisco: McKinsey Global Institute.

Micklethwait, J., & Wooldridge, A. (2013). *The fourth revolution. The global race to reinvent the state.* New York: Penguin Books.

Nahal, B., & Tran, F. (2015). *Robot revolution – Global Robot and AI Primer.* Bank of America Merrill Lynch.

Nowak, B. E. (2017). A polycentric world order and the supply and demand of global public goods. *Yearbook of the Institute of East-Central Europe, 15*(4), 30–45.

OECD. (2016). *Ministerial declaration on the digital economy: Innovation, growth and social responsibility.* OECD, Cancun, 21-23.06.2016.

OECD. (2017). *OECD digital economy outlook 2017.* Paris: OECD.

OECD. (2019). *The future of work. OECD employment outlook 2019.* Paris: OECD.

Peinhardt, C., & Sandler, T. (2015). *Transnational cooperation. An issue-based approach.* New York: Oxford University Press.

PwC. (2017). *Sizing the price. What's the real value of AI for your business and how can you capitalise?* PwC.

Rasmussen, A. F. (2019). The West's dangerous lack of tech strategy. *Politico, 11*(03), 2019.

Scholte, J. A. (2017). Polycentrism and democracy in internet governance. In U. Kohl (Ed.), *The net and the nation state. Multidisciplinary perspectives on internet governance* (pp. 165–184). Cambridge: Cambridge University Press.

Schwab, K. (2016). *The fourth industrial revolution.* Geneva: World Economic Forum.

Sheetz, M. (2017). Technology killing of corporate America: Average life span of companies under 20 years. Retrieved December 16, 2019, from https://www.cnbc.com/2017/08/24/technology-killing-off-corporations-average-lifespan-of-company-under-20-years.html

Slaughter, A.-M. (2017). *The chess-board & the web. Strategies of connection in a networked world*. New Haven, CT: Yale University Press.

State Council of China. (2015). *Made in China 2025*, 19.05.2015.

The Economist. (2015). *The trust machine – The promise of the blockchain*, 31.10.2015.

UNCTAD. (2017). *Information economy report 2017. Digitalization, trade and development*. Geneva: United Nations Conference on Trade and Development.

UNCTAD. (2018). *Technology and innovation report 2018. Harnessing frontier technologies for sustainable development*. Geneva: United Nations Conference on Trade and Development.

UNESC. (2019). *The impact of rapid technological change on sustainable development. Report of the Secretary-General*. ECN.16/2019/2, 4.03.2019.

Wright, N. (2018, July 10). How artificial intelligence will reshape the global order. *Foreign Affairs*.

WTO. (2018). *World trade report 2018. The future of world trade: How digital technologies are transforming global commerce*. Geneva: World Trade Organization.

In Pursuit of Better Economic Governance: The Contribution of the G20 and BRICS

Marina Larionova

1 Introduction

The Group of 20 (G20) and the BRICS grouping of Brazil, Russia, India, China, and South Africa were born in a crowded world of international institutions in the wake of the 2008 financial and economic crisis. The G20 was intended to manage the crisis, reform international financial institutions (IFIs) (G20 Leaders 2008), and devise a new global consensus (G20 Leaders 2009a). Designated by its members as a premier forum for international economic cooperation, the G20 has become transformed into the 'hub of a global network' (Kirton 2013: 46–47) operating on the universal principles of rationality, norms building, and openness.

BRICS committed to fostering cooperation, policy coordination, and political dialogue on international economic and financial matters and also to promoting reform of international institutions to reflect changes in the world economy (BRIC Leaders 2009). Set up to tighten economic ties and promote a fair and more equitable multipolar order and system of global governance, BRICS entered its second 'golden decade' (People's Republic of China, Ministry of Foreign Affairs 2018) as a concert of rising powers rapidly institutionalising and gradually generating stronger political influence.

However, 10 years after their birth, the pursuit by the G20 and BRICS of international monetary and trade system reform has produced no fundamental change. The international community's frustration over the *impasse* in the reform of the global governance architecture is exacerbated by a rapid transition of the world to a new era of globalisation. The Fourth Industrial Revolution coupled with

M. Larionova (✉)
Centre for International Institutions Research (CIIR), Russian Presidential Academy of National Economy and Public Administration (RANEPA), Moscow, Russia

Faculty of World Economy and International Affairs, National Research University Higher School of Economics, Moscow, Russia
e-mail: larionova-mv@ranepa.ru

© Springer Nature Switzerland AG 2020
M. Rewizorski et al. (eds.), *The Future of Global Economic Governance*,
https://doi.org/10.1007/978-3-030-35336-0_5

persistent ecological constraints, the increasingly multipolar international order, and rising inequality open the way to 'Globalisation 4.0'. Whether Globalisation 4.0 will work for all depends on how corporate, local, national, and international governance structures can adapt and respond to persistent challenges of protectionism, geopolitical tensions, isolationism, and increasing imbalances between globally integrating markets and still-fragmented policymaking. What should the G20 and BRICS prioritise to help the current crisis of multilateralism, promote long-overdue global economic governance reform, and make Globalisation 4.0 work for all?

The structural disparity between the weight of emerging and developing countries in the global economy and their role in the global governance architecture has a long history. This chapter reviews the failure of global negotiations on the new international economic order in the United Nations General Assembly (UN GA). It then explores the efforts of the G20 and BRICS to reform the international institutions set up at the beginning of the Globalisation 2.0 era, focusing on the International Monetary Fund (IMF), the multilateral development banks (MDBs), and the World Trade Organization (WTO). The chapter concludes with reflections on priorities for the future agendas of the G20 and BRICS.

2   A Long Story Without a Happy Ending

The economic recession, high rates of interest, inflation and mounting deficits, the problems of liquidity and balance of payments, protectionism, and structural imbalances in the world economy required a comprehensive decision on the reform of the international monetary system as early as the beginning of the 1970s. In 1972 the growing burden of external debt exceeded $7 billion according to World Bank estimates (UN 1972). Trying to tackle the problems of debt, inflation, and the limited access of developing countries to the financial markets of developed countries, the Group of 77 (G77) put the reform of the international monetary system high on the GA's agenda. Taking account of the interests of developing countries in revising IMF quotas, ensuring greater international liquidity, and creating a link between special drawing rights (SDRs) and additional resources for financing development were issues discussed at each session of the GA (UN 1971). However, due to the principled position of the USA, reforms of the international monetary system were limited to measures within the IMF. The International Development Strategy for the Third United Nations Development Decade did postulate the need to restructure the international monetary system:

> The international monetary system should provide for the equitable and effective participation of developing countries in decision making, taking into account, inter alia, their growing role in the world economy, as well as a symmetrical and efficient adjustment process, stability of exchange rates of international currencies, and further strengthening and expansion of the special drawing rights as the central reserve asset in order to ensure better international control over the creation and equitable distribution of international liquidity. (UN 1980a: para. 26)

In the debate on the strategy, the G77 stressed that:

> a large number of reservations and interpretative declarations ... indicate not just a lack of political will on the part of many developed countries, but their real opposition to measures for restructuring the international economic system in order to ensure equity, justice and stability in world economic relations, which are unquestionably the fundamental objectives of the new international economic order. (UN 1980b: 93)

By the end of 1970s the G77 had initiated global negotiations for 'the establishment of a new system of international economic relations based on the principles of equality and mutual benefit' and a comprehensive solution to such problems as 'generalized inflation; unemployment; protectionism; the inadequacy of the financial and monetary systems, the continuing deterioration in the balance of payments and the disorder in trade in raw materials and energy' (UN 1979a). At the 34th session of the GA, the USA and its partners objected (UN 1979b: 450) and subsequently practically blocked the proposals of the G77 to consider a programme of action for further development of the international monetary system so that 'progress in this area could contribute to the establishment of the new international economic order' (UN 1979c).

Formally agreeing to the process, the USA opposed its essence:

> Regarding paragraph 2, we appreciate the strong desire of many nations to ensure that the global negotiations take place in the United Nations system and that they cover many categories of subjects. We support this general concept. But we want to make unambiguously clear that there are certain subjects that can be, and in fact must be, negotiated in their appropriate forums. International monetary issues must be negotiated in IMF; matters related to the General Agreement on Tariffs and Trade must be negotiated in GATT. We can certainly conceive of a structure that would permit the work of these forums and other active specialized forums to be part of the entire process. In this connection, we emphasize that the final phrase of paragraph 2 (a) "without prejudice to the central role of the General Assembly", does not alter the respective roles and powers of the various organizations of the United Nations system that are spelled out in their relationship agreements with the United Nations, nor does it change the recommendatory nature of United Nations General Assembly resolutions and decisions as established in the Charter. We are pleased that paragraph 3 states that global negotiations should neither interrupt nor adversely affect ongoing negotiations. It is our view, for example, that the duplication of active negotiations being held in other forms would represent such an adverse impact. (UN 1979d: 1930)[1]

Despite the political will of the G77 a constructive dialogue did not begin due to opposition from the USA and its group of 7 (G7) partners. Following the crisis in the early 1980s, which the GA assessed was the result of the disruption of the structural balance and the functioning of international relations, the GA called again for global negotiations on international cooperation. Yet at the 37th session (UN 1982a) the discussion on the launch of global negotiations was actually blocked by the USA and other G7 members taking the position that the formula adopted in the G7 Versailles Declaration should be the basis for global negotiations:

> The launching of global negotiations is a major political objective approved by all participants in the Summit. The latest draft resolution circulated by the Group of 77 is helpful, and

---

[1] From the speech of the US representative, Mr. Vanden Huevel.

the discussion at Versailles showed general acceptance of the view that it would serve as a basis for consultations with the countries concerned. We believe that there is now a good prospect for the early launching and success of the global negotiations, provided that the independence of the specialized agencies is guaranteed. (G7 1982)

The G77's objection that 'the Versailles communique, instead of facilitating the negotiations which we would have believed to be a rational and logical response, has instead created a stalemate' (UN 1982b: 2058) faced a formal US response: 'Realism requires that we recognize remaining differences on global negotiations and that we candidly discuss and try to co-operate in reconciling them' (Ibid: 2060). At the 38th session, the G7 pushed the Versailles formula as the basis for negotiations, but even after their launch, the condition of guaranteeing the independence of the specialised agencies created an insurmountable obstacle to finding comprehensive solutions to the restructuring of international economic relations, taking into account the growing role and needs of developing countries.

Thus, the three-decades-long struggle of the G77 to restructure international economic relations and establish a new world order was, in fact, initially doomed to failure. Despite efforts by the G77 to deal comprehensively with the full range of economic issues, the G7's insistence on the 1982 Versailles summit formula blocked global negotiations, defining the system's rigidity for many years to come and contributing to its failure to prevent the 1998 and 2008 crises. The twenty-first century inherited the systemic problems of the international monetary and trading systems.

3 The Old Story Revisited by the New Actors

The G20 and BRICS explicitly committed to reform the global architecture to meet the needs of the twenty-first century. Both have consistently engaged with international institutions (IOs). The IMF, the IFIs, and the WTO are the top 10 most frequently referenced IOs in the discourse of both the G20 and BRICS by the share of references. For both institutions, 2009 was the year of the highest engagement intensity[2] as the crisis activated their pursuit of a collective response (Fig. 1).

The G20 is third in BRICS discourse, confirming its support for the G20's central role in advancing the reform of the international monetary system, curbing protectionism, and improving the international environment for trade and investment (Fig. 2). In their joint statement following the second summit BRIC leaders underlined:

we welcome the fact that the G-20 was confirmed as the premier forum for international economic coordination and cooperation of all its member states. Compared to previous

---

[2]Intensity is expressed as a ratio of the number of references to the institution to the number of characters (including spaces and punctuation) in the documents as follows: $D_I = M_1/S_1$, where D_I is the intensity of references to an international institution for a given year (period), M_1 is the number of references made to this institution during the given year (period), and S_1 is the total number of characters in the documents for the given year (period). To make the findings more easily understood, D_1 is multiplied by 10,000.

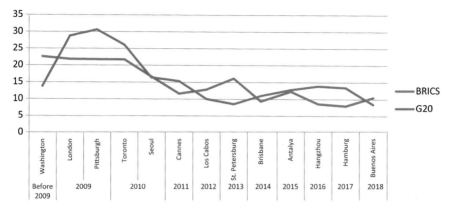

Fig. 1 Intensity of G20's and BRICS' engagement with IOs

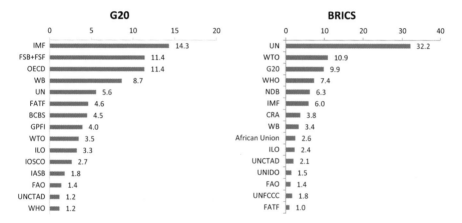

Fig. 2 Shares of the 15 most-referenced IOs in G20 and BRICS discourse

arrangements, the G-20 is broader, more inclusive, diverse, representative and effective. We call upon all its member states to undertake further efforts to implement jointly the decisions adopted at the three G-20 Summits. We advocate the need for the G-20 to be proactive and formulate a coherent strategy for the post-crisis period. We stand ready to make a joint contribution to this effort. (BRIC Leaders 2009)

What has been achieved? And where do we stand now?

4 The IMF

The G20 Washington summit set the course for enhancing IMF resources and building its capacity for surveillance. In London the leaders promised to treble the resources available to the IMF and endorsed new lending instruments to enable it to perform its critical role in promoting global financial stability and rebalancing growth. Under pressure from BRICS at their Seoul meeting, the G20 committed to a doubling of IMF members' quotas and completion by the annual meetings in 2012 of 6% shifts in quota shares to dynamic emerging markets, developing countries, and under-represented countries. The G20 and BRICS consistently applied pressure to carry out the IMF reforms agreed in 2010, urging the USA to ratify them. It took 6 years for the decision to take force. It became effective in January 2016 following the approval by the US Congress in December 2015 (United States Government, Department of the Treasury 2016). The positive outcome of this reform includes a redistribution of 2.8% of the quotas in favour of the developing countries and a 14.18% increase of BRICS' total share.

The 2010 Seoul decision to complete a comprehensive review of the IMF quota formula by January 2013 to better reflect the countries' economic weight in global trading and financial systems has not been implemented. Despite the steadfast push by the G20 and BRICS for conclusion of the IMF's 15th general review of quotas, it has been repeatedly delayed and is now expected to be achieved by the 2019 spring meetings and no later than the 2019 annual meetings.

BRICS' calls for the study of developments in the international monetary system, including the role of reserve currencies (BRIC Finance Ministers 2009a), and a 7% shift of IMF quotas in favour of emerging market and developing countries (BRIC Finance Ministers 2009b) have been futile. And though the G20 2016 chair China and its BRICS partners managed to forge an agreement to include in the G20 Hangzhou declaration a statement on support of the 'ongoing examination of the broader use of the SDR, such as broader reporting in the SDR and the issuance of SDR-denominated bonds, as a way to enhance resilience' (G20 Leaders 2016), the G20 has been silent on the issue since then. In April 2018 the IMF published a policy paper on the role the SDR could play in smoothing the functioning and stability of the international monetary system (IMS). It considered official SDR, the reserve asset administered by the IMF (O-SDR); SDR-denominated financial instruments, or 'market SDRs' (M-SDR); and the SDR as a unit of account (U-SDR). The study concluded that the O-SDR could potentially buffer external adjustment and help reduce precautionary reserve accumulation, and could provide a flexible source of finance to bolster the Fund's lending capacity, for example to respond to large-scale events. The M-SDR and U-SDR would likely make more limited contributions to systemic stability. However, the changes would require a revision of the articles of agreement (AoAs). The paper did not propose any specific reform options (IMF 2018) (Fig. 3).

5 The World Bank and the Multilateral Development Banks (MDBs)

In Washington and London the G20 leaders pledged to make available resources for social protection for the poorest countries, including 'through voluntary bilateral contributions to the World Bank's Vulnerability Framework, the Infrastructure

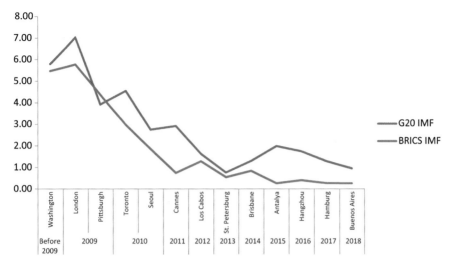

Fig. 3 Intensity of G20's and BRICS' engagement with the IMF

Crisis Facility and the Rapid Social Response Fund' (G20 Leaders 2009a: para. 25). At Pittsburgh the G20 emphasised that:

> additional resources must be joined to key institutional [the WB and MDBs] reforms to ensure effectiveness: greater coordination and a clearer division of labor; an increased commitment to transparency, accountability, and good corporate governance; an increased capacity to innovate and achieve demonstrable results; and greater attention to the needs of the poorest populations. (G20 Leaders 2009b: para. 26)

They also called for a significant increase of at least 3% of voting power for developing and transition countries in the WB (Ibid.: para. 27). In Toronto the leaders endorsed the agreement by the WB shareholders to increase the voting power of developing and transition countries by 4.59%. These decisions ensured an increase of emerging markets' and developing countries' share in the International Bank for Reconstruction and Development (IBRD) by 4.59% and a total increase of voting power to 47.19%. Their share in the International Finance Corporation (IFC) increased from 6.07% to 39.48%. The IBRD's capital expanded by $86.2 billion, and IFC capital rose by $0.2 billion.

As part of international institutional reform and the G20's contribution to development, the G20 committed at its first summits to support a substantial increase in lending of at least $100 billion by the MDBs, including to low-income countries (LICs), and to ensure that all MDBs have appropriate capital (G20 Leaders 2009a: para. 17). By the Toronto summit the G20 had delivered on the promise with a $350 billion capital increase for the MDBs (G20 Leaders 2010: para. 25) (Fig. 4).

However, the increase in the resources of the MDBs by itself is not sufficient. To avert regular systemic crisis, to secure resources for financing developing countries' current account balances, to mobilise resources for sustainable infrastructure investment, and to bridge the digital divide gap the global financial architecture and

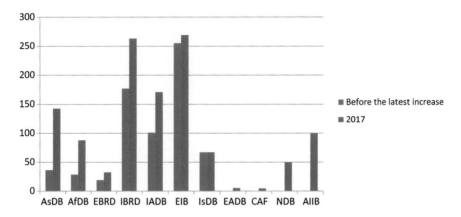

Fig. 4 MDBs' subscribed capital (USD billion). Source: Engin and Prizzon (2018)

governance of the system of international financial institutions should be reformed. The process of its transformation has been launched. At the request of the G20 the MDBs developed the Action Plan to Optimize Balance Sheets (MDBs 2015). Responding to the G20's push for joint actions to foster infrastructure investment, in 2016 the MDBs issued a Joint Declaration of Aspirations on Actions to Support Infrastructure Investment. They also launched the Global Infrastructure Connectivity Alliance to enhance the synergy and cooperation among various infrastructure connectivity programmes, with the WBG serving as a secretariat of the alliance (G20 Finance Ministers and Central Bank Governors 2016: para. 6). But these changes are very minor and incremental so far.

BRICS set up its own New Development Bank (NDB) for mobilising resources for infrastructure and sustainable development projects in BRICS and other emerging economies and developing countries. Though often viewed as an alternative to the existing system of MDBs, the NDB supplements the existing efforts of multilateral and regional development banks for global growth and development. It became fully operational in 2017 and by the end of March 2019 it had approved 30 projects in infrastructure and sustainable development with $8 billion in credit finance, had received an AA+ rating from Fitch and S&P, had become a member of the Global Infrastructure Connectivity Alliance, and had become a party to the MDBs' Joint Declaration of Aspirations on Actions to Support Infrastructure Investment. However, despite making important contributions to the global financial architecture, it has not had a catalytic influence over the international financial institutions system governance.

Thus, progress in the reform of the MDB system is tardy. The G20 and BRICS should lead the multi-stakeholder transformation process for making the system work as a system rather than a set of individual agencies, achieving a significantly higher impact for sustainable and inclusive development, enabling countries to preserve financial stability and secure the benefits of interconnected financial markets as proposed by the G20 Eminent Persons Group on Global Financial Governance (2018) (Fig. 5).

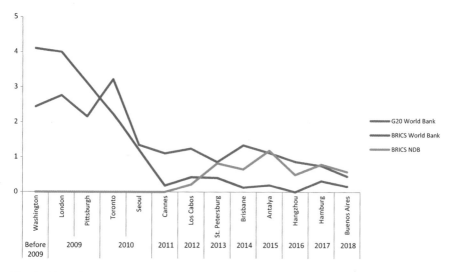

Fig. 5 WB and NDB intensity dynamics in G20 and BRICS discourse

6 The WTO

Both G20 and BRICS committed to curbing protectionism, pursuing comprehensive and balanced results of the WTO's Doha development agenda, and maintaining the stability of the multilateral trading system (BRIC Leaders 2009). In Washington G20 leaders pledged to 'strive to reach agreement this year (2008) on modalities that leads to a successful conclusion to the WTO's Doha Development Agenda with an ambitious and balanced outcome' (G20 Leaders 2008). While the G20's catalyst push for a successful outcome at the WTO ministerial conference (MC9) on trade facilitation in Bali in December 2013 can be perceived as a contribution to the Trade Facilitation Agreement, progress on the other tracks is modest. The WTO is weakened by trade tensions, a successful conclusion to the Doha development round is elusive, and the strengthening of the WTO dispute settlement system and crisis resolution in its appellate body seems unattainable. Monitoring reports by the WTO, the United Nations Conference on Trade and Development (UNCTAD), and the Organisation for Economic Co-operation and Development (OECD) which were mandated at the G20 London summit show a continuous rise in the number of trade-restrictive measures. From 2008 to 2018, G20 members introduced 1750 restrictive measures, with 565 liberalising measures undertaken over the 2012–2018 period (Fig. 6).

The Trump administration's assault on the multilateral trade system brought changes to the G20's collective stance on international trade. Though at their 2017 Hamburg summit the G20 pledged to continue to fight protectionism, including all unfair trade practices, they also recognised the role of legitimate trade defence instruments, asking the OECD, WTO, World Bank Group, and IMF to monitor trade policies and assess their impacts on growth (G20 Leaders 2017: 12). On the positive side is a

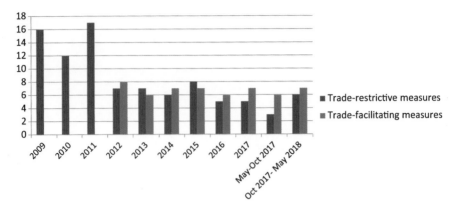

Fig. 6 Number of restrictive and liberalising measures taken by the G20 (an average per month in 2009–2018). Note: Data on liberalising measures are available since 2012. Source: WTO (2018)

relatively high level of compliance (78%) with the G20 Hamburg commitment to keep markets open given 'the importance of reciprocal and mutually advantageous trade and investment frameworks and the principle of non-discrimination, and continue to fight protectionism including all unfair trade practices'. BRICS' compliance with their Xiamen pledge for standstill and rollback of protectionist measures, which reiterated BRICS' earlier commitments to fight protectionism, was also high.

Amid rising tensions in the multilateral trading system at the Johannesburg summit, BRICS leaders reaffirmed the commitment to strengthen the WTO and urged all WTO members to engage constructively to address the *impasse* in the appellate body and develop the legal framework of multilateral trade within the WTO (BRICS Leaders 2018). Despite a tough struggle within the G20, in Buenos Aires the leaders stated support of the necessary reform of the WTO to improve its functioning and agreed to review progress at the next summit.

Though the catalytic efforts of the G20 and BRICS have failed so far, the WTO remains central to the G20 and BRICS trade agenda. The WTO comes second in BRICS discourse by the share of references and intensity (10.9% and 1.16%) and ninth in G20 discourse with a 3.49% share of references and intensity of 0.45. Expectations for progress on the G20 Buenos Aires commitment are very modest, but the thrust for reform should not be weakened (Fig. 7).

7 Conclusion

The G20 and BRICS have been exerting catalytic influence—stimulating, endorsing, compelling, and supporting reform of the IMF, the MDB, and the WTO. However, their pursuit of the reform of international monetary and trade systems has not brought fundamental changes. The causes of the structural disparity between the weight of emerging and developing countries in the global economy and their role in global

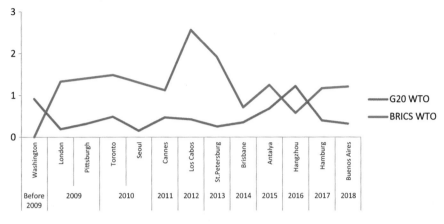

Fig. 7 WTO intensity dynamics in G20 and BRICS discourse

governance architecture are rooted in the foundation of the western-centric international institutions system. As the past 10 years have shown, the G20 alone cannot ensure its transformation into a truly multilateral system given the G7's influence in the G20. BRICS supports the G20's central role in advancing IMS reform, curbing protectionism, and improving the international environment for trade and investment. But BRICS should consolidate coordination within the G20 and beyond. Otherwise the international community faces the risk of repeating the failure of global negotiations for restructuring the international economic system initiated in the late 1970s by the G77 and stifled by the G7. BRICS should consolidate its strategy of combining catalytic influence on IOs and setting up its own institutions, especially in those spheres where the gap between increasing multipolarity in international relations and persistent unilateralism in the system of governance is widening.

Consolidation of efforts to reform financial institutions should be supplemented by building up the resources and competencies of the NDB, transitioning the contingency reserve arrangement into the BRICS Monetary Fund, increasing resources, decoupling loans from the IMF programme, developing surveillance capacities, and fostering closer cooperation between BRICS' central banks. Efforts to strengthen the multilateral trading system should be augmented by negotiations on a BRICS trade and investment agreement open to other countries. Strategically important is that the new institutions should be collectively owned and open to other participants, with an international agenda targeted at creating global public goods. These processes are long term and complex, but they will demonstrate BRICS' capability for political leadership and capacity to contribute to global governance development. The new institutions—the established IOs, BRICS, and the G20—should step up concerted efforts to create a global governance system which reflects the new economic and technological realities, responds effectively to persistent challenges and new risks, and creates conditions for a balanced and inclusive growth.

References

BRIC Finance Ministers. (2009a, 14 March). *Joint communiqué*. Horsham. Retrieved April 1, 2019, from https://www.ranepa.ru/images/media/brics/ruspresidency1/finance%202009%201.pdf

BRIC Finance Ministers. (2009b, 4 September). *Communiqué*. London. Retrieved April 1, 2019, from https://www.ranepa.ru/images/media/brics/ruspresidency1/finance%202009.pdf

BRIC Leaders. (2009, 16 June). *Joint statement*. Yekaterinburg. Retrieved April 1, 2019, from http://www.ranepa.ru/images/media/brics/ruspresidency1/First%20Summit.pdf

BRICS Leaders. (2018, July). *Johannesburg declaration*. Johannesburg, 25–27. Retrieved April 1, 2019, from https://www.ranepa.ru/images/media/brics/sapresidency2/JOHANNESBURG_DECLARATION.pdf

Engin, L., & Prizzon, A. (2018). *A guide to multilateral development banks*. Overseas Development Institute. Retrieved April 1, 2019, from https://www.odi.org/sites/odi.org.uk/files/resource-documents/12274.pdf

G20 Eminent Persons Group on Global Financial Governance. (2018, October). *Report of the G20 Eminent Persons Group on Global Financial Governance*. Retrieved April 1, 2019, from https://www.globalfinancialgovernance.org/report-of-the-g20-epg-on-gfg/

G20 Finance Ministers and Central Bank Governors. (2016, July). *Communiqué*. Chengdu, 23–24. Retrieved April 1, 2019, from https://www.ranepa.ru/images/media/g20/2016Hangzhou/Communiqué%20G20%20Finance%20Ministers%20and%20Central%20Bank%20Governors%20Meeting%20July%202016.pdf

G20 Leaders. (2008, 15 November). *Declaration of the summit on financial markets and the world economy*. Washington DC. Retrieved April 1, 2019, from http://www.ranepa.ru/images/media/g20/2008washington/Declaration%20of%20the%20Summit%20on%20Financial%20Markets.pdf

G20 Leaders. (2009a, 2 April). *Global plan for recovery and reform. Statement issued by the G20 leaders*. London. Retrieved April 1, 2019, from http://www.g20.utoronto.ca/2009/2009communique0402.html

G20 Leaders. (2009b, September). *Leaders' statement*. Pittsburgh, 24–25. Retrieved April 1, 2019, from https://www.ranepa.ru/images/media/g20/2009pittsburgh/G20%20Leaders%20Statement.pdf

G20 Leaders. (2010, 27 June). *Summit declaration*. Toronto. Retrieved April 1, 2019, from https://www.ranepa.ru/images/media/g20/2010toronto/g20_declaration_en.pdf

G20 Leaders. (2016, 5 September). *Communiqué*. Hangzhou. Retrieved April 1, 2019, from https://www.ranepa.ru/images/media/g20/2016Hangzhou/G20%20Leaders%E2%80%99%20Communique%20Hangzhou%20Summit.pdf

G20 Leaders. (2017, July). *Declaration*. Hamburg, 7–8. Retrieved April 1, 2019, from http://www.ranepa.ru/images/media/g20/2017hamburg/G20%20Hamburg%20leaders_%20communiqu%C3%A9.pdf

Group of 7 (G7). (1982, June). *Declaration of the seven heads of state and government and representatives of the European Communities*. Versailles, 4–6. Retrieved April 1, 2019, from http://www.g8.utoronto.ca/summit/1982versailles/communique.html

International Monetary Fund (IMF). (2018, April). *Considerations on the role of the SDR*. IMF Policy Paper. Retrieved April 1, 2019, from https://www.imf.org/en/Publications/PolicyPapers/Issues/2018/04/11/pp030618consideration-of-the-role-the-sdr

Kirton, J. J. (2013). *G20 Governance for a globalized world*. Farnham: Ashgate.

Multilateral Development Banks (MDBs). (2015). *Multilateral Development Banks action plan to optimize balance sheets*. Retrieved April 1, 2019, from https://www.ranepa.ru/images/media/g20/2015Antalya/Note-on-Action-Plan- for-MDB-Balance-Sheet-Optimization.pdf

People's Republic of China, Ministry of Foreign Affairs. (2018, 26 July). *Full text of Chinese president's speech at plenary session of BRICS Johannesburg summit*. Johannesburg. Retrieved April 1, 2019, from http://www.fmprc.gov.cn/mfa_eng/zxxx_662805/t1580849.shtml

United Nations General Assembly. (1971). *The increasing burden of debt services.* /A/RES/2807/ (XXVI). Retrieved April 1, 2019, from https://undocs.org/en/A/RES/2807(XXVI)

United Nations General Assembly. (1972). *External debt servicing by the developing countries.* /A/ RES/3039(XXVII). Retrieved April 1, 2019, from https://undocs.org/en/A/RES/3039(XXVII)

United Nations General Assembly. (1979a). *Global negotiations relating to international economic co-operation for development.* /A/RES/34/138. Retrieved April 1, 2019, from https://undocs. org/en/A/RES/34/138

United Nations General Assembly. (1979b). Proposals for the new international development strategy. /A/RES/34/211. Retrieved April 1, 2019, from https://undocs.org/en/A/RES/34/211

United Nations General Assembly. (1979c). *International monetary reform.* /A/RES/34/216. Retrieved April 1, 2019, from https://undocs.org/en/A/RES/34/216

United Nations General Assembly. (1979d). *Official records of the General Assembly, thirty-fourth session.* Retrieved April 1, 2019, from https://undocs.org/en/A/34/PV.104

United Nations General Assembly. (1980a). *International development strategy for the third United Nations (UN) development decade.* /A/RES/35/56. Retrieved April 1, 2019, from https://undocs. org/en/A/RES/35/56

United Nations General Assembly. (1980b). Official records of the General Assembly, thirty-fifth session. Retrieved April 1, 2019, from https://undocs.org/en/A/35/PV.84

United Nations General Assembly. (1982a). *Launching of global negotiations on International Economic Cooperation for Development.* Resolution A/37/Add.1 adopted on September 19, 1983.

United Nations General Assembly. (1982b). *Official records of the General Assembly, thirty-seventh session.* Retrieved April 1, 2019, from https://undocs.org/en/A/37/PV.122

United States Government, Department of the Treasury. (2016, 15 April). Remarks by Treasury secretary Jacob J. *Lew at IMF-World Bank Spring meetings.* Washington. Retrieved April 1, 2019, from https://www.treasury.gov/press-center/press-releases/Pages/jl0427.aspx

World Trade Organization (WTO). (2018, 4 July). *Report on G20 trade measures.* Retrieved April 1, 2019, from https://www.wto.org/english/news_e/news18_e/g20_wto_report_july18_e.pdf

Multilateralism in Peril? Murky Protectionism and the Populist Backlash Against Globalisation

Marek Rewizorski

1 Introduction

Since the mid-1990s the World Trade Organisation (WTO) has been the headquarters of the multilateral trade system, which resembles a fortress besieged by numerous enemies. Discriminatory liberalisation of trade, protectionism and populism—the latter tinged by more or less imaginary threats to national security and programmes of economic revival in the neo-mercantile vein—have formed a three-pronged alliance. This alliance is gaining strength as trade multilateralism is crumbling, and attracting all those disappointed with the outcome of trade negotiations, including the activists of non-governmental organisations, entrepreneurs whose businesses are included in Global Value Chains (GVCs) and also politicians elected in their respective national election cycles. Awaiting a rescue, the Directors-General of the WTO have been unwaveringly reassuring those who are losing hope that every successive ministerial meeting, whether it is held in Geneva (2008), Bali (2013), Nairobi (2015) or Buenos Aires (2017), is the 'moment of truth' and the 'to be or not to be' of the global trading system. However, it transpires even from the conclusions of these ministerial conferences that more and more WTO members are not concealing their doubts about whether the goals of multilateral negotiations are achievable. WTO members are rejecting the 'single undertaking principle' (nothing is agreed unless everything is agreed) (Wolfe 2009) and opting for a *WTO à la carte* (allowing them to focus on selected issues during negotiations), or for a *menu de jour*, whereby groups or clubs of states enter into preferential trade agreements or plurilateral agreements (Hoekman and Mavroidis 2015). Both these forms of discriminatory liberalisation of trade allow

This chapter is part of the 'Global Economic Governance—Actors, Areas of Influence, Interactions' research project (OPUS, 2016/23/B/HS5/00118) funded by the National Science Centre, Poland.

M. Rewizorski (✉)
Institute of Political Science, University of Gdańsk, Gdańsk, Poland

© Springer Nature Switzerland AG 2020
M. Rewizorski et al. (eds.), *The Future of Global Economic Governance*,
https://doi.org/10.1007/978-3-030-35336-0_6

them to overcome gridlocks in trade negotiations, but they also support the trend of bilateralisation and regionalisation of modern trade relations, departing from the multilateral trade system promoted by the WTO.

The proliferation of preferential trade agreements is additionally related to the increasing importance of emerging economies in the global trade system, with China at the helm. This geoeconomic phenomenon poses an enormous challenge for the WTO and multilateral trade system. Mark Wu, an expert on trade from Harvard University, is of the opinion that the expansion of 'China Inc.', understood as China's economy, which transcends the model of state capitalism (Wu 2016), or as the unique organisation of the Chinese economy (Powell 2016), has become the root cause of misunderstandings between China and its trading partners. While the WTO's system of dispute resolution has helped to alleviate tensions related to the spread of preferential trade agreements and has reduced the destructive influence that different groups of interests have on the deteriorating trade relations between Beijing and Washington, the system has a limited capacity. This has been taken advantage of by populist leaders with an anti-liberal agenda, and by those who are active supporters of trade liberalisation. They treat mega-regional trade agreements, which the US economist Jagdish Bhagwati has dubbed as 'termites' responsible for the erosion of the global trade system (Bhagwati 2008), as a means to overcome the limitations imposed by the WTO system, the exclusion of China from trade nego-tiations aiming to liberalise trade, and an attempt at correcting the mistake of having admitted China to the WTO without indicating its foreign currency rate policy, thereby providing China's economy with a powerful instrument to build its trade power (Wróbel 2015: 288).

The analysis presented in this study, however, does not concern the challenges that the global system of economic governance is facing due to the increasing importance of China in international trade, nor the relatively weakened position of Washington which was outpaced in 2013 by Beijing as the champion of international trade. Instead, the main purpose is to examine the character of two phenomena that may impact upon the global trade system members' faith in the value of maintaining this system. The phenomena concerned are post-crisis, murky protectionism on the one hand, and populism on the other, both of which undermine and subvert the tenets of multilateralism. The first section of this chapter analyses murky protectionism as a challenge for trade multilateralism. The empirical–analytical review of structural and non-cyclical factors which result in the deceleration of trade is based on the statistics provided by the *Global Trade Alert* database and content analysis of documents, complemented by the studies by Simon J. Evenett, Johannes Fritz and Bernard Hoekman, among others. The second section is dedicated to populism and enhances conventional economic analysis by including subjects from political science and psychology, in particular those related to questions about the importance of the redistribution of benefits from international trade and the character of this trade (When can we talk about fair trade? How is fair trade perceived?). This section also provides an opportunity to seek answers to the questions of why international trade is becoming such a sensitive and important political matter, and why populists have made free trade the main reason for political opposition to globalisation. The chapter is concluded with general observations and the call for further research to be carried out.

2 In a Maelstrom of Protectionism

Protectionism is one of the most significant challenges that the global system of trade governance has faced in the times of the gravest financial crisis since the 1930s. Although international trade has visibly slowed down since 2008, as demonstrated by a nosedive in the value of global exports (exceeding 22% in 2009), and shrinking international trade in 2015 (a drop of 14% compared to 2009), WTO members have not decided to implement any instruments that would radically increase import tariffs, as occurred in 1930 when the Smoot–Hawley Tariff Act was passed. That was most likely the source of the optimism demonstrated by the WTO Director-General Roberto Azevêdo, who said in 2017 that the multilateral trading system 'was constructed as the world's response to the chaos of the 1930s, when rising protectionism wiped out two thirds of global trade', and that 'in the 2008 crisis the system was put to the test, and it passed. We did not see a significant rise in protectionism' (Azevêdo 2017). His statement can be viewed as a typical expression of content with the continued operation of the multilateral trading system from the transnational elite, as well as a manifestation of the WTO's limited efficiency in monitoring post-crisis trade distortions, described as murky protectionism. In the opinion of some economists, this form of protectionism—whose virulence for the global trading system is difficult to measure—is one of the structural and non-cyclical factors (and thus one which is not directly related to the current macroeconomic situation) which have resulted in the deceleration of trade and undermined people's trust in the non-discriminatory system of trade liberalisation (Wojtas 2015; 2017). According to Simon J. Evenett and Johannes Fritz, who used the *Global Trade Alert* (GTA) database, diverse forms of murky protectionism are not so much about setting import tariffs, applying protection clauses and trading protection ensured by dispute settlement mechanisms but rather about foreign trade practices, such as subsidising exports, setting quotas, non-automatic import licencing, public procurement, price control and finance measures, environmental, sanitary and phytosanitary measures and many other instruments that are difficult to clearly classify (Evenett and Fritz 2017). Murky protectionism can therefore be defined as a set of measures which do not necessarily breach the obligations of the WTO's trading regime but nevertheless abuse the freedom of applying such measures as financial aid packages, sanitary and phytosanitary regulations, and even labour standards, which may be harmful to trading partners and their employees (Baldwin and Evenett 2009: 5; Cernat and Madsen 2011).

Successive GTA reports have revealed that, since 2008, individual states have increasingly resorted to employing murky protectionism measures, first and foremost state aid, trade defence and import tariffs (see Fig. 1). Over the following 5 years (2011–2016), merchandise trade increased by no more than 3% annually,

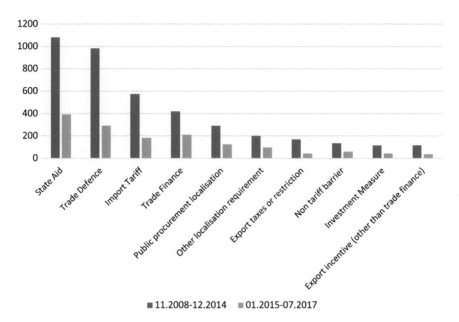

Fig. 1 Ten measures of murky protectionism most frequently implemented by the G20 as the 'trading weapon of mass destruction' 2008–2017. Source: Global Trade Alert, 2009–2017, https:// www.globaltradealert.org/reports, retrieved on 20 Sept 2018

which was a regression compared to the period preceding the global financial crisis, when the volume of merchandise trade went up by c. 7% per annum (1987–2007). Protectionist measures were primarily employed in sectors that are traditionally considered sensitive, in particular steel, mechanical and chemical industries, transport, energy and electricity and agriculture (see Fig. 2).

Even though Roberto Azevêdo tried to convince those in doubt that it was possible to maintain, or even accelerate, the pace of growth of world merchandise trade which in 2017 was the strongest since 2011 at 4.7%, and was forecast by the WTO to increase to ca. 5%, mainly as a result of increased investment and consumption expenditure (WTO 2018a), the threat produced by protectionist measures remains considerable. It may dramatically impede international trade in the medium term. Global demand is a relatively weak engine of growth, which is a legacy of the crisis in developed countries, deteriorating conditions for merchandise exporters and the decelerating pace of the economic growth in China, among other things. Contrary to the WTO's conviction that '[w]orld merchandise trade growth is expected to remain strong in 2018 and 2019 [. . .], but continued expansion depends on robust global economic growth and governments pursuing appropriate monetary, fiscal and especially trade policies' (WTO 2018b), the prospects are not optimistic.

The issue of a global trade slowdown in the aftermath of the crisis is addressed, inter alia, by the renowned expert in trade Bernard Hoekman, who asks a provocative question of whether the global slowdown is a 'new normal' (Hoekman 2015:

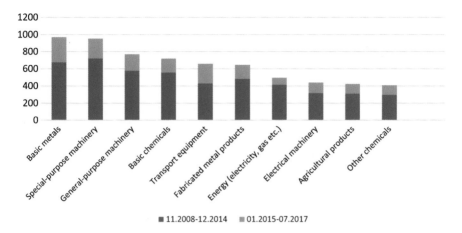

Fig. 2 Ten industries in G20 countries where protectionist measures (interventions) occurred on at least 400 occasions between November 2008 and July 2017. Source: Global Trade Alert, 2009–2017, https://www.globaltradealert.org/reports, retrieved on 20 Sept 2018

9–12). Looking for its reasons, Hoekman stresses the importance of the above-mentioned structural factors which, in the long run, may reduce global income trade elasticity. Alongside protectionism, expressed by excessive government support for domestic industry and by discouraging businesses and households from purchasing goods and services from foreign suppliers (e.g. Donald Trump's 'Buy American'), Hoekman, the above-mentioned Simon J. Evenett and Johannes Fritz, as well as Douglas Irwin, Cristina Constantinescu, Aaditya Mattoo and Michele Ruta, all point to the importance of transformations that have taken place in the structure of international trade, opting for investment goods and fixed assets (which depend on demand and the broader condition of the economy to a much larger extent than consumption goods). Hoekman also emphasises the slowing down of global value chains, within which businesses fragment their manufacturing internationally, and stresses the importance of the Chinese government's strategy aiming at achieving a sustainable economy. This is done by increasing the national absorption of capital while curbing economic growth based on developing exports.

Pessimism about the medium- and long-term development prospects of world merchandise trade is further augmented by the occurrences of hidden forms of protectionism and disappointment with the outcomes of multilateral trade negotiations. As demonstrated by the WTO ministerial conference in Buenos Aires (2017), such negotiations did not even result in an agreement (Hannah et al. 2018). The data collected by Evenett and Fritz for 2009–2018 makes it possible to put forward the hypothesis that a protectionist spiral exists, whereby various forms of murky protectionism replace traditional instruments of foreign trade policy. In 2009–2018, the G20 countries, which account for 86% of the global economy, 78% of global trade and two-thirds of the population, recorded ca. 800 interventions resulting in trade distortion (Evenett and Fritz 2017). These can hardly be avoided for political reasons, although they are expensive as they reduce the benefits generated by the

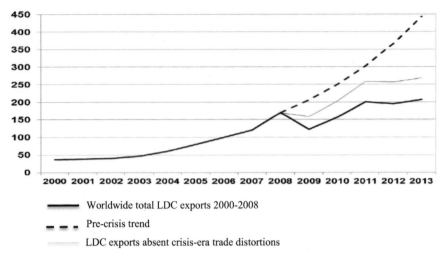

Fig. 3 Trade distortions reduced total LDCs' export growth by 5,5% per annum ($ billions, years). Source: Estimates based on Evenett and Fritz (2015) and the COMTRADE data

exchange of goods. Such measures are a political price that needs to be paid to enable the 'open trading system' to continue operating, although this narrative is contented by right- and left-wing anti-establishment movements alike. The price is steep and is paid primarily by the least developed countries (LDCs), as evidenced by the results of studies published by Evenett and Fritz in 2015. On the basis of statistics in the GTA database, the two scholars identified murky protectionism, which distorts trading streams, as the root cause of the dramatic decrease in economic growth, and consequent drop in employment, pay cuts and the 'vanishing' chances of individuals and families in underdeveloped countries, which rely heavily on exports of strategic merchandise, to be lifted from poverty. Compared to 2000–2008, a record-breaking period in terms of the growth of the LDCs' exports (spiking at 20.6% annually), 2009–2013 saw externally rooted distortions of their exports which brought their average annual growth down to 5.7% (Evenett and Fritz 2015: 275). The LDCs' exports dropped by 31.5% in 2009–2013. These econometric evaluations by Evenett and Fritz, which are actually the only source of knowledge about the extent of the harm murky protectionism has inflicted on the poorest countries, made it possible to find that the most adverse impact on the LDCs' exports in 2009–2013 was exercised by such measures of murky protectionism as state aid (15%) and export taxes or restrictions (14%). Together with a traditional protectionist instruments of increasing tariffs (21%), we find three policy instruments accounting for 50% of damages to commercial interests of the LDCs in the period concerned (Evenett and Fritz 2015: 270).

Estimates in Fig. 3 demonstrate that, if it had not been for the foreign trade distortions, LDCs' exports would have grown by 11.2% per annum. Although the WTO Director-General Roberto Azevêdo argued that 'in the 2008 crisis the system was put to the test, and it passed. We did not see a significant rise in protectionism'

(Azevêdo 2017), the GTA estimates make this test look rather superficial. Both G20 countries and the LDCs witnessed considerable slowdowns in economic growth, exports were limited, and problems were generated by protectionist measures which appear to be immune to trade remedies (understood as all available types of response aimed to eliminate practices which are detrimental to the benefits generated by WTO agreements). The problem is that murky protectionism measures frequently are not so much about inserting inconspicuous regulations into respective national taxation systems, but rather they are manifested by individual government's inclinations to substitute transparent trade protection measures with ambiguous regulations which restrict the redistribution of profits generated by economic globalisation, and even strengthen populist leaders who use the language of contempt and exclusion and 'pass blame to enemies' in public discourse.

3   Populism *ante portas*

The second challenge faced by the global system of trade governance after 2008 is the growing anti-market, antiglobalisation and anti-establishment sentiments which fuel social movements or even political parties, described as 'populism'. Adopting an aggregated definition of populism as 'a form of political thinking, or policy which refers to social fears and resentment, and pertains to such social movements whose leaders seek popularity among the public in order to manipulate people and lead them towards nebulous albeit attractively formulated goals' (Marczewska-Rytko 1995: 16; Olszyk 2007: 237), it should be noted that populism is widespread in many countries at different levels of social, political and economic development. We are not talking here only about the breeding grounds of populism, such as South American countries where anti-establishment movements date back to the 1930s. Modern populism is characterised by its criticism of closer international political integration (the UK), opposition to the regulations of the economic and monetary union of the EU (Greece, Spain and Portugal), a programmatic fight against the intellectual elite and a negative attitude to migrants who are considered a threat to national security (Hungary and Poland), anti-trade nativism (the USA), and economic populism (numerous Latin American countries), to name just a few. What diverse populist movements share is their anti-establishment attitude, claiming their right to speak on behalf of 'the people' against elites, their opposition to the liberal market economy and against globalisation as a set of institutions and processes that allegedly destroy labour markets, and finally (although not universally) a penchant for authoritarian governance.

It may appear surprising to examine relations between populism and international trade, since the liberalisation of trade and protectionism are not the only two influences in labour markets. The position of employees is the outcome of serious supply shocks, technological change, and increasing competition, alongside the pursuit of higher efficiency and the race to the bottom in labour standards. All these result in the mobility of employees (or maybe 'modern nomads') between labour markets to a much larger extent than even imports of goods, services and the inflow of foreign labour. This has been noted by many scholars who have focused on the issues of falling employment and the salaries of medium-qualified employees caused by labour outsourcing (Acemoglu 1998; Acemoglu and Autor 2011; Autor and Dorn 2013). Other researchers have undertaken to explain the polarisation of North American (Katz and Margo 2013) and European (Goos et al. 2010) labour markets, while focusing on the role of technology, globalisation and institutions. Of particular interest in this respect are the findings by Lawrence F. Katz and Robert A. Margo, who have discussed the historical aspects of technological transformations and the demand for skilled labourers. Having examined statistics from the late nineteenth century, they found that the majority of technological changes which had occurred in manufacturing processes since the nineteenth century were related to the development of 'special purpose, sequentially implemented' machinery. The machines were 'special purpose' because they were designed to accomplish specific production tasks that had previously been performed by artisans. The second feature, being 'sequentially implemented', meant that successive manufacturing tasks were performed by one machine after another, each performing strictly defined tasks in an orderly process, or sequence. Over time, sequentially implemented special purpose machines became much cheaper than skilled labour. As a result, manufacturing process became much more capital intensive, which gradually replaced the labour factor (Katz and Margo 2013). To summarise, since the 1980s, a majority of studies that address the relationship between automation and globalisation emphasise the influence that especially the former has had on falling employment in industry. Since the global financial crash, the interrelations between the outcomes of economic globalisation and the frequently dramatic transformations in national labour markets have been increasingly stressed. A study by Hicks and Devtaj (2017) can serve as an example. The authors estimate that 13% of jobs in the North American industrial sector were liquidated in 2000–2010 due to increased imports. Autor et al. (2016) in turn attribute the 10% drop in employment in US industrial plants in 1991–2011 to the 'import shock' triggered by excessive competition from imports from China. These researchers estimate that, over the period in question, import shock directly caused the liquidation of 2–2.4 million jobs in US industrial plants. Interestingly, the adverse impact of trade globalisation on employment prospects is the leitmotiv of both leftist and right-wing populists who, at the same time, typically do not campaign against technological transformation and workers being replaced by automated manufacturing. This is the key issue of this part of the chapter—namely, what makes international trade such a sensitive and important political matter, and why populists have made free trade the main reason for political opposition to globalisation.

It seems hardly satisfactory to look for answers in conventional economic analyses based on the tenets of trade theory, such as the Stolper–Samuelson theorem (which is limited to only two goods and two factors of production) (Rodrik 2018). This quest should therefore be extended to include matters brought to public debate by scholars representing the social sciences, in particular by social psychologists, political scientists and sociologists. Extending the debate to include the issues of the redistribution of profits from international trade (and by the same token from economic globalisation), the character of this trade (When can we talk about fair trade? How is fair trade perceived?) and protection from 'import shocks' and trade agreements evolving towards what is called 'deep integration' becomes essential in the context of the dual nature of populism, which to a certain extent is an outcome of the interaction between the demand and supply factors. 'Demand populism' is generated by the inadequate redistribution of benefits from economic globalisation which results in increased support for social movements that are outside the political mainstream and contest the rules of the political game in a given country. Being a by-product of globalisation, demand populism is driven by insecurity caused by increasing precarisation, dissatisfaction, the delegitimisation of political institutions and growing concerns about fair play in the market. With regard to the above-quoted definition of populism, its demand-related aspect is used by the leaders of social movements who set vague objectives which are detached from the instruments and strategies of their implementation. The fact that political decision makers fail to address accusations thrown at them by populist movements is in turn important for 'supply populism', which aims to create narratives whereby discontented people concentrate around key issues, concerns and anxieties. These narratives are presented as stemming from disregarded needs, and neglected demand for benefits that result, for instance, from the global trade system. They strongly resonate with the public when populist leaders give the reasons for the lack of economic security, falling income and unemployment, and pointing to who should be blamed.

One of the main 'perpetrators' is unjust international trade, confined within the a global system shaped by rivalry between the values, ideals and material interests of the electorate on the one hand and the preferences of lobbying groups, who have access to decision makers with a direct influence on wealth distribution, on the other. Helen Milner (1997) painted a highly intuitive yet accurate picture of this. Pondering who the true beneficiary of economic globalisation in individual countries is (*cui bono?*), Milner said that 'cooperation among nations is affected less by fears of other countries' relative gains or cheating than it is by the domestic distributional consequences of cooperative endeavours. Cooperative agreements create winners and losers domestically; therefore they generate supporters and opponents' (Milner 1997: 9).

The opponents of cooperative agreements (and of deep trade integration), who join the ranks of populist movements in great numbers, intuitively point to international trade as a politically sensitive issue. As a result, they choose international trade as the target of their attacks. This is the mechanism of finding a 'scapegoat', which is employed with delight by populist leaders who readily blame all economic mishaps on the 'foreigners': the Chinese who generate the 'import shock', Germans who export unemployment to neighbouring countries where they establish their assembly plants and chain stores, or Mexicans who take jobs away from Americans under the NAFTA agreement. This quite obvious explanation conceals another, much less clear one, which is related to the problem of the redistribution of benefits generated by international trade, which apparently raises much more emotions than the challenges related to the above-mentioned technological transformation, including automated manufacturing. The problem here is that sometimes international trade involves forms of competition which are banned at the national level (what the US philosopher Michael Walzer termed 'blocked exchanges', cf. Walzer 1983), because they violate employment standards (social dumping), environmental protection agreements (use of substances that damage the ozone layer), or the rules of social order. Pursuing projects which are deemed to be prohibited by law or stigmatised in the area of trade emphasises its political nature, which is associated with the difficult matters of distributive justice that political decision makers need to resolve. What is meant here in the broad sense is justice, defined as fair and comparable distribution of both economic and non-economic benefits among beneficiaries (Cohen and Greenberg 1982). The purpose of economic benefits is to improve the financial well-being of their recipients, while non-economic benefits refer to improved working conditions and access to social benefits (Deutsch 1985). For the most part, the allocation of benefits is based on the equality principle (Leung and Bond 1982; Leung and Bond 1984). Benefits are allocated primarily in relation to results achieved by a group rather than individual achievements (Sampson 1975).

What triggers social dissatisfaction and fuels populism, however, is not inequality as such but unfairness, which is often mistaken for inequality. A survey was published in 2017 in which a group of social psychologists asked respondents why people choose to live in societies based on the principle of the lack of equality (Starmans et al. 2017), demonstrating that people opt for equality when they are members of small groups. When asked about an ideal model of distributing benefits and resources for large groups (including countries) they preferred that the principle of inequality be kept. This survey considerably updates our knowledge of preferences concerning the optimal benefit distribution model from the 1970s and 1980s, leading to the conclusion that, while no evidence has been found that inequality at the international level raises protests (pertaining to a multilateral trading system), economic inequalities are erroneously identified with economic (including trading) unfairness. These concerns are deeply rooted in people's experience and result in adopting a certain strategy to prevent opportunistic behaviour.

4 Conclusions

Among the numerous challenges faced by multilateral trade, murky protectionism and populism are a relatively infrequent object of analysis which would combine topics addressed by different social sciences. Reflecting on these difficult-to-interpret 'borderline issues' is more worthwhile the more it focuses on the dimension of the distributive effects of economic globalisation, and the influence it has on the political balance of integrating international capital and commodity markets. In other words, the fundamental issue when developing global economic governance is that of the 'political space' available to governments, which seek to adopt political solutions which they find optimal for the purpose of achieving their economic objectives and experiment with regulations without fear that national decision-making will be 'handcuffed' by supranational institutions. This search for a country's 'own place in the world' is accompanied by criticism of trade multilateralism and of politicians opting for plurilateral solutions. This comes as no surprise given the series of tremors which have recently shaken global trade and triggered questions about its future. The picture of the economic and political turbulence shaking the western hemisphere is painted, inter alia, by Donald Trump's protectionist decisions, in particular the USA withdrawing from the Trans-Pacific Partnership (TPP), the USA seeking to renegotiate the NAFTA agreement, bilateralisation of trade (e.g. modifications to the USA–South Korea agreement on free trade), the 'devaluation' of the crown jewel of the multilateral trading system—namely the dispute settlement system—due to the USA blocking the appointment of judges to the WTO's appellate body, increasing trading tensions between neighbours (the USA–Canada dispute concerning the aviation, lumber and paper industries), and the trade war between the USA and China. In Europe, a selection of challenges for the multilateral trade system involves Brexit, the consequences of which for the single market and the euro area are hard to predict, troublesome trading relations with the USA, and the atmosphere of mutual accusation between the European Union and China, concerning currency exchange manipulations, China's illegal support for its national industry and the lack of agreement on granting the status of market economy to China. The lack of unity among the trading system's members, profound divisions between them and the limited decision-making potential of the system's *sacrum palatium,* the WTO, was demonstrated by the ministerial conference in Buenos Aires. Its outcome was essentially a single decision on fisheries subsidies. Never before have negotiations revealed such a deep cleft between elite decision makers and civil society, as symbolised by the government of Argentina, the conference's host, withdrawing the accreditations of 63 non-governmental organisations before the conference, thereby transforming the WTO into a fortress surrounded by a wall of non-transparency.

Among this turmoil and a multitude of challenges, murky protectionism and populism can appear inconspicuous, yet they have a disastrous impact on trade multilateralism in economic, political and psychological terms. Firstly, they undermine people's faith that maintaining the system makes sense, since populists (but not only populists) claim it is far from transparent, unfair and has been 'appropriated' by the political and business elites of respective national establishments and transnational bureaucracies. Both these threats to the global trading system, treated as an organism, are inconspicuous and operate at a slow pace, like 'bad cholesterol' which builds up in the arteries leading to a blockage. Murky protectionism measures are not only about inserting concealed regulations into national taxation systems, but they are also manifested by individual governments' inclinations to substitute transparent trade protection measures with ambiguous regulations which restrict the redistribution of profits generated by economic globalisation, and even strengthen populist leaders who use the language of contempt and exclusion and 'pass blame to enemies' in public discourse. They rely on demand populism, generated by inadequate redistribution of profits from economic globalisation, which results in increased support for social movements that are outside the political mainstream and contest the rules of the political game in a given country. Demand populism is linked with supply populism. Since political decision makers fail to address accusations thrown at them by populist movements, they are responsible for the emergence of narratives whereby discontented people concentrate around key issues, concerns and anxieties. These narratives are presented as stemming from disregarded needs, and neglected demand for benefits that result, for instance, from the global trading system. They strongly resonate with the public when populist leaders give reasons for the lack of economic security, falling income and unemployment, and pointing to who should be blamed.

Concluding these considerations and outlining further reflections which will soon follow, one can ask the question of whether being aware of the fact that trade multilateralism is crumbling, and its *sacrum palatium*—the WTO—is failing, should result in changing the tack from global to national governance, expanding the realm of decisions made by individual governments and, by the same token, 'resetting' and reprogramming our attitude to politically balanced democratic capitalism. Or maybe it should be the opposite: global governance should be reinforced and the forces which emerge in the right conditions and were once dubbed by Polanyi (1944) as 'social protection' should be disarmed? Although it is impossible within the confines of this chapter, due to its essential significance in understanding the relationship between hyper-globalisation, democracy and sovereignty (Rodrik 2011), this issue deserves to be re-examined in the context of the 'second unbundling', viewed as the transition from the earlier stage of globalisation to the post-industrial economy which is characterised by new links forming between regional production centres, rapidly developing small service providers and the expansion of global value chains involving even the largest transnational corporations.

References

Acemoglu, D. (1998). Why do new technologies complement skills? Directed technical change and wage inequality. *Quarterly Journal of Economics, 113*(4), 1055–1089.

Acemoglu, D., & Autor, D. (2011). Skills, tasks and technologies: Implications for employment and earnings. In *Handbook of labor economics* (Vol. 4b). Amsterdam: Elsevier-North.

Autor, D., & Dorn, D. (2013). The growth of low-skill service job and the polarization of the US labor market. *American Economic Review, 103*(5), 1553–1597.

Autor, D., Dorn, D., & Hanson, G. (2016). The China shock: Learning from labor market adjustment to large changes in trade. *Annual Review of Economics, 8*, 205–240.

Azevêdo, R. (2017). *Reenergising the multilateral trading system.* Accessed September 18, 2018, from http://www.eastasiaforum.org/2017/05/21/reenergising-the-multilateral-trading-system/

Baldwin, R., & Evenett, S. (2009). *The collapse of global trade, murky protectionism, and the crisis: Recommendations for the G20.* London: Centre for Economic Policy Research.

Bhagwati, J. (2008). *Termites in the trading system: How preferential agreements undermine free trade.* Oxford-New York: Oxford University Press.

Cernat, L., & Madsen, M. (2011). *"Murky protectionism" and behind-the-border barriers: How big an issue? The €100 billion question.* Retrieved September 20, 2018, from https://voxeu.org/article/murky-protectionism-how-big-issue

Cohen, R. L., & Greenberg, J. (1982). *The justice concept in social psychology*. New York: Academic Press.

Deutsch, M. (1985). *Distributive justice: A socio-psychological perspective*. New Haven: Yale University Press.

Evenett, S., & Fritz, J. (2015). Crisis-era trade distortions cut LDC export growth by 5.5% per annum. In B. Hoekman (Ed.), *The global trade slowdown: A new normal?* London: Centre for Economic Policy Research. *A VoxEU.org eBook*.

Evenett, S., & Fritz, J. (2017). The WTO's next work program – As if the global economic crisis really mattered. In C. A. Primo Braga & B. Hoekman (Eds.), *Future of the global trade order*. EUI: Florence.

Goos, M., Manning, A., Salomons, A. (2010). *Explaining job polarization in Europe: The roles of technology, globalization and institutions*. Centre for Economic Performance Discussion Papers. No. 1026.

Hannah, E., Scott, J., & Wilkinson, R. (2018). The WTO in Buenos Aires: The outcome and its significance for the future of the multilateral trading system. *The World Economy, 41*(10), 2578–2598.

Hicks M. J., Devtaj S. (2017). *Myth and reality of manufacturing in America*. Ball State Center For Business and Economic Research.

Hoekman, B. (2015). Trade and growth – End of an era. In B. Hoekman (Ed.), *The global trade slowdown: A new normal?* London: Centre for Economic Policy Research. *A VoxEU.org eBook*.

Hoekman, B., & Mavroidis, P. C. (2015). WTO 'a la carte' or 'menu du jour'? Assessing the case for more plurilateral agreements. *The European Journal of International Law, 26*(2), 319–343.

Katz, L. F., & Margo, R. A. (2013). *Technical change and the relative demand for skilled labor: The United States in historical perspective*. National Bureau of Economic Research No. w18752.

Leung, K., & Bond, M. H. (1982). How Chinese and Americans reward taskrelated contributions: A preliminary study. *Psychologia, 25*(1), 32–39.

Leung, K., & Bond, M. H. (1984). The impact of cultural collectivism on reward allocation. *Journal of Personality and Social Psychology, 47*(4), 793–804.

Marczewska-Rytko, M. (1995). *Populizm. Teoria i praktyka polityczna*. Lublin: Wydawnictwo UMCS.

Milner, H. (1997). *Interests, institutions, and information. Domestic politics and international relations*. Princeton: Princeton University Press.

Olszyk, S. (2007). "Vox populi vox Dei": Teoria populizmu politycznego. *Annales Universitatis Paedagogicae Cracoviensis. Studia Politologica, 46*(3), 236–247.

Polanyi, K. (1944). *The great transformation: Economic and political origins of our time*. New York: Rinehart.

Powell, B. (2016). China, Inc. is on a spending spree abroad. *Newsweek*. Retrieved from September 14, 2018, http://www.newsweek.com/chinese-foreign-investments-starwoodhotels-443706

Rodrik, D. (2011). *The globalization paradox: Democracy and the future of the world economy*. New York/London: W.W. Norton.

Rodrik, D. (2018). Populism and the economics of globalization. *Journal of International Business Policy*, 1. https://doi.org/10.1057/s42214-018-0001-4

Sampson, E. E. (1975). On justice as equality. *Journal of Social Issues, 31*(3).

Starmans, C., Sheskin, M., & Bloom, P. (2017). Why people prefer unequal societies. *Nature Human Behaviour, 1*(4).

Walzer, M. (1983). *Spheres of justice: A defence of pluralism and equality*. Oxford: Martin Robertson.

Wojtas, M. (2015). Międzynarodowa polityka handlowa w XXI wieku – główne trendy. *Zeszyty Naukowe Uniwersytetu Szczecińskiego. Studia i Prace Wydziału Nauk Ekonomicznych i Zarządzania, 41*(1).

Wojtas, M. (2017). Przyczyny spowolnienia światowego handlu. *Zeszyty Naukowe Uniwersytetu Szczecińskiego. Studia i Prace Wydziału Nauk Ekonomicznych i Zarządzania, 49/2.*

Wolfe, R. (2009). The WTO single undertaking as negotiating technique and constitutive metaphor. *Journal of International Economic Law, 12*(4), 835–858.

Wróbel, A. (2015). Implikacje negocjacji TTIP dla wielostronnego systemu handlowego. In E. Stadmuller & Ł. Fijałkowski (Eds.), *Normy, wartości i instytucje we współczesnych stosunkach Międzynarodowych*. Rambler: Warszawa.

WTO. (2018a). *WTO trade forecasts: Press conference.* Retrieved November 10, 2018, from https://www.wto.org/english/news_e/spra_e/spra218_e.htm

WTO. (2018b). *Strong trade growth in 2018 rests on policy choices*, PRESS/820 Press Release. Retrieved November 10, 2018, from https://www.wto.org/english/news_e/pres18_e/pr820_e.htm

Wu, M. (2016). The 'China, Inc.' challenge to global trade governance. *Harvard International Law Journal, 57*, 1001–1063.

Protectionism as Challenges for the Global Trade Governance

Sang-Chul Park

1 Introduction

After the General Agreement on Tariffs and Trade (GATT) in 1947, the World Trade Organization (WTO) was established in 1995. Building a new trade system with WTO was a cornerstone for a gradual process of global liberalization that started since the Second World War. Under GATT, average tariff for many countries in 1950 accounted for nearly 30%, and a wide variety of nontariff barriers (NTBs) existed. However, under WTO, average tariffs declined up to 5% in 2010 although NTBs still existed broadly. These dropped continuously to lower than 3% in 2015. It reflects a process of economic liberalization that stated in the 1980s. Moreover, technological development in telecommunication and transportation contributed to reducing trade costs and strengthening globalization of trade (Hoekman 2013; World Bank 2017; Park 2017; Dicken 2015).

The global trade system played important roles in strengthening economic globalization by providing a framework for countries to exchange trade policy commitments and establishing a mechanism that enforced the commitments between countries. The scope of policy disciplines expanded gradually and steadily since the GATT and the WTO established a dispute settlement mechanism in order to adjudicate global trade disputes that recommend losing parties to comply with the regulation of WTO. The global trade system based on WTO tried to prove its resilience during the global financial crisis (GFC) in 2008 by asking major trade countries not to implement protection measures such as increasing tariffs and NTBs (Hoekman 2013).

Trade protectionism led by the Trump administration in the USA has been intensified since the end of 2017 and negated the Trans Pacific Partnership (TPP)

S.-C. Park (✉)
Graduate School of Knowledge based Technology and Energy, Korea Polytechnic University, Siheung-si, South Korea
e-mail: scpark@kpu.ac.kr

© Springer Nature Switzerland AG 2020
M. Rewizorski et al. (eds.), *The Future of Global Economic Governance*,
https://doi.org/10.1007/978-3-030-35336-0_7

Agreement although the Japanese Prime Minister Abe had restored it as Comprehensive and Progressive Trans Pacific Partnership (CPTPP) without the US participation in 2018. Even in 2019, the trade conflicts between China and the USA as well as the EU and the USA are still ongoing processes and nobody can estimate exactly what the final result will be in the global economy although the USA and China negotiation for trade deal approaches near to the end. Eventually, trade protectionism is regarded as one of the most sensitive issues of global economic cooperation along with political and military conflicts in the world such as nationalistic populism in the EU and the USA pullout in the Middle East such as Iraq and Syria.

Under such circumstance based on economic and political instability around the world, the global trade environment has become worsened since the GFC in 2008. The GFC escalated the existing anti-globalization sentiments and created views of opposition in liberalized trade resulting from neoliberalism. Under this condition, many countries have attempted to increase tariffs for imports of goods and services and set nontariff barriers on trade as well. As a result, the G20 Leaders Summit, and the meetings of finance ministers and central bank governors agreed to fight against all forms of protectionism in trade and maintain open trade since the Seoul Summit in 2010. Despite such a clear political economic statement of the major countries, the WTO addressed its official views on the new trend of increased trade protectionism as a result of deepening global economic crisis (Park 2016; WTO 2018).

Although the recent global protectionism on trade started to spread rapidly, global trade has contributed to high economic growth in the world since the second part of the twentieth century. However, the trade growth started to slow down in the global economy particularly since the GFC in 2008 and the EU's sovereign debt crisis in 2010/2011. Additionally, the Trump administration started to set high tariffs on trade with its major trade partners such as Canada, China, the EU, Mexico, Russia, South Korea, Turkey, and others in the end of 2017 that affected the global economy negatively. The impacts of trade could be longer than expected if patterns followed during the last trade conflicts in the 1930s. In fact, the impacts of rising protectionism between 1929 and 1932 lasted until the 1960s that are four decades long (Martin 2018).

Given the estimation, the full scale of trade conflict could cause a tenfold increase in the average tariff for US exporters from 3% to 30%. For Chinese exporters, the tariff increases up to 36%, while it rises to 32% for EU exporters. However, it is unclear how the tariff increase faced on export bundle could lead to any country to gain more profits than other. Additionally, the present trade conflicts could cause the increasing total cost continuously. It was estimated up to $800 billion that was about 4% of the world trade and 0.4% of the global GDP in 2018 (Edwards 2018; Nicita et al. 2018).

2 Global Trade Governance

2.1 Development of Global Trade System

The genesis of multilateral trade system came from the experience of protectionism and capital controls that was put in place by governments as they used policy tools to stimulate domestic economic activity and employment. In the USA, Smoot–Hawley Act of 1930 was adopted and it increased average US tariffs from 38% to 52%. US trade partners imposed retaliatory trade measures. As a result, a domino effect resulted in declining trade flows and ensuring further retaliation. Due to such a negative impact on the world economy, political leaders sought to establish international institutions in order to reduce similar experiences even before the Second World War was ended.

On the basis of such a historical experience, new international organizations such as the United Nations (UN) and International Monetary Fund (IMF) were created for managing international relations and monetary and exchange policies, respectively. Furthermore, the World Bank (WB) and the International Trade Organization (ITO) were also established. The roles of the former assisted in financing reconstruction and promoting economic development, while those of the latter focused on managing trade relations. The basic idea of creating the ITO was that increasing trade could support the rising real incomes, and non-disciplinary access to markets could reduce the scope for political and trade conflicts spilling over into other areas (Hoekman 2013; Hoekman and Kostecki 2009).

After the Second World War, the ITO Charter was negotiated to regulate trade in goods and commodity agreements. It was also discussed to regulate subjects such as employment policy and restrictive business practices. However, the ITO was never established because the US Congress did not ratify the Charter. In parallel to the ITO negotiations, a group of 12 developed and 11 developing countries started to negotiate the General Agreement on Tariffs and Trade (GATT) and tariff reduction commitments that entered into force on January 1, 1948 on a provisional basis. As a result, the GATT became the only result of trade negotiation that applied for 47 years until it became a part of the WTO in 1995. Over time, the GATT gradually evolved into an international institution representing trade issues although it was formally a treaty.

During most of the GATT period (1948–1994), the USA played roles as a hegemon and concerned little for free riding or noncooperative behavior of developing countries because they were mostly non-influential actors in the global trade system. At that time, rulemaking and major negotiations were made by the Organization for Economic Cooperation and Development (OECD) member nations in particular the four nations such as the USA, the EC, Japan, and Canada. However, it started to change since the end of the 1980s as a number of developing countries gained their economic significance. In the end of the 1980s, China emerged, while Brazil and India took a more positive position as rising powers in the global economy, and Russia became a member of G8 in the political forum in the 1990s. These new emerging economies started to defy the old global trade order (Duggan 2015; Heldt 2017).

The evolution from the GATT to the WTO is regarded as the result of political bargaining influenced by both governmental and nongovernmental actors. The reason is that a set of interest groups expanded while attention shifted from falling average tariffs to nontariff policies affecting trade more severely than ever. Therefore, the WTO included agreements on services and intellectual property rights

(IPRs) that reflected the interests of the industry in OECD member nations. These were mainly telecommunication, financial and pharmaceutical industries seeking access to foreign markets (Hoekman 2013).

2.2   The WTO as New Global Trade Governance

Since the WTO was established in 1995, it has played a central role in the global trade governance. The reason why the WTO has played the central role is that it established ground rules for economic operators and governments. As a result, mutually agreed rules embodied in the WTO agreements could reduce uncertainty for companies to trade in foreign markets. In the open global economy, preserving an effective multilateral trade system is regarded as very significant for countries to cooperate in managing rapid structural change and transformation.

Despite the WTO's central role, the global trade system faces difficulties because of rapidly changing trade structure that hinders from agreements among WTO member nations regarding the priorities for the multilateral trade system. The core point of trade structural change is based on a shift from agricultural and manufacturing activities taking place predominantly national in nature toward geographically dispersed global production networks and a rising share of total value added in services. It requires updating the prevailing governance framework. While updating it, disagreements between WTO member nations arise because these inhibit the scope for the WTO to perform its role in rulemaking, monitoring, and enforcing mutually agreed policy commitments (Bluth and Hoekman 2018).

Decision-making in the WTO is consensus based. It means that any decision can be rejected if any member nation objects. This principle ensures that no member nation can be pressed to accept decisions or agreements although the large players carry more weight than do small ones in practice. It means that the decision-making of the WTO is a package deal, take it all or leave it. In order to overcome such disadvantage, small member nations can build coalition in decision-making processes. With the Doha Round of multilateral trade negotiations in 2001, rising powers built several coalitions such as G20, G11, and G33. The G20 was an alliance including Brazil, China, and India, while G11 was a group of developing countries having national interests in nonagricultural market access in the Doha Round. The G33 aimed at having the issues more relevance to them included in the negotiating agenda. In practice, they blocked negotiations effectively by refusing to accept the compromise suggested by existing powers at ministerial meetings such as Cancun in 2003 and Bali in 2013. As a result, the Doha Development Agenda failed (Narlikar and Tussie 2004; Heldt 2017; Hoekman 2013).

The failure of the first multilateral round of trade negotiation under the WTO auspices generated significant global welfare losses that are more than no discipline of using trade distorting policy based on agricultural support and tariff escalation. Furthermore, it has prevented WTO member nations addressing new sources of policy and engaging in a collaborative effort to update WTO rules reflecting changes in the global economy (Bluth and Hoekman 2018).

The other important principle of the WTO is nondiscrimination principle called as most favored nation (MFN). It requires that any concession or commitment must be accorded to all member nations. Based on the principle, the WTO member nations may not provide any grants or better treatment to a subset of countries negotiating concessions than other countries offering no concessions. The only exception is to conclude free trade agreements (FTAs) with each other or negotiate a plurilateral agreement. Under these agreements, the subset member nations are able to agree specific disciplines applying only to them and not applying the associated benefits to nonmember nations (Hoekman 2013).

Due to the failure of Doha Round, the WTO has had difficulties to make progress in negotiating new agreements. As a result, many member nations of the WTO started to negotiate preferential trade agreements (PTAs), called also as free trade agreements (FTAs). The number of FTAs has been rising steadily since the early 2000s, and over 400 FTAs entered into force in 2018. Some of FTAs cover more than one region in the world that is called Mega FTAs. Resort to FTAs stems from several motivations. However, the common element is a strong willingness of participating countries to engage in deeper economic integration than desirable multilateral trade negotiation. Such agreements are complement of the WTO although they are a partial substitute for multilateral cooperation on trade policy (Bluth and Hoekman 2018; Park 2018).

In order to govern the global trade system properly, the WTO has the following five major functions: firstly, to facilitate the implementation, administration and operation of the agreements; secondly to provide a forum for negotiations between member nations; thirdly to administer the Dispute Settlement Understanding; fourthly to administer Trade Policy Review Mechanism; and last but not least to cooperate with the global institutions such as the IMF and the World Bank Group to achieve coherence of global economic policy making. These major functions are carried by the consensus principle combined with a dispute settlement mechanism. Owing to such functions and the mechanism, it is extremely difficult to amend the WTO and to conclude multilateral trade negotiations on time (Jones 2010; Hoekman 2013).

2.3   Challenges for the WTO

Scholars discussed intensively possible disputes between existing and rising powers since the 2000s. They widely disagree whether rising powers so called BRIC nations such as Brazil, Russia, India, and China are to contest or accept the rules and institutions of the existing world order. Some scholars urged that BRIC nations could exercise their actions as revisionists and be a de facto threat to the existing global order, while others argued that the emerging powers would use the global order as an opportunity for them to rise by seeking incremental adaptations of existing rules and institutions (Chin 2015; Stephen 2012; Barma et al. 2014).

Focusing on the success of rising powers' challenges that is based on an institutionalist power shift theory developed by Zangl et al., they argue that it is fully dependent on rising powers' ability whether institutional adaptation can succeed or fail how to deal with international institutions or to make credible threats to this effect. Accordingly, it is wise to examine rising powers' negotiations and coalition building efforts in international organizations such as the IMF, the WB, the UN in general, and the WTO in particular (Zangl et al. 2016; Heldt 2017).

The behaviors of the rising powers are regarded as similar to those of incumbent powers. In the all IOs, they approach to extract their benefits as much as possible from international cooperation, while conceding to other members their autonomy as little as possible. They also have clear preferences on how to reform global governance and structure of decision-making that influences to shape global trade governance rules (Kahler 2013).

A wrong perception of trade also threats the activity of the WTO. The role of trade and trade liberalization has been regarded as a driver of inequality and stagnation in average household incomes of the middle class in many countries. However, empirical research demonstrated that trade is not a major driver of these trends. The major drivers are primarily the results of technological change and domestic policy choices. Despite the fact, trade agreements are criticized as the major reason of inequality and low economic growth. As a result, arguments against trade agreements and trade system spread out in businesses, NGOs, and citizens more generally. Moreover, the idea and value of rules-based trade has been questioned in the WTO (Bluth and Hoekman 2018).

Different perceptions between major emerging economic powers such as China and India and existing economic powers such as OECD member nations are deep seated. The former believes that the WTO is unbalanced and treats them unfairly, while the latter regards the emerging economies engaging in trade distorting policy that is in favor of their national companies and violates fair competition in the domestic and global markets. Therefore, consumers concern about the fairness of trade whether or not they can ensure national governments to regulate economic activities in order to meet the fundamental societal goals for their economic benefits and welfares (Wu 2016).

These perceptions have raised the question confronting in the WTO how to restore trust in the global rules-based trade system. An effective multilateral trade system plays a critical role in supporting the governments of member nations that is able to sustain the global trade order generating the economic growth for both parties. Therefore, reversal of trade liberalization and rejection of trade policy commitments agreed in the WTO and regional trade agreements can create negative impacts by increasing trade costs and rising price of products for consumers.

Additionally, wide-spreading protectionism in the WTO member nations, particularly in major member nations also challenges the global rules-based trade system. Protests against the recent EU trade negotiations with Canada and the USA as well as the USA withdrawal from Trans Pacific Partnership (TPP) and the US revision of

Table 1 Top 10 major countries imposing discriminatory measures in 2015

Rank	Countries	No. of measures imposed in 2015	Share of world imports in 2014
1	USA	90	13.5
2	Russia	86	1.6
3	India	67	2.6
4	Brazil	42	1.3
5	Indonesia	42	1.0
6	Argentina	36	0.4
7	Japan	36	4.5
8	UK	36	3.8
9	Italy	34	2.6
10	Canada	27	2.6

Source: Global Trade Alert Report 2016

North America Free Trade Agreement (NAFTA) and Korea–USA Free Trade Agreement (KORUS FTA) represent a severe challenge of global trade system (See Table 1).

3 Protectionism Against Global Trade Governance

3.1 Background

The globalization trend is not a new phenomenon. Its first movement started in the mid nineteenth century through the early twentieth century that is the first wave of the globalization. During the period, the impact was rather very significant on various levels. The international trade increased rapidly, and at the same time the share of GDP for trade in many countries also grew sharply. The reason for the rapid growth of world trade resulted from declining transportation costs and tariffs that eliminated cross-border price differences on many basic commodities. As a result, markets became truly global in the early twentieth century.

The powerful globalization forces united many parts of the global economy particularly between the Atlantics and Oceania. Free trade, capital flows, and international migration enabled to provide countries benefits of specialization and to distribute resources to be deployed to where they were most needed and searched for the highest returns. At the same time, the globalization also created negative impacts that widened income inequality within wealthier countries and fall in poor countries in the Atlantic areas (O'Rourke and Williamson 2001). As a result, a strong political backlash against the globalization took place, and political pressure increased to restrict globalization. The USA started to raise tariffs in order to increase revenues during the Civil War and kept them high for decades. Following the change of the US trade policy, the UK, protectionist claimed high tariffs in the early twentieth century when the UK's industrial bases started to be challenged from abroad. After that, the first round of the globalization turned to protectionism (Feinman 2016; Park 2018).

The second wave of the globalization began after the end of the Cold War. Many closed economies such as China, India, and Eastern Europe opened up and liberalized their economies so that they became a part of global economic system adopting standards of global rules-based trade system agreed in the WTO. Since the new global trade order established by the WTO in 1995, the average tariff has declined continuously till the GFC in 2008, while the nontariff barriers (NTBs) remained. Due to the increasing NTBs particularly since the GFC, political leaders worldwide started to concern about the global trade system that affected developed and developing economies experiencing a simultaneous downturn. At the same time, the number of unemployed in the world increased more than doubled in 2009 that caused income inequality and political instability in many nations. Under such a circumstance, protectionist sentiment emerged strongly. Similar to the first wave of the globalization, the global leaders of second wave of the globalization such as the USA and the UK initiated protectionism represented by the America First Policy and the Brexit, respectively.

3.2 Reasons for Protectionism

During the high economic growth period till the global financial crisis in 2008, most of the nations adopting the global rules-based trade system were strongly pro-globalization. However, large income inequality particularly after the crisis caused a political populism in the EU and the USA that resulted in the Brexit referendum and the Trump administration in the USA. Paradoxically, pro-globalization leaders such as the USA and the UK turned to the de-globalization process based on the protectionism so that the world witnesses a combination of economic and political risks at present that could affect the global economy negatively (Park 2018).

The global trade sentiment turned to protectionism since the GFC, and the USA has led this trend that has affected to the global economies severely. In fact, the protectionist trade policy has always existed even in the global free trade system. The largest difference of the US protectionism is to impact on the global economy seriously due to its economic size compared with other small- or medium-sized economies. The US protectionism has three major reasons as follows.

Firstly, the US protectionism has caused the income inequality and distribution in the USA that has risen since the 2000s although economists are not fully sure yet whether the free trade has created the income inequality or not. The fact is that the average of real wage of production per hour has been stagnant since the 1980s. As a result, the wage increase in production has lagged behind the growth in real GDP per capita. Furthermore, the share of pretax income in the top 1% increased from 10.5% in 1980 to over 20% in 2015, while its share of bottom 50% declined from 20.5% to 13% during the same period that led the USA to the second most inequality nation

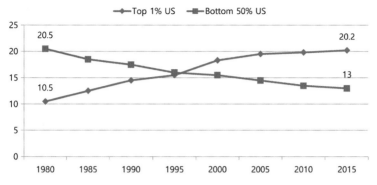

Fig. 1 Share of pretax income in the USA (as of 1980–2015). Source: Alvaredo et al. (2017)

among the OECD after Mexico (OECD 2015; Piketty 2014; Alvaredo et al. 2017) (See Fig. 1).

Secondly, the rise of East Asia changes trade relationships between the USA and East Asia. The East Asian economy has been mostly developed by the trade expansion based on comparative competitiveness. Certainly the US market has also played significant roles for the rapid development of East Asian economy. While trading between the two economies, trade surplus of the East Asian economy has continuously grown that accounted for 72% of the total trade deficit in the USA in 2015. Therefore, the US government and public possess strong impression that the East Asian economy carries out unfair trade policies and its comparative advantage weakened the US manufacturing sectors and industrial bases that could disturb the domestic production of weaponry in time of war. It is the reason why several trade restriction measures were implemented even in the Obama government that were tariff based, but frequently regulatory. The Obama government set Buy American clause in the economic stimulus program in 2009. This trend has persisted, and it has been strengthened in the Trump government in the name of America First Policy (CCGA 2010; Hillebrand et al. 2010; Genereux 2017).

The last, but not least may be the less dependency of US economy on the global trade. The USA is the second least dependent economy on the global trade system after Brazil. Its trade share based on GDP in 2015 accounted only for 28%, while Chinese share of GDP was 40%. Countries depending on exports as primary source of growth could be directly and negatively impacted by import tariffs and other trade restrictions. In protectionism, small open economies can be more vulnerable than large closed economies. It means that the US economy as the largest economy and the second least dependent on the global trade can be the least affected along with Brazil in the protectionist movement (Hofschire et al. 2017; Park 2018).

The UK's protectionism known as Brexit also has mixed several reasons that are mainly composed of economy, sovereignty, and political elitism. Firstly, in the EU economy, opponents of the EU regarded the EU's economy as a dysfunctional entity because the EU failed to solve its economic problems caused by the high unemployment rate in Southern European member nations and the low economic growth in the Euro zone. Secondly, rising nationalism worldwide influenced Brexit. There has been a growing distrust of multinational financial, trade, economic, and defense organizations such as the IMF, the WB, the WTO, the EU, and the NATO because they take control away from individual nations. As a result, the opponents of the EU voted for Brexit as a reasonable solution to keep their sovereignty. Thirdly, the British political leadership faced a fundamental loss because the third political party, the Liberal Party rejected both the Conservative and Labor parties although both parties endorsed remaining with the EU. Accordingly, it was a three-way struggle between two established parties and the third faction. Under such circumstance, British voters thought politicians, business leaders, and intellectuals had lost their rights to control the political system so that they voted for Brexit. It means that Brexit was a vote against the British elite. Besides that, immigrant issue in the EU, dissatisfaction of the UK's budget contribution to the EU, EU's burdensome regulations can be pointed out for the reasons of Brexit (Lee 2016; Friedman 2016).

3.3 Possible Impacts of Protectionism on Global Trade Governance

There are worrying indications of protectionism rising again since the GFC. While trends with respect to agricultural support in many OECD member nations, Foreign Direct Investment (FDI) and services supplied by local establishment are regarded as a positive direction. However, tariff liberalization is not working properly and several types of NTBs increased in recent years. As a result, restrictions on data flows and the risk of backlash against the movement of persons have emerged although G20 agreed to refrain from raising new barriers to investment and trade in goods and services after the GFC. It adds a growing concern in the global trade system (Altenberg 2016).

The concept of protectionism varies widely between institutions. However, the two core features of protectionism are regarded as discrimination and trade restrictiveness although these overlap in many cases. Tariffs discriminate against foreign exporters and at the same time restrict trade. However, export subsidies discriminate against foreign economic operators, but do not restrict the imports. On the contrary, specific measures such as technical barriers to trade (TBT) and sanitary and phytosanitary (SPS) measures restrict trade, but do not discriminate between domestic and foreign economic operators. Protectionist regards the free trade model as a reversed protectionism in disguise using trade policy for tariffs to protect foreign economic operators from domestic competition. A government becomes fully to rely on domestic taxation in order to provide its revenue if it rules out revenue tariffs on foreign products. As a result, it burdens heavily domestic manufacturing disproportionately. It is the reason why protectionism is needed that is the logic of protectionist. Despite the evidence of damage caused by trade restrictions, pressure on anti-free trade movement persists because specific interests groups such as big corporations, labor unions, and farmers influence politicians to pass laws favorable to them (Ngono Fouda 2012).

Protectionism will cost for the global economy. Historically, the costs from the USA completing ban on overseas shipping during the Napoleon War were estimated to reduce the US real income by 8%, while the Smooth–Hawley Act for tariffs in 1930 reduced US imports by 5% that resulted in an annual income loss of 0.3% of GDP. It was a substantial reduction from the only one legislation. During the 1990s, estimates of the cost of protectionism ranged between 1% and 7% of GDP in the major economies and East Asian economies such as the EU, the USA, Japan, Korea, and China. In the recent period, US exports to other countries are estimated to decline by 70% or more and US imports from foreign countries would drop by 50% to 60% or more if the protectionist US trade policy in the Trump administration with a 20% increase in all customs duties against all WTO member nations is carried out. It means that all protectionist measures carried out by the US government would lead to negative economic consequences not only for US trade partners, but also for the US economy itself. Furthermore, this trade policy could cause a long-run decline in global trade volumes, FDI, and economic growth (Irwin 2011; Altenberg 2016; Petersen et al. 2017; Yalcin et al. 2017).

Protectionist measures influence not only economic dimensions, but also political and social aspects. The USA has played major roles in developing the global economic system with the three pillars of global institutions such as the IMF, the WB, and the WTO. Moreover, integration into the Western economic system made possible that developing and newly industrialized nations could evolve their economies and democratize their political system as well as advance liberal values that has created them economic prosperity, political development, and social welfare. Therefore, protectionist measures to restrict global market accesses spreading out worldwide could harm the multilateral trade system against all WTO member nations severely that could limit the role of WTO (Yalcin et al. 2017).

Additionally, protectionism could damage the global value chain that has been created by the global trade order based on the three pillars since the Second World War. Given different flows in the global economy such as goods, services, investment, labor, knowledge, and technology, firms do not perceive trade in a compartmentalized way. In reality, different barriers and liberalizing measures interact and influence firms in terms of production costs and let them decide on cross-border trade, local establishment, or digital platforms. Protectionism influences the behavior of firms trade negatively so that the global value chain can be weakened that could result in declining competitiveness and productivity of firms at a global scale and global trade growth in all WTO member nations (Altenberg 2016; Park 2018).

4 Conclusions

As explained, global trade has contributed to creating global economic growth longer than five decades since the Second World War. It has grown average twice higher than global GDP growth in the same period. During this period, trade liberalization represented globalization and played major roles in creating global economic system. However, such a trend shifted to trade protectionism since the GFC in 2008 although G20 vowed to prevent from tariff barriers and NTBs in the Washington Summit.

Protectionism leads to global economic slowdown instead of global economic growth theoretically and in practice because the total trade volumes decline worldwide. It also reduces investment and technology transfer that could result in declining productivity if the knock-on effect continues at a global scale. Consequently, few nations can generate profits from it in the short run, but most of the nations will lose their economic benefits in the long run that the global economy had already experienced during the Great Recession in the early 1930s. It is the reason why protectionism must be prevented by the close cooperation between global economic institutions such as the IMF, the WB, and the WTO that govern the global economy.

In terms of the global trade, the WTO plays a major role in dealing with the multilateral trade system based on nondiscrimination and consensus principles. However, these principles have made the WTO member nations difficult to conclude negotiations in time due to various national interests. It is the reason why the Doha Round failed and the WTO faced difficulties to govern the global trade system based on the multilateral trade system. As a result, many member nations in the WTO have competed regional trade agreements that are bilateral and plurilateral trade agreements. Accordingly, the WTO must reform by itself first in order to meet member nations' economic goals. Otherwise, it will face even more difficulties to govern the global trade system if protectionism spreads out and continues at a global scale longer than expected. If such a global trade environment is intensified, the global value chain will change rapidly that will affect to the global economy extremely negatively. Therefore, protectionism must be solved wisely, and the global trade governance has to be restored properly.

References

Altenberg, P. (2016). *Protectionism in the 21st century, Kommerskollegium 2016:2*. Stockholm: National Board of Trade.

Alvaredo, F., Chancel, L., Piketty, T., Saez, E., & Zucman, G. (2017). *World inequality report 2018*, executive summary. Retrieved March 23, 2019, from http://wir2018.wid.world/

Barma, N., Ratner, E., & Weber, S. (2014, 12 November). Welcome to the world without the west, *The National Interest*. Retrieved March 21, 2019, from http://www.naazneenbarma.com/uploads/2/9/6/9/29695681/welcome_to_the_world_without_the_west_tni_web_nov2014.pdf

Bluth, C., & Hoekman, B. (2018). *Revitalizing multilateral governance at the World Trade Organization*. Gutersloh: Bertelsmann Stiftung.

Chicago Council on Global Affairs (CCGA). (2010). *Global views 2010: Detailed findings*. Chicago, IL: CCFR.

Chin, G. T. (2015). The state of the art: Trends in the study of the BRICS and multilateral organizations. In D. Lesage & T. V. de Graaf (Eds.), *Rising powers and multilateral institutions* (pp. 19–41). London: Palgrave Macmillan.

Dicken, P. (2015). *Global shift*. London: The Guildford Press.

Duggan, N. (2015). BRICS and the evolution of a new agenda within global governance. In M. Rewizorski (Ed.), *The European Union and the BRICS. Complex relations in the era of global governance* (pp. 11–26). London/New York: Springer.

Edwards, J. (2018, 4 July). Trump's trade war could destroy 4% of global trade: The treat to world growth is significant. *Business Insider.* Retrieved September 17, 2018, from https://www.businessinsider.com/statistics-trump-trade-war-global-trade-world-growth-gdp-2018-7

Feinman, J. N. (2016). *Backlash against globalization: Déjà vu? Deutsch asset management, Dec.* Chicago: Deutsch AM Distributors.

Friedman, G. (2016, 5 July). *3 Reasons Brits voted for Brexit.* Retrieved March 23, 2019, from https://www.forbes.com/sites/johnmauldin/2016/07/05/3-reasons-brits-voted-for-brexit/

Genereux, F. (2017, 17 February). *Protectionism: A brake on economic growth.* Economic Studies.

Heldt, E. (2017). Shaping global trade governance rules: New powers' hard and soft strategies of influence at the WTO. *European Foreign Affairs Review, 22*(Special Issue), 19–36.

Hillebrand, E. E., Lewer, J. J., & Zagardo, J. T. (2010). Backtracking from globalization. *Global Economy Journal, 10*(4), 1–17.

Hoekman, B. (2013). *Global trade governance.* In T. Weiss, & R. Wilkinson (Eds.), International organization and global governance. London: Routledge. Retrieved March 14, 2019, from http://globalgovernanceprogramme.eui.eu/wp-content/uploads/2012/11/Hoekman-Global-Trade-Governance_FINAL.pdf

Hoekman, B., & Kostecki, M. (2009). *The political economy of the world trading system* (3rd ed.). Oxford: Oxford University Press.

Hofschire, D., Emsbo-Mattingly, L., Dourney, C., & Wilde, J. (2017). *For now, the risks of trade protectionism are offset by global reacceleration. Leadership Series, Febraury.* New York: Fidelity Investment.

Irwin, D. A. (2011). *Peddling protectionism: Smoot-Hawley and the great depression.* Oxford and Princeton: Princeton University Press.

Jones, K. (2010). *The Doha blues: Institutional crisis and reform in the WTO.* Oxford: Oxford University Press.

Kahler, M. (2013). Rising powers and global governance: Negotiating change in a resilient status quo. *International Affairs, 89*(3), 711–729.

Lee, T. B. (2016). *Brexit: The 7 most important arguments for Britain to leave the EU.* Retrieved March 23, 2019, from https://www.vox.com/2016/6/22/11992106/brexit-arguments

Martin, W. (2018, 15 July). A troubling lesson from the 1930s suggests Trump's trade war will damage the world for decade, *Business Insider.* Retrieved September 15, 2018, from https://www.businessinsider.com/oxford-economics-trump-trade-war-protectionism-great-depression-2018-7

Narlikar, A., & Tussie, D. (2004). The G20 at the Cancun Ministerial: Developing countries and their evolving coalition in the WTO. *The World Economy, 27*(7), 947–966.

Ngono Fouda, R. A. (2012). Protectionism and free trade: A country's glory or doom? *International Journal of Trade, Economics and Finance, 3*(5), 351–355.

Nicita, A., Olarreaga, M., & da Silva, P. (2018, 5 April). *A trade war will increase average tariffs by 32 percentage points,* VoxEU. Retrieved March 15, 2019, from https://voxeu.org/article/trade-war-will-increase-average-tariffs-32-percentage-points

O'Rourke, K. H., & Williamson, J. G. (2001). *Globalization and history: The evolution of nineteenth century atlantic economy.* Cambridge, MA: The MIT Press.

Organization for Economic Cooperation and Development (OECD). (2015). *Factbook 2015.* Paris: OECD.

Park, S.-C. (2016). Korea's trade strategies for mega free trade agreements in regional and global economic integration. *International Organizations Research Journal, 11*(4), 19–40.

Park, S.-C. (2017). Can trade help overcome economic crisis? Implications for Northeast Asia creating regional FTA between Korea, China, Japan and mega FTAs such as RCEP and TPP. *International Organizations Research Journal, 12*(2), 104–128.

Park, S.-C. (2018). U.S. protectionism and trade imbalance between the U.S. and Northeast Asian countries. *International Organizations Research Journal, 13*(2), 76–100.

Petersen, T., Shoof, U., Yalcin, E., & Felbermayr, G. (2017). *Global impact of protectionist U.S. trade policy*. Gutersloh: Bertelsmann Stiftung.

Piketty, T. (2014). *Capital in the twenty first century*. Cambridge, MA: Belknap Press.

Stephen, M. D. (2012). Rising regional powers and international institutions: The foreign policy orientations of India, Brazil and South Africa. *Global Society, 26*(3), 289–309.

World Bank. (2017). *World Bank data base*. Retrieved March 14, 2019, from http://data.worldbank.org/indicator/BX.KLT.DINV.WD.GD.ZS

World Trade Organization (WTO). (2018). *World trade report 2018*. Geneva: WTO.

Wu, M. (2016). The China, Inc.: Challenge to global trade governance. *Harvard International Law Journal, 57*(2), 261–324.

Yalcin, E., Felbermayr, G., & Steininger, M. (2017). *Global impact of a protectionist U.S. trade policy*. Ifo forschungsberichte 89, Munich: Ifo Institute.

Zangl, B., Heussner, F., Kruck, A., & Lanzendorfer, X. (2016). Imperfect adaption: How the WTO and the IMF adjust to shifting power distribution among their members. *The Review of International Organization, 11*(2), 171–196.

Part II
From Global to Regional Challenges

From Global to Regional Financial Governance? The Case of Asia-Pacific

Karina Jędrzejowska

1 Introduction

Both the Asian financial crisis (1997–1998, AFC) and the global financial crisis (2007–09, GFC) unfolded serious deficiencies in global financial governance (GFG). The inability of global actors to provide credible crisis prevention and crisis management mechanisms encouraged the development of alternative solutions in the form of regional and plurilateral financial arrangements. As a result, in spite of the emergence of new global financial actors (e.g., Financial Stability Forum and subsequent Financial Stability Board), the last two decades have witnessed an unprecedented rise in the scope and intensity of regional financial cooperation. In particular, many Asia-Pacific[1] countries have become involved in various forms of regional financial cooperation (Sohn 2005; Amyx 2005; Boughton et al. 2017).

The chapter takes a closer look at financial arrangements in Asia-Pacific. It represents an attempt to "map" various forms of financial governance in the region. By doing so, it does not intend to provide an in-depth analysis of individual institutions. In line with the analytical model deployed in this volume, the chapter addresses the relationship between global and regional institutions of financial governance. The author assumes that following the Asian financial crisis and global financial crisis, multilayered financial governance structures have developed with regional financial arrangements (RFAs) complementing and partially substituting for global arrangements. Given the relatively insufficient theorization of regional financial governance,

---

[1]For the purpose of this study Asia-Pacific is defined as a region limited to Northeast Asia, South Asia, Southeast Asia, as well as Australasia.

K. Jędrzejowska (✉)
University of Warsaw, Warsaw, Poland
e-mail: k.jedrzejowska@uw.edu.pl

© Springer Nature Switzerland AG 2020
M. Rewizorski et al. (eds.), *The Future of Global Economic Governance*,
https://doi.org/10.1007/978-3-030-35336-0_8

the chapter contributes to the deepening of the existing literature in this field. It is based mostly on literature review backed by analysis of official documents.

The chapter is organized as follows. The first section introduces the analytical framework for the study by presenting the concept of global financial governance and the rationale behind its regional dimension. The second section looks at the evolution of financial cooperation and its drivers in Asia-Pacific from the financial governance perspective. The third section presents an overview of the Asia-Pacific regional financial architecture. A more functional approach toward the regional financial governance is used in the fourth section that deals with the forms of financial cooperation mechanisms in Asia-Pacific.

2   Between Global and Regional Financial Governance

As indicated in the introduction to this volume, the global economic governance framework remains far from perfect and fully efficient. This statement is true also for its financial dimension where globalization of money and finance and recurring financial crises have brought new challenges for policymakers at all governance levels: global, regional, and national (Woo et al. 2016: 270–271).

Over recent years, several attempts have been made at the conceptualization of global financial governance. Randall Germain defines global financial governance as "broad fabric of rules and procedures by which internationally active financial institutions are governed" (Germain 2010) together with mechanisms leading to the creation of these rules (Germain 2001: 411). In line with this approach global financial governance may be seen as a complex of standards, market access arrangements, and coordination structures supporting the global financial market (Moloney 2017). By applying the concept of global public goods Kern Alexander et al. (2004) focus on the provision of financial stability as the main purpose of global financial governance.

The concept of financial governance is closely linked with that of monetary governance. According to Benjamin Cohen (2007), monetary governance focuses on currency and can be defined as the creation, regulation, and management of money as currency. In the modern era, the area of monetary governance has been almost exclusively handled by central banks and other public actors. This feature distinguishes it from financial governance which includes both public and private actors and covers mostly the creation of credit and exchange of financial assets (McNamara 2016). In practice, the spheres of money and finance cannot be separated, and many financial governance initiatives can be analyzed from the monetary governance perspective, and the other way round.

Although none of the abovementioned analytical frameworks excludes national and regional financial arrangements, the majority of GFG analysis focuses on global financial institutions and regulations. In most cases, the financial governance at the global level can be seen as a unique hybrid of institutions and regulations inherited from the Bretton Woods regime and those established (or reformed) as a result of the financial crises of the last three decades. From the institutional perspective, it can be argued that the contemporary system of global financial governance is based on five institutions with differently defined objectives, diverse legal and international status, and heterogeneous membership. These are, respectively, the G20-led Financial Stability Board (FSB), the International Monetary Fund (IMF), the World Bank (or rather the World Bank Group), the Bank for International Settlements (BIS), and the Organization for Economic Co-operation and Development (OECD).

All of the global financial governance institutions have their limitations. Jose Antonio Ocampo indicates that there is an undersupply of services by international financial institutions that have become more glaring due to the growing economic linkages created by the process of financial globalization. As a result, at least two of the global public goods associated with the financial sphere remain undersupplied as the global governance system lacks the ability to provide adequate mechanisms for preventing and managing financial crises, as well as for guaranteeing global macro-economic and financial stability (Ocampo 2016: 1).

As the odds for comprehensive reform of the global financial architecture in the foreseeable future remain low, it is important to seek alternatives to the global financial arrangements. Even though the strongest financial and monetary governance mechanisms are usually provided at the national level (McNamara 2016), they also can prove insufficient. Hence, the recommendation to build or reinforce regional institutions mandated with preventing or mitigating crises for countries in their regions (Culperer 2016: 41).

Development of regional financial arrangements can be attributed to the broader concept of financial regionalism, i.e., regional-level cooperation in the field of economic and financial policies.[2] The role of regional institutions—often seen as complementary to global arrangements (Hirata et al. 2013: 7)—is to prevent, manage, and resolve crises as well as to provide conditions for stable development of the region. According to Kathleen McNamara (2016) regional financial governance encompasses two parallel processes: regional financial (and/or monetary) integration and regional financial (and/or monetary) cooperation. This type of governance is built upon regional financial arrangements that rely on a network of agreements "rather than having a set of rules generated by one regulatory global body" (McNamara 2016: 352).

In most cases, regional financial governance is limited to regional financial cooperation. According to Gordon de Brouwer and Yunjong Wang (2004), financial cooperation "relates to the mechanisms by which countries can provide financial

---

[2]Until recently the bulk of literature on regionalism in global economic governance has focused on trade-related issues. In contrast, financial cooperation on a regional basis has been relatively underdeveloped. This relative lack of interest in regional financial structures might be partially attributed to the fact that the global financial institutions—in spite of their numerous shortcomings—still represent a primary forum for intergovernmental cooperation. Another factor constitutes a rather unequal development across different regions with only Europe (or the European Union to be precise) promoting more advanced regional forms of regional financial governance (McNamara 2016: 352).

support to each other, regionally or globally, in the event of the financial crisis" (de Brouwer and Wang 2004: 1). It can be understood as the development of policy networks aimed at reducing risks associated with cross-border financial transactions. As such, monetary cooperation and integration can be—to some extent—included in the concept of financial cooperation.[3] Financial integration, on the other hand, can be seen as the process in which financial markets in neighboring economies become closely linked together and their participants acquire the same level of privileges (Stavarek et al. 2011: 2–4).

Changyong Rhee et al. (2013: 3) identify two generations of regional financial arrangements. The first generation was launched in response to the fall of the Bretton Woods in 1971 and subsequent shocks generated by the oil crisis of 1973. Regional responses to global financial instability included the Arab Monetary Fund created in 1976, the Association of Southeast Asian Nations (ASEAN) Swap Arrangement in 1977, and the Latin American Reserve Fund (established as the Andean Reserve Fund) in 1978. The second generation of regional financial arrangements—which includes new cooperation mechanisms in Asia-Pacific (e.g., the Chiang Mai Initiative, CMI)—was the result of recurring financial crises since the 1990s (Rhee et al. 2013: 5).

A well-designed regional financial framework can contribute to the provision of financial stability for three main reasons. First, the global efforts in this field are still inadequate and national efforts take more time to become effective. Second, as regional trade linkages and financial flows grow, an efficient regional framework for policy coordination allows for better adjustment. Third, as economic contagion tends to begin with a geographic focus, a regional framework for financial cooperation allows for more efficient crisis prevention, management, and resolution solutions. According to Ocampo (2016: 4–7) more active use of regional financial arrangements can strengthen the international financial architecture. He indicates that due to the heterogeneity of the international community the global and regional institutions can play complementary roles, following the principle of subsidiarity that has been central to the integration processes in Europe. Moreover, regional financial arrangements can "fill the gaps in the world's current highly incomplete international financial architecture." Furthermore, regional and subregional institutions may be better placed to capture and respond to specific regional needs and demands.[4]

The relationship between global and regional financial governance is well presented in the case of the global financial safety net (GFSN). GFSN can be described as "the set of arrangements to provide international liquidity to countries facing sharp reversals in capital inflows despite following sound economic and financial policies" (Truman 2013). It incorporates the liquidity assistance provided through the IMF and regional financing arrangements (RFAs), as well as bilateral or

---

[3]Such an approach is adopted in this chapter.

[4]For more political and economic arguments in favor of regional financial governance see Culperer (2016).

multilateral central bank swap arrangements (Volz 2016b: 3). Substantial input to the GFSN constitute mechanisms developed within Asia-Pacific.

3 Regionalization of Financial Governance in Asia-Pacific: Origins and Drivers

Over the last 30 years, regionalization processes in Asia-Pacific have been characterized by high level of dynamics: New institutions and forms of cooperation have been established and existing ones have undergone significant changes. This also applies to financial governance, where the region's typical paradox is in place. On the one hand, there is a widespread belief that Asia-Pacific is a region characterized by an insufficient level of institutionalization. On the other hand, it is a region where a number of more or less formalized forms of cooperation with overlapping goals and areas of competence are present (Hamanaka 2010: 1).

Both developed and developing countries of Asia-Pacific participated in the post-World War II financial and monetary regime being active members of the IMF and the World Bank Group. Yet only a few players from the region (e.g., Japan and Australia) could have been regarded as integrated with global financial structures and having an impact on their governance. In the case of the majority of developing representatives of the region participation in global financial governance had been limited to preferential loans offered by multilateral development banks.

As for the regional financial architecture, at the first glance, it might seem that it has been largely shaped only in the last two decades as a response to consecutive financial crises and the inability of global financial institutions (IMF in particular) to address them. Yet financial cooperation in the region is not unprecedented and its elements can be traced back as far as to the 1950s first central bank cooperation organizations and the Asian Development Bank (ADB) have been created. Another early input into regional financial cooperation constituted the creation of the Association of Southeast Asian Nations (ASEAN) in 1967. Although ASEAN initial goals only indirectly related to money and finance, today the organization can be named one of the main drivers of financial regionalism.

Significant changes in the region's financial architecture began after the end of the Cold War when the then Deputy Minister of Finance of Japan, Tadao Chino, proposed cyclical meetings of the Ministers of Finance of Asia-Pacific region. In 1992, this initiative took the form of the so-called Four Markets Group (FMG) that included Japan, Australia, Singapore, and Hong Kong. Since 1997, the meetings have been extended to include China and the USA (the Six Markets Group). Given the similar level of financial development of participating countries, this group seemed to have been an optimal forum for discussion on cooperation in the region, but the initiative froze after the Asian financial crisis (Hamanaka 2010: 7–9).

Since the early attempts at creating regional financial governance structures in Asia-Pacific, several factors have been affecting financial cooperation in the region.

After the fall of the Bretton Woods regime in the 1970s, it was mostly the dynamic socioeconomic development of the countries of the region together with the growing trade linkages that shaped financial cooperation mechanisms. Export-oriented development policies fostered deepening of trade linkages within the region and beyond. This process has been accompanied by the gradual removal of capital controls and subsequent liberalization of financial sectors. As a result, some countries in the region have become relatively well integrated with international capital markets (Kuroda and Kawai 2003: 2).

Although geographical proximity is not imperative for financial cooperation and integration, the specifics of Asia-Pacific significantly affects the forms of regional financial governance in place (Pacific 2002: 9–10). The region brings together both highly industrialized countries and representatives of the least developed countries with diverse levels of economic and financial development (Arner and Park 2011: 129). This differentiation in terms of financial development has often been seen as a barrier to regional financial integration and cooperation (Auster and Foo 2015: 24). Among very few similarities of the Asia-Pacific financial system, it is their bank-oriented nature that is usually underlined (Szilagyi and Batten 2004: 58).

Characteristic for the financial cooperation in Asia-Pacific prior to the Asian financial crisis was the fact that most regional financial arrangements could have been classified as spillovers from integration and cooperation processes in other areas, most notably trade liberalization. Initiatives of exclusively financial nature were almost nonexistent. Even nowadays financial integration and cooperation in the region are considered to be side effects of financial integration at the global level rather than products of a coherent strategy for regional cooperation. Thus, the early development of financial governance structures in Asia-Pacific has often been described as a market-led process rather than a policy-led process (Nair 2008: 114–115). It was a long process before regional governance mechanisms have undergone a shift from market-driven regionalization to institutionalized regionalism (Langhammer 1995). Nevertheless, the regionalization processes in the region and Asia-Pacific regionalism continue to represent the case of "open regionalism." Countries of the region attempt to be part of the global financial governance structures, and simultaneously pursue regional cooperation policies together with developing financial and monetary relations with countries from outside of the region (e.g., Americas or Europe) (Drysdale 1998).

This "open" (or hybrid) nature Asia-Pacific regionalism contributes to unequal and asymmetrical development of regional governance structures with East Asia being the major "hub" for financial cooperation and the most financially integrated subregion. However, many financial initiatives that begin in East Asia are subsequently extended to include other countries of Asia-Pacific (Mayes 2009: 1; Milner 2003: 285).

Another factor affecting the regionalization of financial governance in Asia-Pacific is the role of individual economic (and political) powers in the region. Back in the 1980s, many regional initiatives were stalled because they were proposed by Japan whose domination was feared by many countries in the region. Today concerns about Japan taking over control over the region have been replaced by the anxiety caused by the rapid growth of Chinese presence in the region. Moreover, the regional geoeconomic and geopolitical situation remains very much affected by the USA (Kangyu 2011: 72; Yuan and Murphy 2010: 131). The US presence in the region is manifested inter alia through the dominance of the US dollar as a reserve currency in the region. Hence, efforts to reduce reliance on the US dollar provide another incentive to expand regional financial cooperation.

Regional financial cooperation is fueled also by the proliferation of free trade agreements (FTAs) that usually include clauses liberalizing trade in financial services. A good example of a comprehensive FTA in the region constitutes the FTA between ASEAN and China (Zhang and Li 2010: 3). Intensification of financial cooperation in the coming years will be further facilitated by a number of initiatives concerning economic cooperation, both of an intra-regional nature and covering a much wider area. These include the implementation of the Comprehensive and Progressive Agreement for Trans-Pacific Partnership (CPTPP) and the completion of negotiations on the Regional Comprehensive Economic Partnership (RCEP) (Yuechun 2013: 109–114; Ravenhill 2003: 302–303; Khan et al. 2018).

Xiaoyan Zhang and Haitao Li (2010: 4) describe the institutionalization of regional financial governance as a crisis-driven process: The consecutive financial crises have increased demand for insurance against economic shocks as the gaps in the insurance mechanisms provided mostly by the Bretton Woods institutions have been exposed. As a result, alternative insurance mechanisms—both national and regional—have been developed over the years and regional safety nets established as necessary complements to the global financial safety net. This statement holds true also for Asia-Pacific where the Asian financial crisis constituted a significant turning point in terms of regional financial governance (Rhee et al. 2013: 3).

The Asian financial crisis can be regarded as a catalyst accelerating financial integration and cooperation processes in Asia-Pacific. It provided a direct impetus for countries to recognize the value of financial regionalism. Many economies in the region found themselves subject to similar shocks and contagion, leading to volatile capital movements and the risk of "sudden stops" and reversals of capital flows. Despite the fact that the crisis affected mostly East Asia, many of the initiatives taken during the struggle with its effects included a much wider membership. In the aftermath of the crisis, many policymakers in the region assumed that only the strengthening of regional financial stability mechanisms can protect Asia-Pacific from further crises. This belief was fueled by the failure of the international financial institutions, IMF in particular, to meet the region's demand for short-term liquidity. Thus, the aim of regional cooperation became not the only provision of financial stability but also gaining independence from global financial institutions (Rajan 2008: 31–32; Park and Wyplosz 2008).

Individual financial cooperation efforts with Asia-Pacific subregions that followed the Asian financial crisis can be regarded as part of a global tendency toward the strengthening of regionalism. These developments include the launch of the European Economic and Monetary Union (EMU) as well as the advancement of economic integration in the Americas (Yuan and Murphy 2010: 129). Furthermore, the formation of regional financial arrangements can be interpreted as a consequence of dissatisfaction with the stalled process of reform of the international financial system (Park 2016: 228).

The global financial crisis of 2007–2009 and the subsequent Eurozone sovereign debt and banking sector crisis of 2011–2012 added to the urgency for greater financial cooperation. In the aftermath of the GFC, the multilayered international financial governance regime has been strengthened in order to address three major forms of cooperation: crisis prevention, crisis management and resolution, and market strengthening. In Asia-Pacific, the crisis effects differed across countries depending on the degree of economic and financial openness, as well as on dependency on external demand and credit. Relative resilience to the crisis displayed by some of the markets proved that the development of national and regional financial arrangements can constitute a viable anti-crisis measure that led to further advances in developing regional financial architecture (Park 2011: 2).

4 Mapping Financial Governance Institutions in Asia-Pacific[5]

Within almost seven decades of financial development, Asia-Pacific countries managed to build numerous governance mechanisms that encompass a significant number of institutions with duplicate and often purely defined competencies and differentiated membership. Although East Asian countries constitute a center of monetary and financial cooperation in the region, most of the arrangements—directly or indirectly—also include South Asian countries, Australia, or even the USA.

In terms of institutionalization financial cooperation in Asia-Pacific was developing in two major tracks. Firstly, it was cooperation between central banks which dates back to the 1950s. The second direction was intergovernmental cooperation, which can be exemplified by the financial cooperation mechanisms pursued within ASEAN (Mayes 2009: 4).

There are currently three financial cooperation organizations of central banks in Asia-Pacific. These are (1) the South East Asia, New Zealand and Australia Forum of Banking Supervision (SEANZA); (2) the South East Asian Central Banks (SEACEN); and (3) the Executives' Meeting of East Asia and Pacific Central Banks (EMEAP). Among the three, SEANZA is the most comprehensive in terms of membership. Its activity is mainly focused on the exchange of information between central banks and training for central bank employees. In addition to that SEACEN is more of a technical institution conducting research on the financial systems of the region. The youngest of the central bank cooperation bodies—EMEAP (established in 1991 following the initiative of Japan and Australia)—appears currently to be the most influential unit of this type in the region. Apart from information exchange and staff training, its objectives include supervision over financial institutions in the region or supporting the development of financial markets (Kuroda and Kawai

---

[5]This section constitutes a shortened and updated version of the analysis provided in Jędrzejowska (2016).

2003: 17). Because of its involvement in establishment of regional emergency liquidity provisions and development of regional bond markets EMEAP is often regarded as a leader of regional financial cooperation (Jung 2008: 121).[6]

With the exception of ASEAN most intergovernmental financial cooperation organizations in Asia-Pacific have not been directly involved in specific financial projects until the AFC. In spite of the fact that financial cooperation constitutes only a small share of ASEAN's activities, it is one of the first organizations in the region to have taken a closer interest in financial cooperation. From the institutional perspective, ASEAN's contribution to Asia-Pacific financial governance is twofold. First, it contributed to the creation of the regional expanded cooperation platform in form of ASEAN+3 (ASEAN plus China, Japan, and the Republic of Korea) that—in turn—developed regional emergency liquidity support mechanism (CMI). Next, together with Australia, New Zealand, and India ASEAN+3 became ASEAN+6 which is a driving force behind both the RCEP as well as the East Asia Summit (EAS). Second, since the Asian financial crisis ASEAN has initiated several cooperation mechanisms (e.g., ASEAN Surveillance Forum and a permanent crisis monitoring team). It also attempted at developing regional integration strategies for the banking sector, capital markets, and insurance services markets. These initiatives have resulted in countless strategies, road maps, working groups, and committees (e.g., 2020 ASEAN Banking Integration Framework, Roadmap for Financial Integration) (Almekinders et al. 2015). Another ASEAN-led initiative constitutes the ASEAN Economic Community (AEC) which is the most advanced regional framework for financial regulatory harmonization in Asia (Kawai and Morgan 2014).

Further intergovernmental cooperation processes that are taking place in Asia-Pacific—the Asia-Pacific Economic Co-operation (APEC) and the Asia–Europe Meeting (ASEM)—address financial governance on a limited scale and work mostly through meetings of member states' finance ministers. APEC's contributions to regional financial cooperation include the establishment of the Asia-Pacific Financial Forum (APFF) which is meant to coordinate financial integration processes in Asia-Pacific (Jung 2008: 121).

Another group within the intergovernmental cooperation mechanisms constitute regional multilateral development banks providing development financing. Until recently, ADB was the most influential development finance institution in the region. In addition to development assistance, it provided also comprehensive research in terms of financial cooperation and development as well as contributed to the establishment of the Association of Credit Rating Agencies in Asia (ACRAA) (Kanamori 2005: 5) or the creation of the Asian Financial Stability Dialogue (AFSD) (Kawai 2011: 139; Berger 1999: 1015). Yet with the progressing reform of the development finance architecture, the ADB position in the region appears to

---

[6]In addition to the specialized central bank organizations, since 1997 there is also ASEAN+3-based platform for central bank cooperation in the form of the meetings of central bank governors and (since 2015) meetings between monetary authorities and finance ministers.

be challenged. First, China and India have been instrumental in establishing the BRICS' (Brazil, Russia, India, China, South Africa) New Development Bank (NDB). Next, it is the possible developmental impact of the Chinese Belt and Road Initiative together with the establishment of the Asian Infrastructure and Investment Bank (AIIB). Finally, ADB's financial mechanisms need to be adjusted to the new development finance framework based upon the "Maximizing Finance for Development" principle.

In addition to central bank cooperation organizations and intergovernmental organizations and cooperation platforms in Asia-Pacific, there is a number of organizations and initiatives that do not fit into this framework. These include—among others—some public–private organizations and think tanks. A good example of such a forum constitutes the Pacific Economic Cooperation Council (PECC). It is an unofficial organization gathering representatives of business, academia, and government officials. PECC can be considered a leader in initiating (and—indirectly—implementing) economic norms and regulations in the region, including financial ones (Aggarwal 1993: 1033; PECC 2003).

Finally, strengthening regional structures does not equal rejecting global structures (McNamara 2016). In line with this statement, since the AFC and GFC most Asia-Pacific countries have significantly improved their position in the international financial system through involvement in the works of the G20, FSB, BIS, G10 Committees, or the International Organization of Securities Commissions (IOSCO) Asia-Pacific Regional Committee (Sohn 2007: 2).

5   Selected Forms of Financial Cooperation in Asia-Pacific

From the functional perspective, the regional financial governance system includes financial regulations adopted by regional financial cooperation bodies and the specific cooperation mechanisms they have established. Masahiro Kawai and Yung Chul Park (2015: 33–44) indicate that regional financial cooperation in East Asia has been pursued on three fronts: (1) regional economic surveillance; (2) regional short-term liquidity support mechanisms; and (3) local currency bond market development. This classification of regional financial cooperation mechanisms allows its application also to the broader region of Asia-Pacific. It has to be stressed that all the presented mechanisms have their functional equivalents both at the national and global levels. Moreover, the role of RFAs in crisis prevention and management is seen as complementary to global arrangements (Darvas 2017: 44).

Regional Economic Surveillance   At the global level, economic surveillance relies mostly on the IMF's Article IV consultations which include also Asia-Pacific. Regional surveillance mechanisms in Asia-Pacific constitute another element in the regional governance network that developed in the aftermath of the AFC. The beginning of regional surveillance cooperation dates back to November 1997 when the so-called Manila Framework Group was created (Wang and Yoon 2002: 98). In the same year, ASEAN launched its Surveillance Process (ASP). Yet the most advanced surveillance and information exchange mechanisms were developed within the ASEAN+3 framework. In May 2000 ASEAN+3 members launched the Economic Review and Policy Dialogue (ERPD). As part of this process, ASEAN+3 Finance Ministers meet once a year to exchange information and discuss the harmonization of indicators. ERPD focuses on macroeconomic risk management, corporate finance, monitoring of capital flows in the region, strengthening of national financial and banking systems, reform of international financial architecture and strengthening of regional cooperation mechanisms (Kuroda and Kawai 2003: 15).

After the GFC it was determined that the EPRD shows two major shortcomings: (1) lack of involvement of central bank governors and (2) limited institutional support to the process (Kawai and Park 2015: 34). Hence, in the aftermath of the global financial crisis, the ASEAN+3 authorities established the ASEAN+3 Macro-economic Research Office (AMRO). Initiated in May 2012 AMRO combines meetings of central bank governors and finance ministers. It benefits from the support of the IMF, ADB, Bank for International Settlements, or OECD. It aims to directly support the functioning of the CMIM, in particular by supporting the decision-making process of the Chiang Mai Initiative (Arner and Park 2011: 138).

Short-Term Liquidity Support The AFC was to some extent a liquidity crisis resulting from the outflow of foreign capital. Given the IMF's failure to provide sufficient liquidity to the region (East Asia in particular) a number of Asia-Pacific countries have chosen to limit their reliance on IMF financing and focus on the accumulation of foreign exchange reserves. Further actions included the implementation of regional liquidity provisions (Fritz and Mühlich 2019: 99–101). Origins of this type of financial cooperation in Asia-Pacific can be traced back to 1977 when the ASEAN Swap Agreement (ASA) was concluded. After the AFC, in addition to several bilateral swap arrangements (BSAs) in the region, the main step toward regional short-term liquidity support constituted the CMI (Kawai and Park 2015: 35).

Initially, CMI was no more than a network of BSAs between the ASEAN+3 countries. Yet after the global financial CMI was converted into "the form of self-managed reserved pooling arrangement governed by a single contractual agreement" (Kawai and Park 2015: 37) instead of a network of BSAs. CMI Multilateralization (CMIM) became effective as of March 2010. Since then its initial size of USD 120 billion has been doubled. Contrary to CMI its multilateralized form includes both crisis prevention and crisis response tools. It is also partially separated from the IMF.

Even though the ASEAN+3-led CMI and CMIM have become the most comprehensive regional crisis prevention tools, they are not the only representatives of this type of cooperation in the region. Even before the AFC, a system of cooperation based on repo agreements existed between EMEAP and the US Federal Reserve. Another initiative in the region was the so-called New Miyazawa Initiative (NMI) proposed by Japan during the 1997 crisis. Moreover, in 1998, the ASEM Trust Fund (ATF) was launched (Yeo 2003: 50).

Local Currency Bond Markets The idea of regional bond markets started with the realization that the underdevelopment of bond markets in the region and the resulting excessive dependence on bank-intermediated financing and foreign short-term financing were major causes of the Asian financial crisis of 1997–1998 (Park et al. 2016: 264–265; Volz 2016a: 9). The crisis showed that even though some of the Asia-Pacific countries were relatively well integrated with international financial markets, the financial integration within the region was either highly asymmetrical or nonexistent (Mercereau 2006).

A direct response to the Asian crisis was a series of initiatives aimed at strengthening the regional debt market. Analogically to the abovementioned forms of cooperation, the most important projects were launched by EMEAP and ASEAN +3. Back in 2003 EMEAP supported the creation of the Asian Bond Fund (ABF) Initiative (Jung 2008: 126; Zhang and Li 2010: 6–8). The current edition of the ABF (ABF2), comprising the Pan-Asia Bond Index Fund (PAIF) and eight single-market funds, is managed by private sector fund managers with the BIS as the administrator (Government of Hong Kong 2018). In turn, the Asian Bond Market Initiative (ABMI) has been launched by ASEAN+3. Initially, it was meant to increase the liquidity of the regional bond markets, but later shifted more toward assistance in developing regional market infrastructure (Dent 2005: 392).

One of the drawbacks of both ABF and ABMI constitutes insufficient involvement of private sector actors in the form of investors, financial intermediaries, stock exchanges, or credit rating agencies. These should be included in the ASEAN+3 Asian Bond Market Forum (ABMF) (Kawai and Park 2015: 43). ASEAN+3 established the ABMF in 2010 as a common platform to foster standardization of market practices and harmonization of regulations relating to cross-border bond transactions in the region. Among other initiatives, ABMF is developing an ASEAN+3 Multi-currency Bond Issuance Framework, a common regional bond issuance program in the ASEAN+3 region (Villafuerte and Yap 2015: 35–36).

In addition to the abovementioned mechanisms of crisis prevention and management other dimensions of financial cooperation in Asia-Pacific can be listed. One of them constitutes broader efforts to increase regional economic and financial integration both through intra-regional trade linkages and further advances in financial market integration.[7] Another issue is the deepening of monetary cooperation. Last but not least several regional developments have been taking place within the architecture of development financing (Ocampo 2016: 5).

6 Conclusions

This chapter has shown that financial governance both at the global and regional level is characterized by a high degree of diversity and complexity. The regional financial arrangements can complement the global regulatory and institutional framework by addressing its shortcomings, most notably undersupply of liquidity

---

[7]Initiatives in Asia-Pacific include also broader framework of capital market integration coordinated by the ASEAN Capital Markets Forum (ACMF). See Tamaki (2013).

provisions. As a result, global and regional financial governance structures can jointly contribute to the provision and maintenance of financial stability.

In the case of Asia-Pacific processes of regional financial cooperation have been accelerated by the Asian financial crisis and—to a lesser extent—global financial crisis. As of today, two organizations seem to be the leading financial cooperation in the region. These are the Executives' Meeting of East Asia and Pacific Central Banks (EMEAP) and the ASEAN+3 Cooperation (ASEAN plus China, Japan, and the Republic of Korea). It was prevalently within these frameworks that the regional surveillance mechanisms, short-term liquidity provision mechanisms, or initiatives aimed at deepening of local currency bond markets developed.

Yet even though financial and monetary governance in Asia-Pacific has been significantly strengthened over the last 30 years, its construction cannot be regarded as a completed process. It remains a "work in progress" as the governance processes and membership structure in regional cooperation bodies remain asymmetrical and the financial cooperation process in the region appears to be missing precise long-term strategy. Moreover, it is uncertain whether the present institutional arrangements are adequate to preserve stability in Asia-Pacific. This question together with the monetary cooperation and national financial sector development requires further analysis.

Acknowledgments This chapter is part of the "Global Economic Governance—Actors, Areas of Influence, Interactions" research project (OPUS, UMO-2016/23/B/HS5/00118) funded by the National Science Centre, Poland.

References

Aggarwal, V. K. (1993). Building international institutions in Asia-Pacific. *Asian Survey, 33*(11), 1029–1042.

Alexander, K., Dhumale, R., & Eatwell, J. (2004). *Global governance of financial Systems: The international regulation of systemic risk*. CERF Monographs on Finance and the Economy. Oxford University Press.

Almekinders, G., Fukuda, S., Mourmouras, A., & Zhou, J. (2015). *ASEAN Financial Integration*. IMF Working Paper No. 15/34.

Amyx, J. (2005). *What motivates regional financial cooperation in East Asia today?* Asia Pacific Issues. Analysis from the East-West Center No. 76.

Arner, D. W., & Park, C.-Y. (2011). Developing Asia and the global financial regulatory agenda. *Journal of Banking Regulation, 12*(2), 119–143.

Auster, A., & Foo, M. (2015). *Financial integration in the Asia-Pacific: Fact and fiction*. Financial Services Institute of Australia.

Berger, M. T. (1999). APEC and its enemies: The failure of the new regionalism in the Asia-Pacific. *Third World Quarterly, 20*(5), 1013–1030.

Boughton, J. M., Lombardi, D., & Malkin, A. (2017). The limits of global economic governance after the 2007–09 international financial crisis. *Global Policy Special Issue: Europe and the World: Global Insecurity and Power Shifts, 8*(4), 30–41. https://doi.org/10.1111/1758-5899.12430

Cohen, B. J. (2007). *Global monetary governance*. Oxon and New York: Routledge.

Culperer, R. (2016). Reforming the global financial architecture: The potential of regional institutions. In J. A. Ocampo (Ed.), *Regional financial cooperation* (pp. 40–67). Baltimore, MD: United Nations Economic Commission for Latin America and the Caribbean, Brookings Institution Press.

Darvas, Z. (2017). *Regional and global financial safety nets: The recent European experience and its implications for regional cooperation in Asia.* Bruegel Working Paper, Issue 06.

De Brouwer, G., & Wang, Y. (2004). Policy dialogue, surveillance and financial cooperation in East Asia. In G. De Brouwer & Y. Wang (Eds.), *Financial governance in East Asia: Policy dialogue, surveillance and cooperation* (pp. 1–14). London: Routledge.

Dent, C. M. (2005). Taiwan and the new regional political economy of East Asia. *The China Quarterly, 182,* 385–406.

Drysdale, P. (1998). Japan's approach to Asia Pacific economic cooperation. *Journal of Asian Economics, 9*(4), 547–554. https://doi.org/10.1016/S1049-0078(98)90062-8

Fritz, B., & Mühlich, L. (2019). Regional financial arrangements in the global financial safety net: The Arab monetary fund and the Eurasian fund for stabilization and development. *Development and Change, 50*(1), 96–121.

Germain, R. (2001). Global financial governance and the problem of inclusion. *Global Governance, 7*(4), 411–426.

Germain, R. (2010). *Global politics and financial governance.* Basingstoke and New York: Palgrave Macmillan.

Government of Hong Kong. (2018). *EMEAP Central Banks announce the launch of PAIF securities lending.* Press Release. Retrieved June 28, 2019, from https://www.hkma.gov.hk/eng/key-information/press-releases/2018/20180626-3.shtml

Hamanaka, S. (2010). *Regionalism cycle in Asia (-Pacific): A game theory approach to the rise and fall of Asian regional institutions.* ADB Working Paper Series on Regional Economic Integration No. 42.

Hirata, H, Kose, M. A., &Otrok, C. (2013). *Regionalization vs. globalization.* IMF Working Paper WP/13/19.

Jędrzejowska, K. (2016). Ewolucja współpracy finansowej w regionie Azji i Pacyfiku (Evolution of the monetary cooperation in Asia-Pacific region). In A. Jarczewska & J. Zajączkowski (Eds.), *Region Azji i Pacyfiku w latach 1985–2015: ciągłość i zmiana w regionalnym systemie międzynarododowym* (pp. 436–460). Warsaw: Scholar.

Jung, J. (2008). *Regional financial cooperation in Asia: Challenges and path to development.* BIS Papers No. 42, pp. 120–135.

Kanamori, T. (2005). *Emerging issues for regional cooperation in Asia-Pacific.* ADBI Research Policy Brief no. 14.

Kangyu, R. (2011). Exploring financial cooperation between China and ASEAN countries under CAFTA. *International Journal of China Studies, 2*(1), 71–95.

Kawai, M. (2011). G-20 financial reforms and emerging Asia's challenges. In K. Dervi, M. Kawai, & D. Lombardi (Eds.), *Asia and policymaking for the global economy* (pp. 105–150). Tokyo: ADB.

Kawai, M., & Morgan, P.J. (2014). *Regional financial regulation in Asia.* ADBI Working Paper Series No. 460.

Kawai, M., & Park, Y. C. (2015). Financial and monetary cooperation in East Asia: An overview. In M. Kawai, Y. C. Park, & C. Wyplosz (Eds.), *Monetary and financial cooperation in East Asia* (pp. 11–51). Oxford: Oxford University Press.

Khan, A., Mukhopadhyay, K., & Zada, N. (2018). Economic implications of the comprehensive and progressive agreement for trans-Pacific partnership (CPTPP) on Pakistan: A CGE approach. *Journal of Economic Structures, 7*(1). https://doi.org/10.1186/s40008-017-0103-x

Kuroda, H., Kawai, M. (2003). *Strengthening regional financial cooperation in East Asia,* PRI Discussion Paper Series, nr 03A-10.

Langhammer, R. (1995). Regional integration in East Asia. From market-driven regionalisation to institutionalised regionalism? *Review of World Economics (Weltwirtschaftliches Archiv), 131*(1), 167–201.

Mayes DG (2009). Financial integration in Asia. *Archive of European Integration*. Retrieved June 28, 2019, from http://aei.pitt.edu/33109/1/mayes._david.pdf

McNamara, K. R. (2016). Regional monetary and financial governance. In T. Risse & T. A. Börzel (Eds.), *The Oxford handbook of comparative regionalism* (pp. 351–373). Oxford: Oxford University Press.

Mercereau, B. (2006). *Financial integration in Asia: Estimating the risk-sharing gains for Australia and other nations*, IMF Working Paper WP/06/267.

Milner, A. (2003). Asia-Pacific perceptions of the financial crisis: Lessons and affirmations. *Contemporary Southeast Asia, 25*(2), 284–305.

Moloney, N. (2017). The European Union in international financial governance. *RSF: Russell Sage Foundation Journal of the Social Sciences, 3*(1), 138–152.

Nair, D. (2008). Regionalism in the Asia Pacific/East Asia: A frustrated regionalism? *Contemporary Southeast Asia, 31*(1), 110–142.

Ocampo, J. A. (2016). Regional financial cooperation: Experiences and challenges. In J. A. Ocampo (Ed.), *Regional financial cooperation* (pp. 1–39). Baltimore, MD: United Nations Economic Commission for Latin America and the Caribbean, Brookings Institution Press.

Park, C-J. (2011). *Asian financial system: Development and challenges*. ADB Economics Working Paper Series No. 285.

Park, Y. C. (2016). Regional financial integration in East Asia: Challenges and prospects. In J. A. Ocampo (Ed.), *Regional financial cooperation* (pp. 227–263). Baltimore, MD: United Nations Economic Commission for Latin America and the Caribbean, Brookings Institution Press.

Park, Y.C., & Wyplosz, C. (2008). *Monetary and financial integration in East Asia: The relevance of European experience*. European Economy Economic Papers 329.

Park, Y. C., Park, J. H., Leung, J., & Sangsubhan, K. (2016). Asian bond market development: Rationale and strategies. In J. A. Ocampo (Ed.), *Regional financial cooperation* (pp. 264–290). Baltimore, MD: United Nations Economic Commission for Latin America and the Caribbean, Brookings Institution Press.

PECC. (2003). *Financial and monetary cooperation in East Asia: A road map*. PECC Issues. Retrieved June 28, 2019, from https://www.pecc.org/resources/finance-1/203-financial-and-monetary-cooperation-in-east-asia-a-road-map/file

Rajan, R. S. (2008). Monetary and financial cooperation in Asia: Taking stock of recent ongoings. *International Relations of the Asia-Pacific, 8*, 31–45.

Ravenhill, J. (2003). The new bilateralism in the Asia Pacific. *Third World Quarterly, 24*(2), 299–317.

Rhee, Ch., Sumulong, L., & Vallée, S. (2013). *Global and regional financial safety nets: Lessons from Europe and Asia*. Bruegel Working Paper 2013/06.

Sohn, I. (2005). Asian financial cooperation: The problem of legitimacy in global financial governance. *Global Governance, 11*, 487–504.

Sohn, I. (2007). *East Asia's counterweight strategy: Asian financial cooperation and evolving international monetary order*. G-24 Discussion Paper Series, no. 44.

Stavarek, D., Repkova, I., & Gajdosova, K. (2011). *Theory of financial integration and achievements in the European Union*. MPRA Paper No. 34393.

Szilagyi, P. G., & Batten, J. A. (2004). Corporate governance and financial system development, Asia-Pacific in comparative perspective. *Journal of Corporate Citizenship, 11*, 49–64.

Tamaki, R. (2013). The future of the Asian economic and financial community. *OECD Journal: Financial Markets Trends, 2012*(2).

Truman, E. (2013). The global financial safety net needs better tools to cope with future crises. *Realtime Economic Issues Watch*. Peterson Institute for International Economics. Retrieved June 28, 2019, from https://www.piie.com/blogs/realtime-economic-issues-watch/global-finan cial-safety-net-needs-better-tools-cope-future

Villafuerte, J., & Yap, J. T. (2015). *Managing capital flows in Asia: An overview of key issues*. ADB Economics Working Paper Series No. 464.

Volz, U. (2016a). *Regional financial integration in East Asia against the backdrop of recent European experiences.* SOAS Department of Economics Working Paper No. 194. London: SOAS, University of London.

Volz, U. (2016b). *Toward the development of a global financial safety net or a segmentation of the global financial architecture?* SOAS.

Wang, Y., & Yoon, D. R. (2002). Searching for a better regional surveillance mechanism in East Asia. KIEP Discussion Paper 02-01. Korea Institute.

Woo, J. J., Ramesh, M., Howlett, M., & Coban, M. K. (2016). Dynamics of global financial governance: Constraints, opportunities, and capacities in Asia. *Policy and Society, 35*(3), 269–282. https://doi.org/10.1016/j.polsoc.2016.10.002

Yeo, L. H. (2003). *Asia and Europe. The development and different dimensions of ASEM.* London and New York: Routledge.

Yuan, W.J., & Murphy, M. (2010). Regional monetary cooperation in East Asia. Should the United States be concerned? A Report of the CSIS Freeman Chair in China Studies. Retrieved June 28, 2019, from https://www.csis.org/analysis/regional-monetary-cooperation-east-asia

Yuechun, J. (2013). Asia-Pacific regional economic cooperation and CJK cooperation. *China International Studies, March/April,* 109–128.

Zhang, L., & Li, J. (2010, September 23–24). *Regional financial cooperation in East Asia: Recent developments and prospects.* Background paper for "regional financial and regulatory cooperation – A Chinese – European dialogue", Beijing.

Societal Dynamics in European Economic Governance: A Comparative Analysis of Variation in British and German Governmental Stances

Aukje van Loon 🅘

1 Introduction and Puzzle

In times of crisis, European governments are confronted with a significant necessity to act in a very limited time to push for substantial reforms in order to change things for the better. During this opportunity to make up for past mistakes and previous reluctances, these governments are obliged to take their constituencies' demands carefully into account when formulating reform stances to be promoted at EU level negotiations. Since in the first phase of EU decision-making, national preference formation, governmental responsiveness is of utmost importance if punishment at the voting booth for not having defended public concerns is to be avoided, governments cannot act in a domestic political vacuum. This argument is reflected in the societal approach to governmental preference formation: Office-seeking governments align positions according to their constituencies' demands, or more specifically, societal dynamics shape governmental stances, thus indicating the presence of responsiveness (Schirm 2009, 2011, forthcoming). Due to the crisis putting governments under close scrutiny by instantly affected countries' societies, i.e. economic sectors and voters, this proficient approach enables a rigorous comparative explanation of variation in governmental stances in EMU reform proposals.

This chapter applies said approach by analysing European economic governance reform proposals and aspires to contribute to research on European countries'

This chapter is a revised and further developed version of a paper presented at the ECPR Joint Sessions Workshop "Towards the Fiscal Union: The Formation of National Preferences on Eurozone Policies and Lessons for Future Reforms", 8–12 April 2019, Université catholique de Louvain, Mons.

A. van Loon (✉)
Chair of International Politics, Faculty of Social Science, Ruhr University of Bochum, Bochum, Germany
e-mail: aukje.vanloon@rub.de

conflicting stances towards revamping the Economic and Monetary Union (EMU). It thereby analyses two European governments, the UK and Germany and their stances towards two specific reform proposals, the creation of the European Supervisory Authorities (ESAs) and the introduction of a Financial Transaction Tax (FTT). Although the crisis led to a revival of the debate on European economic governance, a broad understanding as well as consensus dominated amongst European governments on the need to reform the EMU governance framework, their stances often reflected diverging perspectives and far-reaching disagreements on what European economic governance should look like (Van Loon 2018). The purpose of this study is to investigate these two most extreme European governmental stances towards the proposals under scrutiny, the UK strictly opposing both reform proposals while Germany resolutely promoting these. This allows (1) to examine two European governments which faced the consequences of the crisis fairly equal, and (2) to go beyond an analytical focus on individual reforms and individual countries. Additionally, whereas research has put member states' positions at centre stage, still very little is known about how and why European *governments*, represented on the EU level by their governments and heads of state, form the stances they advance in overhauling the EMU (Degner and Leuffen 2018; Hardimann and Metinsoy 2018).

Applying the societal approach to governmental preference formation provides this study with a thorough examination of national preferences and illustrates that the process of forming British and German EMU reform stances (dependent variable) were strongly shaped by two societal dynamics, sectoral interests and value-based ideas (independent variables). Governmental responsiveness in times of crisis is tested with a process-tracing (discourse) analysis of national preference formation. Different qualitative sources, including official governmental documents and speeches, statements of business associations, public opinion surveys such as the Eurobarometer, the World Values Survey, as well as quality newspaper articles (e.g. FAZ, Euractiv) are used. The empirical results of the analysis highlight that the British and German governmental stances reflected the immediate circumstances of the crisis: They did not act in a political domestic vacuum as they were obliged to take societal dynamics carefully into account when formulating their stances on controversial reform proposals. The governments' leeway in determining EMU stances thus were clearly constrained by domestic politics.

The chapter is structured as follows. It starts off by presenting the societal approach to governmental preference formation, its further development of the core variants of domestic politics theories is discussed, followed by its innovate elements and concluded by a formulation of its hypotheses. Against this backdrop, the research design introduces the discourse analysis approach and the data used for the empirical analysis. Subsequently the empirical investigation is divided into the two case studies on the creation of the ESAs and the introduction of the FTT. Both sections briefly introduce these EMU reform proposals, followed by a short encounter of the conflicting governmental stances under scrutiny in order to then conduct an analysis of the national preference formation processes by studying the societal dynamics, sectoral interests and value-based ideas, to which the governments are assumed to be responsive. The chapter ends with a comparative summary on the formulated hypotheses and empirical results.

2   The Societal Approach to Governmental Preference Formation

In analysing the puzzle of conflicting British and German governmental stances towards the ESAs and the FTT reform proposals, this chapter follows the societal approach to governmental preference formation. Resting on domestic politics and liberal theories of international relations (IR) its focus is on endogenous societal variables such as interest groups (Milner 1997; Moravcsik 1997), ideas (Goldstein and Keohane 1993) and institutions (Fioretos 2001; Hall and Soskice 2001). Equally in line with these theories, the assumption is that in democratic political systems, while governments seek to stay in office, they are likely to be responsive to 'material and ideational societal foundations', prior to inter-state and international negotiations (Schirm 2018: 64). Contrary to these theories, instead of applying scholars' traditional way of procedure by often employing one of these variables exclusively, the imperative 'refining' (Schirm forthcoming) innovative element of this approach is its inclusion of two variables and subsequent conceptualisation of hypotheses on the conditions (*impact of sector/policy issue at stake*) for these variables' prevalence vis-à vis each other in shaping governments' positions (Schirm 2013: 692).[1] Hence, the question of when either societal dynamic, of material or ideational nature, is thus addressed. In line with said approach and inserted within the context of this chapter, the two societal dynamics are domestic sectoral interests and value-based ideas. Within this study's context, the former is defined as material considerations of German and the UK sectoral interest associations whose short-term cost–benefit calculations tend to alter immediately in response to the proposed reforms due to subsequent potential changed market conditions. This definition encompasses the literature on the above-mentioned domestic politics approaches and liberal theories of IR, which addresses that changes in the international economy subsequently spurs interest groups to lobby their government into (re-)establishing competitive conditions (Milner 1997: 9; Moravcsik 1997: 528). Value-based ideas are defined as collective value-based expectations of the UK and German voters about the appropriate behaviour of the government's role in managing the proposed reforms. These are rooted in the past and cannot alter immediately in response to changed market conditions, thus underlining path dependency. This definition equally corresponds partly to the earlier mentioned literature (Goldstein and Keohane 1993), yet is developed further by considering value-based ideas expressed as long-term fundamental attitudes on appropriate governmental action in steering the economy and does not highlight the causes of ideas nor turns to elite ideas or party ideologies (Schirm 2016: 77).

In an additional embracement of the applied societal approach, it is important to further note that the two societal dynamics, sectoral interests and value-based ideas, can concur and so reinforce each other, yet they can also differ and hence collide with each other in shaping governmental positions (Schirm 2018: 65). This particular mutual complying or competing of variables leads to an advancement of the to date cogent

---

[1] The societal approach to governmental preference formation integrates three independent variables, interests, ideas, and institutions (Schirm 2016). Due to space constraints, this chapter applies the first two actor-centered variables.

aspect ignored by other scholars applying domestic politics theories, which is to inquire the conditions for the prevalence of either material or ideational societal dynamics (Schirm forthcoming). This results in three central hypotheses analysing the variation in governmental stances towards the ESAs and FTT. On the one hand, it is argued here that if the creation of the ESAs and the introduction of an FTT concerned direct *sectoral impacts*, thus implying potential cost–benefit calculations for specific UK and German economic sectors, then the societal dynamic sectoral interests predominated in shaping UK and German governmental stances. Conversely, it is suggested here that if the creation of the ESAs and the introduction of an FTT concerned *policy issues at stake* regarding fundamental long-term societal expectations on the appropriate role of the government in steering the economy, then the societal dynamic value-based ideas was more likely to prevail in shaping UK and German governmental stances. These first two propositions indicate that the societal dynamics can compete. For combining this with the reinforcement aspect, a third premise is formulated in order to account for the interplay of these dynamics. This argues that if the creation of the ESAs and the introduction of an FTT raised both potential cost–benefit calculations for specific economic sectors as well as fundamental long-term societal expectations on the appropriate role of the government in steering the economy, then the two societal dynamics competed or reinforced each other in shaping UK and German governmental stances.

3 Case Study Selection and Operationalisation

The argument that the conflicting governmental stances towards the ESAs and FTT were shaped by two societal dynamics, sectoral interests and value-based ideas, will be examined by analysing the discourse regarding the UK's and Germany's governmental stances from 2005 until 2012. This time period encompasses perspectives of the UK and German government, as well as their society before and during the crisis and the subsequent reform proposals. The selection of these two countries can be justified by (1) being two of the largest countries in the EU, (2) having the largest financial sectors, (3) the obvious contrast in their political systems, (4) both having been crucial players during reform proposals, and (5) the significant differences in terms of their economies with, in the UK case, a tradition of equity-based financing of firms, while Germany has a bank-based financial system. In terms of political economy, the two countries are generally considered to be the classic examples of the two ideal types of varieties of capitalism, with the UK as a liberal market economy (LME) profoundly accommodated by financial services and Germany as a coordinated market economy (CME) substantially shaped by manufacturing (Hall and Soskice 2001). Examining these two European countries is ideal in analysing societal dynamics and implies that an LME tends to rely more on markets' modes of coordination in the financial sphere, while a CME relies more on the existing institutional governance structures of non-market institutions.

Considering differences with regard to value-based ideas, two dyads of ideas on the role of the government in managing the market can be highlighted: 'individual responsibility' versus 'collective solidarity' and 'trust in market forces' versus 'trust in governmental regulation'. Previous research has illustrated that the set of the so-called pro-market ideas 'individual responsibility' and 'trust in market forces' derives more resilient support from the UK than from Germany, whereas in contrast, the set of the so-called pro-regulation ideas 'collective solidarity' and 'trust in governmental regulation' are supported stronger in Germany than the UK (Schirm 2011: 50–51; Van Loon 2018: 250–251).

Governmental responsiveness is tested with a process-tracing discourse analysis of national preference formation. Different qualitative sources will be used, such as (1) quotes and statements from relevant sectoral interest groups (financial, banking, insurance sector) as well as responsible politicians (finance ministers and heads of government); (2) attitudes of voters in public opinion polls, such as the Eurobarometer and the World Values Survey; and (3) analyses and reports from specialised media (e.g. FAZ and Euractiv). Speeches from politicians will be examined to analyse whether governmental stances represent domestic actors' material interests or value-based ideas. Significant here is the fact that politicians' speeches and statements can only provide plausibility but do not prove real motivations behind governmental stances. Public statements and speeches are however testimonials for what governments acknowledge as acceptable to voters and therefore do provide legitimacy (Schirm 2009: 507). Based on the standard assumption of self-interest to remain in office, public statements by politicians accountable to the populace give evidence for what they consider acceptable to crucial to their constituencies.

4   Societal Dynamics in Governmental Stances Towards the Creation of the ESAs and the Introduction of an FTT

The momentum for both the set-up of the ESAs and the introduction of a European FTT was triggered by the global financial crisis in 2007/2008 which led to an outbreak of the Eurozone crisis in early 2010. The crisis revealed the instability of financial markets and, as a result, confidence in their efficiency weakened. In pursuance of alleviating the impact of the crisis on European countries and so prevent recurrence, widespread calls within the EU arose on the future of post-crisis European economic governance, which resulted in a broad consensus among European governments about the essential urgency for reform. Existing frameworks were to be revised and a new system of financial supervision to be adopted. Additionally, in order to ensure that the financial sector was to make a fair and substantial contribution, a debate over the benefits and disadvantages of a tax on financial transactions was revived (Schulmeister et al. 2008: 5). While the crisis advanced this reopening of a European economic governance discussion, the dire situation led the two European governments under scrutiny to agree on the necessity to reform the EMU governance framework, their stances however often reflected opposite perspectives as they largely did not agree on what European economic governance should look like (Van Loon 2018). What follows here are the empirical case studies on the societal dynamics, sectoral interests and value-based ideas, of variation in the UK and German governmental stances. It will be examined whether these stances correspond to these dynamics in a cross-country comparison.

5   Case I: The European Supervisory Authorities (ESAs)

Regarding the creation of the ESAs, the De Larosière Report (2009) included recommendations to strengthen the European financial supervisory framework and increase EU financial stability. Based on its recommendations, the European Commission (henceforth Commission) published a proposal for the creation of more centralised EU supervisory authorities. This was adopted by the Economic and Financial Affairs Council (ECOFIN) as the European Supervisory Framework (European Commission 2009) and consisted out of two supervisory frameworks: the European Systemic Risk Council (ESRC, later renamed European Systemic Risk Board (ESRB)) and the European System of Financial Supervision (ESFS). The latter consists of three European Supervisory Authorities (ESAs) with sectoral responsibilities—the European Banking Authority (EBA), the European Securities and Markets Authority (ESMA), and the European Insurance and Occupational Pensions Authority (EIOPA). This supervisory structure started operating on 1 January 2011 and has been viewed as 'one of the most significant EU legislative responses to the crisis' (Buckley and Howorth 2010: 120). These issues for supervisory reform were fiercely debated among European countries (EU Observer 2010) which highlighted on the one hand, tensions between the need for greater centralisation of financial supervision and regulation at the EU level (Germany, France, Italy) and on the other hand, the reluctance to give up national regulatory autonomy (the UK, Ireland, Luxemburg). As reform efforts were constrained by conflicting governmental stances, this encounter was made visible by a 'conflicts of interests' (Bini Smaghi 2009) as well as 'varieties of strategies' (Schirm 2011), primarily between the UK and Germany.

5.1   UK and Germany: Governmental Stances

UK
Preceding the financial crisis, the British government was highly in favour of light-touch regulation and supervision at home and hostile to almost all developments abroad, apart from those that provided access to international financial markets (Zimmermann 2010). Prime Minister Gordon Brown held this to be 'fair, proportionate, predictable and increasingly risk-based' (Brown 2005). The interpretation of the global financial crisis by the UK government was that it was caused by the failure of individual actors, and not by the system. Brown recalled in his book *Beyond the Crash* where he writes

> this crisis calls for the ability to reason morally. I believe the most stunning revelation of the crisis was this: despite the financial markets infusing every aspect of everyday life, the ethical values that matter in everyday life had never infused the financial market. (Brown 2010: 9)

Equally, Chancellor of the Exchequer Alistair Darling stated that the regulatory and supervisory system was not to blame for the credit crunch but big bosses of financial institutions were responsible (Darling 2009). Darling stated that international coordination and cooperation was necessary (Handelsblatt 2009a) but that 'EU supervisory and regulatory arrangements must not in itself become a barrier to more integrated global markets—or indeed put at risk the integrity of the Single Market' (Darling 2009). The UK persistently argued to stay in line with global developments on financial regulation and supervision reforms. Nevertheless, it welcomed the De Larosière Report (Taylor 2009). With voices from within the country calling for 'no return to light-touch regulation' (The Telegraph 2009) Brown was forced to drop his 'limited touch' approach (The Guardian 2006). Yet, although the UK government supported the establishment of the ESAs, various proposals were viewed as not acceptable. For one, the further strengthening of the powers of these EU micro-prudential authorities was a matter of controversy. Darling warned against attempts to give EU centralised financial market regulators powers over national regulators voicing concerns about possible fiscal burden and loss of sovereignty, posing a competitive threat to the City of London (Darling 2009). The proposed rules were viewed as intrusive and potentially protectionist (Benoit and Tait 2009; Handelsblatt 2009a). The government was also reluctant to grant decision-making powers to EU-level bodies, while public funds to tackle banking crises came from national budgets (The Economist 2009). Hence, at the 2009 ECOFIN meeting, it blocked the agreement. Darling stated 'the bottom line for us is that we couldn't have a situation where a European supervisor could make an order to an institution in our country which could have fiscal consequences'. (O'Donnell 2009)

Germany

Since the mid-1990s and reinforced in 2007 during the G8 Summit in Heiligendamm, the German government had strongly been in favour for stricter regulation and supervision of financial markets (Zimmermann 2010: 121). German efforts and proposals however were most often criticised by the UK as its light-touch regulation was viewed as clearly superior to the German social market economy model (Schirm 2011: 52). Both Chancellor Angela Merkel and Finance Minister Peer Steinbrück criticised the Anglo-American model as being responsible for the financial crisis. In summer 2008, Merkel said that

> Europe has developed a certain independence thanks to the euro [but] in terms of the rules, the transparency guidelines and the entire standardisation of financial markets, we still have a strongly Anglo-Saxon-dominated system. (Barber et al. 2008)

Merkel's support of the social market economy was stressed in a speech in 2008 where she stated that the social market economy is not only the way out of the crisis, but the state as 'Hüter der Ordnung' and the social market economy model should become an export success both in Europe and in the world as it would stem the excesses of the market which would be the key to preventing future crises (Merkel 2008: 12). In an interview in which Peer Steinbrück blamed the USA for the global financial crisis, he stated that financial products became more and more complex, but the rules and safeguards didn't change. I don't know anyone in New York or London who would have asked for a stronger regulatory framework 18 months ago. They were always saying: The market regulates everything. What a historic mistake! (Steinbrück 2008)

In their statements, both Merkel and Steinbrück interpreted the financial crisis as being primarily the result of insufficient regulation. In their views, the social market economy represents an alternative and prioritised model. Faced with re-elections in September 2009, Merkel stated that in future it would be the EU's responsibility to be 'a voice for the social market economy in the international order' (Merkel 2009). The German government endorsed the proposals made in the De Larosière report and was clearly in favour of the ESAs. Together with France, Germany published a statement stating that the EU 'must move resolutely towards a European regulatory framework' (Parker et al. 2009). At a meeting two months before the G20 Summit in London in April 2009, the heads of government and finance ministers agreed on the shared goal to ensure that no financial product, no financial market and no financial operator should remain unregulated, which was endorsed in a joint statement (Bryant 2009). At the EU Summit in June 2009 in Brussels, Steinbrück criticised the UK's 'lack of interest' and 'high abstinence towards regulatory measures' (Handelsblatt 2009b) regarding introducing new rules to give the ESAs binding powers in order to force national regulators to act.

5.2 UK and Germany: Sectoral Interests

UK
UK sectoral interests were generally in favour of the creation of the ESAs, yet they were very sceptical about the role and powers of these EU watchdogs. Archi Kane, Chairman of the Association of British Insurers (ABI), warned against a 'one-size-fits-all' financial regulation and urged to strengthen confidence in this as well as in those who regulate it. 'It is vitally important we get this right for the industry and avoid a direct read-across from the regulation of banking to the insurance sector' (Dunkley 2009). In a position paper, the ABI stated its long-standing support of strengthening the EU supervisory framework before the crisis and thus broadly supported the proposals in the De Larosière report. Two main concerns however were the risk of overregulation and the importance of maintaining open markets.

The response to the financial crisis carries a risk of over-regulation that would stifle innovation and increase costs, excluding consumers from the protection of insurance and other financial products. But we must not stop at Europe's borders, but work to ensure that EU level initiatives are integrated into a global framework. (ABI 2010)

The British Bankers Association (BBA) was equally in favour of reforming EU financial supervision and understood the necessity for some centralisation of power in the ESAs. It was however extremely concerned about the Commission's proposed powers to be assigned to these authorities.

The primary concern we have is the ability of the ESAs to take binding decisions addressed to individual institutions. We believe, in particular that this could give rise to legal uncertainty, if national supervisors can be second guessed and subject to override. This could have a destabilising effect in the market. (BBA 2009)

The BBA did support cooperation between national supervisors and the authorities if this did not come 'at the cost of undermining national powers and creating friction within the European System of Financial Supervision' (O'Grady 2009). The Investment Management Association (IMA) was less critical towards the proposals aiming to reform EU financial market supervision. It stated that it was in favour of improved micro-prudential supervision and supported transforming the current EU committees into EU authorities with greater powers, including the ability to draft binding technical standards (IMA 2009). The IMA's primary issue of concern was potential protectionism and keeping global markets open.

There have been some worrying signs of protectionism, which would be harmful in the long run to Europe's financial markets, its industry and its consumers. Closing Europe's borders is not an option in the globalised economy. We agree that the EU can and should take the lead, but it must act responsibly and in co-ordination with other jurisdictions. (IMA 2009)

Germany

German sectoral interests were equally in favour of the creation of the ESAs and not as sceptical towards this issue compared to its British counterparts (Gamelin 2010). The German Insurance Association (GDV) stated the plans of creating the ESAs as the right way forward towards more stability of financial markets because

the insurance industry itself is also interested in strong supervision, as this ensures that, in a competitive environment, all companies will be operating on a level playing field and that no company will be able to gain a (temporary) advantage by failing to comply with regulations. Moreover, the insurance industry relies on the confidence in the sector and effective supervision strengthens this confidence. (GDV 2012: 12)

Also, while expressing the views of the European Savings Bank Group (ESBG) with regard to the De Larosière report, Mr. Schackmann-Fallis, Executive Board member of the German Savings Bank Association (DSGV), was in favour of an early warning system and to connect national supervisory bodies 'as the creation of European authorities will be a first step towards a full-scale supervisory authority for the system relevant cross-border banks at EU-level'. By stressing the need for supervision, he stated that it 'must be effective and put in place at short notice' (ESBG 2009: 8). Equally, Chief Executive of the Association of German Banks (BDB) Manfred Weber stated that in order to create an efficient and harmonised EU Single Market a more centralised approach regarding supervisory competences on the EU-level needs to be applied. He stated that although an EU-level supervisor cannot be created overnight, convergence of national regulations should be driven forward and closer cooperation between national authorities should become a priority. The ultimate aim should be the creation of a single institution responsible for supervising large banks that operate across the EU, with national regulators responsible only for domestic banks (Weber 2008).

5.3 UK and Germany: Value-Based Ideas

Concerning value-based ideas, a survey conducted in 2012 revealed that a significant majority of UK voters held the banking industry accountable for the financial crisis. Regarding the question 'who is to blame the most for causing the UK financial crash in 2008?' 62% of respondents blamed the banking industry whereas 71% of people did not primarily blame the Labour Government (Survation 2012). With the banking industry having this poor reputation, it would seem that tighter supervision through greater government intervention was to be welcomed by UK voters. The response to the question 'if major public services and industries ought to be in state ownership?' shows however no evidence that greater government intervention was wished by the UK public. This question had been posed in four polls in the years 1994, 1996, 1997 and 2009, respectively. British attitudes resulted in 45, 43, 38 and 41% of respondents agreeing to more government intervention (Curtice and Park 2010: 139). These numbers reveal that attitudes on an increased role of the government in managing the economy had not risen due to the dire crisis situation. Concerning German domestic value-based ideas, a poll conducted 1 year after the financial crisis revealed that 59% of German respondents were of the opinion that 'Germany was a victim of mistakes made pre-eminently in the USA'. Also, 62% of the respondents were in favour that 'the state should in general increasingly intervene in the economy'. Particularly, 51% agreed that 'the state should acquire a stake in significant businesses' (ARD Deutschlandtrend 2008).

The responses of two Eurobarometer opinion polls also show diverging attitudes of the UK and German public wanting a greater role for the state. The 2009 Eurobarometer poll (Eurobarometer 2009: 123), asked UK and German respondents the question 'from the following list of measures, which one should be given priority when it comes to reforming the financial system in the European Union?' Regarding the priority of measures to be undertaken in reforming the financial system in the EU, respondents from the UK and Germany were fairly divided.

From the following list of measures, which one should be given priority when it comes to reforming the financial system in the European Union?

	Transparency of benefits, costs and risks on financial markets (%)	Stronger European system of supervision of financial markets and financial institutions (%)	Accountability of financial managers, including bonuses (%)	Government guarantee for deposits made by individuals (%)	DK (%)
EU	26	26	24	13	9
DE	25	32	27	9	5
UK	19	21	31	13	14

Source: Based on Eurobarometer (2009: 231)

With a choice of four measures, 31% of UK respondents stated that the most urgent measure to be given priority when reforming the EU financial system was to make financial managers accountable (Eurobarometer 2009: 123). This tops the

EU27 average of 24% which is however more in line with German respondents' opinions (27%) that see this as a second priority. The most urgent measure of 32% of German respondents was to strengthen the system of supervision of financial markets and institutions. With the EU27 average being at 26%, UK respondents (21%) were less convinced of the urgency of this measure. Equally, the Eurobarometer poll from 2012 asked UK and German respondents in order to find ways to combat the crisis, whether on the one hand, 'they would be better protected in the face of the current crisis if [our country] adopted measures and applied them in a coordinated way with the other EU countries' or on the other hand, if the country 'adopted measures and applied them individually'. Sixty-two per cent of UK respondents were in favour that their country would adopt measures and apply these individually. Again, this differs from the 67% of German respondents who were in favour of applying the measures in a coordinated manner with other European countries (Eurobarometer 2012a: 11). In the UK, there was thus no sign of increased voters' desire regarding government intervention.

> Although the financial crisis has made people feel a little less secure about their jobs it has not persuaded them to change their attitudes in any more fundamental fashion. The sight of governments rescuing banks or the stories of bankers' bonuses does not seem to have made them question their views about the role that government should play in the market place. There has certainly been no renewal of enthusiasm for more active government. (Curtice and Park 2010: 150)

This statement is supported by results of the 2009 Eurobarometer poll where 74% of UK respondents found that 'the state intervenes too much in our lives' (Eurobarometer 2009: 12). On the other hand, a poll conducted in the same year the ESAs entered into force resulted in 92% of German respondents being in favour of stronger rules for financial markets when asked the question whether 'global financial markets should be subjected to stronger regulation so that states can better control markets' (ARD Deutschlandtrend 2011). Whereas UK respondents were not in favour of relying on the state in managing the economy as approval of regulatory state intervention did not increase, German respondents had the exact opposite opinion. For a way out of the crisis Germans were more in favour of relying on the state as approval of regulatory state intervention increased whereas trust in the market significantly declined reaching a level of 22% in 2009, the lowest level since 1994 (Bundesverband Deutscher Banken 2009: 5).

6 Case II: The European Financial Transaction Tax (FTT)

Concerning the introduction of a European FTT, the failure of the 2010 G20 Toronto Summit to reach agreement on global coordinated action to tax the financial sector led European governments to pursue an FTT at the regional level. The Commission adopted a proposal for a Council Directive on a common FTT in September 2011 in order (1) to avoid fragmentation of the internal market for financial services; (2) to ensure that financial institutions make a fair and substantial contribution to covering the costs of the crisis; (3) to introduce appropriate disincentives for transactions that do not enhance the efficiency of financial markets; and (4) to create complementing regulatory measures to avoid future crises (European Commission 2011: 2). EU governments were, similar to the creation of the ESAs, involved in a heated debate on the benefits and disadvantages this reform proposal would have on financial transactions between financial institutions. Its introduction was strongly supported by some governments, in particular Germany, yet highly opposed by a majority of member governments, most vocally by the UK. In the end, only a minority, 11 of 27 governments, decided to proceed with the implementation of the FTT under voluntary 'enhanced cooperation'.[2]

6.1   UK and Germany: Governmental Stances

UK

Repeatedly pointing to the various negative effects an FTT would have on the EU economy, British Prime Minister David Cameron cited the Commission's 2011 impact assessment by indicating that a European FTT could end up reducing EU GDP by €200 billion and could cost nearly 500,000 jobs and force much of the financial industry out of Europe: 'Even to be considering this at a time when we are struggling to get our economies growing is quite simply madness' (Cameron 2012). The British government further expressed concerns over the negative impact an FTT would particularly have on the UK's large financial industry. Cameron repeatedly insisted that he considered the financial service industry one of Britain's main strengths which it should openly support (Cameron 2013). Chancellor of the Exchequer George Osborne, backed this argument by stating that proposals for a European FTT 'are a bullet aimed at the heart of London, (. . .) economic suicide for Britain and for Europe [and] this government will ensure that our national interests and our voice in the EU are protected' (Falloon 2011). Speaking on the margins of the 2011 G7 Summit in Marseilles, he pronounced this rejection while stating that companies would leave the City of London as well as the EU for financial centres not covered by a financial transaction tax.

> I am against an EU tax. There would be no point introducing a financial transaction tax that led, the next day, to our foreign exchange markets moving to New York or Singapore or anywhere else. (Waterfield 2011)

---

[2]Austria, Belgium, Estonia, France, Germany, Greece, Italy, Portugal, Slovakia, Slovenia and Spain. Although statements of support for this broad-based FTT by the remaining heads of state and government (Euractiv 2018), as well as the respective finance ministers continue, a final agreement is still pending at the time of writing.

Germany

The German government supported an FTT and had reached consensus on this in May 2010 (Tagesschau 2013). The financial sector, among others, was considered responsible for the financial crisis as well as the ensuing economic crisis (Bundesregierung 2012a; Merkel 2011). As a result, German Chancellor Angela Merkel and Finance Minister Wolfgang Schäuble repeatedly demanded that this industry must make a fair contribution to the costs imposed on states and taxpayers during and after the crisis (Bundesregierung 2012b; Schäuble 2012a). It was in turn regarded unacceptable that financial gains were privatised while costs were socialised (Schäuble 2012b). An FTT was furthermore viewed as a proper means to limit high frequency trading, thereby stabilising financial markets (Schäuble 2012c). Chancellor Merkel stated that she was in favour of the tax as this was the 'correct answer' to the crisis: 'we will fight for it'. She furthermore said that if necessary, if there is no common solution for all EU countries, the tax could be proposed only in the euro area as an FTT-light version (Spiegel Online 2012).

Due to these controversial governmental stances, it became clear during the seven meetings of the Council's Working Party on Tax Questions as well as the European Council meeting on 22 June 2012 that unanimous support for an EU-wide FTT could not be reached. Germany (together with France) nevertheless has regularly been putting the FTT on the agenda of the ECOFIN meetings in order to advance the issue and to renew political commitment of the remaining ten member states. Stating in a recent proposal Germany's Finance Minister Olaf Scholz stated that the tax is 'an important element' in strengthening the EU (Süddeutsche Zeitung 2018), if turned 'into a source of European revenue' (Spiegel Online 2018).

6.2 UK and Germany: Sectoral Interests

UK

The examined British business associations voiced their distinct opposition to an FTT. They feared that, unless adopted worldwide, the tax would especially affect the City of London as Europe's largest financial centre and European financial markets in general, putting the EU at a competitive disadvantage with other trading hubs and thereby diverting financial activities to other jurisdictions (CBI 2012: 1; COBCOE 2011: 2). Particular attention was paid to the presumed negative impact of an FTT on the real economy, stressing that this

> would actually weaken both financial sector operators and the economies in which they do business, which would ultimately be detrimental to European tax revenue, to employment and to the citizens of the EU. (BBA 2011: 5)

The Commission's strategy of applying a very low tax rate on a very broad base of transactions was not expected to precisely target speculative trading, especially because it was considered impossible to distinguish between 'good' and 'bad' transaction types (BBA 2011). Rather, as an FTT was expected to be a disincentive to risk hedging in the form of derivatives, according to BBA (2011), systemic risks could actually increase. Accordingly, British business associations under scrutiny openly applauded the British government once the latter had made its refusal of an FTT clear, calling it 'absolutely the right decision not to adopt the European Financial Transaction Tax in the UK' (CBI 2012: 1).

Germany

In the examined period leading up to the Commission's proposal for an FTT under enhanced cooperation, the sectoral interests of Germany's leading business associations, BDI, Bankenverband and DIHK shared the concerns over the negative impact of an FTT on Germany's real economy as well as on private actors. The main concern referred to possible migration of financial institutions such as banks and investment funds to jurisdictions in which transactions were not generally taxed. Furthermore, the business associations voiced concerns that it would become more difficult for German enterprises to borrow money and appropriately hedge risks (DIHK et al. 2011: 3; BDI, BDA 2012: 1). As a result, an FTT was expected to even further decrease growth and employment (DIHK et al. 2011: 4). Germany's cooperative banking association (BVR), not in favour of Chancellor Merkel's idea of applying a financial transaction tax only to the euro area, stated that such a tax would fail to bring stability to markets: 'For all the legitimate efforts at stabilising financial markets, we feel a financial transaction tax which is limited to the euro zone is not effective' (Euractiv 2011).

6.3   The UK and Germany: Value-Based Ideas

As stated above, Germans are generally more regulation friendly, which is considered typical for CMEs, while the British society, more in line with LMEs, is expected to oppose more regulation due to their pro-market ideas. These perceptions are reflected in the public survey data taken from the 2011 and 2012 Eurobarometer, corresponding to society's FTT opposition in Britain and its approval in Germany. Concerning the question whether respondents were in favour of or opposed to a financial transaction tax, in both years, German respondents showed a higher approval rate for a European FTT, whereas the UK was fairly divided over the introduction of such a tax in 2011. In 2012, the approval rate of German respondents increased by 7% which resulted in 81% being the highest approval rate of all countries (together with Austria), with the average of the EU27 being at 63%. The disapproval rate in the UK also increased by 7%, with almost one in five people (48%) being against an FTT. With the EU27 average of 27% opposing the introduction of an FTT, this resulted in the UK positioning itself on rank four after the Netherlands, Malta and Hungary (58, 57 and 56%, respectively).

Thinking about reform global financial markets, please tell me whether you are in favour or opposed to the following measures to be taken by the EU.
The introduction of a tax on financial transactions

2011				2012			
	Totally in favour (%)	Totally opposed (%)	Don't know (%)		Totally in favour (%)	Totally opposed (%)	Don't know (%)
EU	61	25	14	EU	63	27	10
DE	74	16	10	DE	81	14	5
UK	43	41	16	UK	39	48	13

Source: Eurobarometer (2011: 10; 2012b: 144)

One reason for this could be linked to respondents being asked about the major threats to their state's economic well-being. While the lack of jobs tops the list in Britain with 87% of respondents regarding it as a major threat compared to 70% of Germans, the power of banks is perceived as a serious threat to 78% of Germans compared to 65% in the UK (Pew Research 2012: 21). Concerning the question of the appropriate role of the state versus the market, 66.7% of Germans but only 42.5% of British respondents rather support the statement that 'governments should take more responsibility' whereas a majority of 56.6% of British respondents agree that 'people should take more responsibility', compared to only 31% in Germany (WVS 2006). Yet, it must be noted that figures by Pew Research suggest a bigger convergence on a similar subject: A majority of both German (62%) and British respondents (55%) found that it was more important that the state guarantees nobody is in need than the freedom to pursue life's goals without state interference (Pew Research 2012: 1). This relates to different attitudes assigned to individual responsibility as opposed to collective responsibility: While 63.6% of Germans agree that incomes should be made more equal and only 31.3% maintain that large income divides are required as incentives, UK respondents are virtually split on the subject (49 versus 48.8%) (WVS 2006). Also, the fact that governments tax the rich and subsidise the poor is considered rather an essential part of democracy by a vast majority of Germans (71.1%) and, to a lesser extent, British respondents (59.9%) (WVS 2006). The differences expressed in these figures are corresponding to the different types of market economies of the two countries.

Considering the preceding data, although both countries share core assumptions and both agree that the state is to govern markets to a certain extent (Schirm 2011: 50), the argument that the German and the British societies have different attitudes about appropriate governmental behaviour towards markets can be supported. Whereas the more regulation-friendly attitudes of Germans, who maintain the relevance of the role of the state towards the market and largely supported the introduction of an FTT, are expected to have shaped the government's approval of such a measure, in the UK value-based ideas were largely opposed to this reform proposal and are prone to have reinforced the opposition of business associations towards the FTT.

7   Conclusion

This chapter's aim was to contribute to research on European countries' conflicting stances towards revamping the Economic and Monetary Union (EMU) by providing a better understanding of the governmental preference formation processes of the UK and Germany and their conflicting stances towards the two reform proposals, the creation of the ESAs and the introduction of a European FTT. Although the crisis led to a revival of the debate on post-crisis European economic governance and a broad understanding as well as consensus dominated amongst European governments on the need to reform the EMU governance framework, their stances often reflected diverging perspectives and far-reaching disagreements on what European economic governance should look like. With scholarship finding itself largely in a lacuna with regard to both the causes of and variance in governmental stances towards these reform proposals, and finding no answers to the questions which of societal dynamics, sectoral interests and value-based ideas, within the European countries under scrutiny were more prevalent in shaping the respective governmental stances on these reform proposals and why, this chapter applied a comprehensive adoption of the societal approach to governmental preference formation to fill this research gap. Departing from the above-mentioned empirical puzzle, the specific goals of this study were to analyse (1) how and to what extent these dynamics determined conflicting stances, (2) when each of these dynamics mattered, and (3) how they interacted with each other in shaping the two chosen governmental stances to be against (UK) and in favour (Germany) of introduction of the ESAs and an FTT.

The case studies firstly have illustrated that Germany and the UK had interpreted the financial crisis completely different. Whereas Germany viewed the crisis as a failure of the (international) market system, the UK held missing market morals and individual boardrooms responsible for the crisis. Secondly, the chapter's empirical part has shown that the UK and German governmental stances towards the reform proposals clearly correlated to different domestic societal dynamics in a cross-country comparison. The societal approach to governmental preference formation endorses rich theoretical and empirical results and eminently illustrates its contribution in explaining the origins of and variation in governmental stances towards post-crisis European economic governance. Confirming its hypotheses, the above-mentioned high relevance of the UK's dependence on financial markets resulted in disapproving both proposed reforms. On the other hand, the above-mentioned less relevance of Germany's dependence on financial markets resulted in approving the introduction of both reforms. The first case study revealed that UK sectoral interests, although generally in favour of the creation of the ESAs, were strictly opposed to the role and powers of these authorities, whereas German sectoral interests were not as sceptical and largely in favour of these authorities' creation. The case study on the FTT revealed that both UK and Germany sectoral interests, as expressed in leading business associations' publications, proved to be opposed to this reform proposal. Concerning value-based ideas, the above-mentioned pro-market ideas of the UK and the pro-regulation ideas of Germany resulted in disapproval (UK) and approval

(Germany) of both proposed reforms once fundamental long-term societal expectations on the appropriate role of the government in steering the economy were raised. Thus, whereas both societal dynamics played a role in shaping the UK governmental stance towards both reform proposals, sectoral interests and value-based ideas equally formed the German governmental stance in the case study on the ESAs, yet the latter societal dynamic prevailed in shaping the governmental stance towards the FTT reform proposal.

This leads to the results on the relationship between the societal dynamics, sectoral interests and value-based ideas, as they can concur and so reinforce each other, yet they can also differ and hence collide with each other in shaping governmental stances. In fact, the comparatively limited role of financial markets to the German economy facilitated a colliding interdependency between the two societal dynamics, with the more regulation-friendly societal attitudes competing with disapproving material interests in the FTT case. This resulted in the value-based ideas to predominantly have shaped the favourable German governmental stance towards introducing the FTT. Similarly, the interaction between the two societal dynamics within the UK context led to the opposite effect. The more regulation-averse UK attitudes expressed similar concerns to those of the business associations under scrutiny, thus facilitating a reinforcement of these societal dynamics, shaping the opposing UK FTT governmental stance.

Lastly, the case studies have also revealed that the country-specific type of market economy has provided an understanding of both governmental stances being in line with the LME and CME frameworks. Germany's favourable stance towards the ESAs and FTT correlated to both societal dynamics regarding the ESAs and to value-based ideas (and not sectoral interests) in the FTT reform proposal. The German CME framework typically strengthened the effect of sectoral interests and value-based ideas in favour of the introduction of the ESAs. Concerning the FTT reform proposal, this strengthened the effect of regulation-friendly ideas and, in turn, the governmental stance in favour of both reform proposals. Conversely, the opposing governmental stance of the UK correlated to both societal dynamics in both reform proposals. The British LME, 'light-touch', regulatory system typically strengthened the effect of sectoral interests and value-based ideas opposed to the introduction of the ESAs and an FTT and, consequently resulted into an opposed governmental stances towards these.

In sum, this chapter has demonstrated the overall rich explanatory power of the societal approach to governmental preference formation. The argument that in the first phase of EU decision-making, national preference formation, governmental responsiveness is of utmost importance if punishment at the voting booth for not having defended public concerns is to be avoided, can be perfectly reflected and tested by this approach. Therefore, its focus on the domestic level and inclusion of two societal dynamics promises to enrich future research on (1) the origins of as well as the variation in governmental stances, (2) on the reasons why and under which conditions societal dynamics matter in shaping their respective governmental stances, as well as (3) on success and failure of post-crisis European economic governance in general and reforming the EMU framework in specific.

References

ABI. (2010, April 9). *ABI response to the European Commission consultation on the improvement of supervision for the financial services sector.* Retrieved from https://www.abi.org.uk/~/media/Files/Documents/Consultation%20papers/2009/04/De_la_rosiere_vFINAL10Apr09_150409101359.ashx

ARD DeutschlandTrend. (2008, November). *DeutschlandTrend.* Retrieved from http://www.tagesschau.de/inland/deutschlandtrend472.html

ARD DeutschlandTrend. (2011, November). *DeutschlandTrend.* Retrieved from http://www.infratest-dimap.de/uploads/media/dt1111_bericht.pdf

Barber, L., Bernoit, B., & Williamson, H. (2008, June 11). March to the middle. *Financial Times.* Retrieved from http://www.ft.com/intl/cms/s/0/bb9ca588-374f-11dd-bc1c-0000779fd2ac.html#axzz2cdQ5uC5x

BBA. (2009, November 9). *Written evidence submitted by the British Bankers' Association,* House of Commons Treasury Committee. Retrieved from http://www.publications.parliament.uk/pa/cm200809/cmselect/cmtreasy/1088/1088we05.htm

BBA. (2011). *BBA responds to the European Commission's consultations on financial sector taxation.* Retrieved from www.bba.org.uk/policy/financial-and-risk-policy/taxation/fs-taxation/bbaresponse-to-the-european-commissionis-consultation-on-financial-sector-taxation-2/

BDI and BDA. (2012). *BDA und BDI: Keine zusätzlichen Belastungen durch neue Finanztransaktionssteuer.* Retrieved from www.bdi.eu/163_Pressemitteilung_BDI_BDA_zur_Finanztransaktionssteuer_08_06_2012.htm

Benoit, B., & Tait, N. (2009, June 4). Berlin to back Brussels supervisory regime plan. *Financial Times.* Retrieved from http://www.ft.com/cms/s/0/5244f0bc-509f-11de-9530-00144feabdc0.html#axzz2eTFxNbXz

Bini Smaghi, L. (2009). Conflicts of interest and the financial crisis. *International Finance, 12*(1), 93–106.

Brown, G. (2005, October). *Globales Europa: Europa der Vollbeschäftigung, Blickpunkt Großbritannien,* FES London. Retrieved from http://library.fes.de/pdf-files/bueros/london/03631.pdf

Brown, G. (2010). *Beyond the crash: Overcoming the first crisis of globalisation.* London: Simon and Schuster.

Bryant, C. (2009, February 23). EU leaders push sweeping regulations. *Financial Times.* Retrieved from http://www.ft.com/intl/cms/s/0/a896e59e-011f-11de-8f6e-000077b07658.html#axzz2cdQ5uC5x

Buckley, J., & Howorth, D. (2010). Internal market: Gesture politics? Explaining the EU's response to the financial crisis. *Journal of Common Market Studies, 48*(Annual Review), 119–141.

Bundesregierung. (2012a). *Finanzmärkte an den Kosten beteiligen.* Retrieved from www.bundesregierung.de/ContentArchivDE/Archiv17/Artikel/2012/06/2012-06-27-finanztransaktionssteuer-kabinett.html

Bundesregierung. (2012b). *Pressestatements von Bundeskanzlerin Angela Merkel und dem Ministerpräsidenten der Italienischen Republik, Mario Monti.* Berlin. Retrieved from www.bundesregierung.de/ContentArchivDE/Archiv17/Mitschrift/Pressekonferenzen/2012/01/2012-01-11-merkel-monti.html

Bundesverband Deutscher Banken. (2009). *Kraftakt Krisenbewältigung: Was hilft, was ist finanzbar, was gerecht?* Mai. Retrieved from https://bankenverband.de/media/publikationen/kraftakt-krisen.pdf

Cameron, D. (2012). PM Davos speech delivered on 26 January 2012. *World Economic Forum.* Davos. Retrieved from www.gov.uk/government/speeches/pm-davosspeech

Cameron, D. (2013). *Transcript of PM's speech at the global investment conference.* London. https://www.gov.uk/government/speeches/pm-speech-at-opengovernment-partnership-2013

CBI. (2012). *CBI welcomes government decision on financial transaction tax*. Retrieved from www.cbi.org.uk/media-centre/press-releases/2012/10/cbi-welcomes-governmentdecision-on-financial-transaction-tax/

COBCOE. (2011). *To bin or not to bin*. Retrieved from www.cobcoe.eu/wp-content/uploads/2011/10/PP1011.pdf

Curtice, J., & Park, A. (2010). A tale of two crises: Banks, MPs' expenses and public opinion. In A. Park, J. Curtice, E. Clery, & C. Bryson (Eds.), *British social attitudes – the 27th Report: Exploring labour's legacy*. London: Sage. Retrieved from http://www.uk.sagepub.com/upmdata/39537_BSA_27th_Report_FINAL.pdf.

Darling, A. (2009, March 3). *European financial regulation and supervision, letter to Miroslav Kalousek, minister of finance of the Czech Republic*. Retrieved from http://data.parliament.uk/DepositedPapers/Files/DEP2009-0735/DEP2009-0735.pdf

De Larosière Report. (2009, February 25). *The high-level group on financial supervision in the EU*, Brussels. Retrieved from http://ec.europa.eu/internal_market/finances/docs/de_larosiere_report_en.pdf

Degner, H. & Leuffen, D. (2018). *Crisis and responsiveness. Analysing German preference formation during the Eurozone Crisis*. EMU Choices Working Paper Series. Retrieved from https://emuchoices.eu/wp-content/uploads/2019/02/Degner-et-al.-PSR-2018-final.pdf

DIHK/ BDI/ZDH/BDA/BDB/GDV/HDE. (2011). *Öffentliche Anhörung zur Finanztransaktionssteuer*. Retrieved from www.dihk.de/ressourcen/downloads/verbaende-finanztransaktionssteuer

Dunkley, J. (2009, June 10). FSA calls for single EU financial regulator. *The Telegraph*. Retrieved from http://www.telegraph.co.uk/finance/newsbysector/banksandfinance/5489862/FSA-calls-for-single-European-financial-regulator.html

ESBG. (2009, May 7). Statement Dr. *Karl-Peter Schackmann-Fallis, ESBG's view on the De Larosière Report*. Brussels. Retrieved from http://ec.europa.eu/internal_market/finances/docs/committees/supervision/schackmann-fallis_en.pdf

EU Observer. (2010, September 22). Europe seals deal on financial supervision. *EU Observer*. Retrieved from http://euobserver.com/economic/30866

Euractiv. (2011, August 18). Banks, markets oppose financial transaction tax. *Euractiv*. Retrieved from https://www.euractiv.com/section/euro-finance/news/banks-markets-oppose-financial-transaction-tax/818288/

Euractiv. (2018, December 3). *Germany and France to outline EU financial transaction tax proposal*. Retrieved from https://www.euractiv.com/section/economy-jobs/news/germany-and-france-tooutline-eu-financial-transaction-tax-proposal/

Eurobarometer. (2009). *Eurobarometer 72, Public opinion in the European Union, Part 2*, European Commission, Autumn. Retrieved from http://ec.europa.eu/public_opinion/archives/eb/eb72/eb72_vol2_de.pdf

Eurobarometer. (2011, January). *Eurobarometer 74, Economic governance in the European Union*. Retrieved from http://ec.europa.eu/commfrontoffice/publicopinion/archives/eb/eb74/eb74_anx_en.pdf

Eurobarometer. (2012a). *Eurobarometer 77.2, Krise und Wirtschaftspolitische Steuerung*, Europäisches Parlament 21. Mai. Retrieved from http://www.europarl.europa.eu/at-your-service/de/be-heard/eurobarometer/crisis-and-economic-governance-v

Eurobarometer. (2012b, November). *Eurobarometer 78, Public opinion in the European Union*. Retrieved from http://ec.europa.eu/commfrontoffice/publicopinion/archives/eb/eb78/eb78_anx_en.pdf

European Commission. (2009, May 27). *European Financial Supervision, 252 final*, Brussels. Retrieved from http://ec.europa.eu/internal_market/finances/docs/committees/supervision/communication_may2009/C-2009_715_en.pdf

European Commission. (2011). *Council directive on a common system of financial transaction tax and amending Directive 2008/7/EC*. Brüssel. Retrieved from https://eur-lex.europa.eu/legal-content/EN/TXT/PDF/?uri=CELEX:52011PC0594&from=EN

Falloon, M. (2011, November 11). EU financial transaction tax would be "suicide" – Osborne, *Reuters Business News*. Retrieved from https://uk.reuters.com/article/uk-britain-osborne/eu-financial-transaction-tax-would-be-suicide-osborne-idUKTRE7AD1E820111114

Fioretos, O. (2001). The domestic sources of multilateral preferences: Varieties of capitalism in the European Community. In P. A. Hall & D. Soskice (Eds.), *Varieties of capitalism* (pp. 213–244). Oxford/New York: The Institutional Foundations of Comparative Advantage.

Gamelin, C. (2010). Kontrolle der Banken. Die Finanzen sind heilig. *Süddeutsche Zeitung*, 17. Mai. Retrieved from http://www.sueddeutsche.de/geld/kontrolle-der-banken-die-finanzen-sind-heilig-1.441888

GDV (2012, July). *The positions of German insurers*. Berlin. Retrieved from http://www.gdv.de/wp-content/uploads/2012/07/GDV_Positions_of_German_insurers_2012_engl.pdf

Goldstein, J., & Keohane, R. O. (1993). *Ideas and foreign policy: Beliefs, institutions and political change*. Cornell: Cornell University Press.

Hall, P. A., & Soskice, D. (Eds.). (2001). *Varieties of capitalism: The institutional foundations of comparative advantage*. Oxford: Oxford University Press.

Handelsblatt. (2009a, February 12). Darling: Protektionismus wäre fatal. *Handelsblatt*. Retrieved from http://www.handelsblatt.com/politik/international/interview-mit-alistair-darling-darling-protektionismus-waere-fatal/3109968.html

Handelsblatt. (2009b, July 1). Finanzmärkte: Steinbrück knöpft sich Briten vor. *Handelsblatt*. Retrieved from http://www.handelsblatt.com/politik/deutschland/regulierung-finanzmaerkte-steinbrueck-knoepft-sich-briten-vor/3210678.html

Hardimann, H., & Metinsoy, S. (2018, November 2). Power, ideas and national preferences: Ireland and the FTT. *Journal of European Public Policy*.

IMA. (2009, November 9). *Written evidence submitted by the Investment Management Association*. House of Commons Treasury Committee. Retrieved from http://www.publications.parliament.uk/pa/cm200809/cmselect/cmtreasy/1088/1088we07.htm

Merkel, A. (2008). *Rede der CDU-Vorsitzenden*, Bundeskanzlerin Angela Merkel, Parteitag in Stuttgart, 1 Dezember. Retrieved from http://www.stuttgart08.cdu.de/wp-content/uploads/2008/12/081201-rede-merkel-stbericht.pdf

Merkel, A. (2009). *Rede der Bundeskanzlerin auf dem Kolloquium "Neue Welt, neuer Kapitalismus"*, Paris 8. Januar. Retrieved from http://www.bundesregierung.de/Content/DE/Bulletin/2009/01/02-2-bk-paris.html

Merkel, A. (2011). *Pressestatement von Bundeskanzlerin Angela Merkel beim G20-Gipfel*. Cannes. Retrieved from www.bundesregierung.de/ContentArchivDE/Archiv17/Mitschrift/Pressekonferenzen/2011/10/2011-11-03-bkln-cannes.html

Milner, H. V. (1997). *Interests, institutions and information: Domestic politics and international relations*. Princeton: Princeton University Press.

Moravcsik, A. (1997). Taking preferences seriously: A liberal theory of international politics. *International Organization, 51*(4), 513–553.

O'Donnell, J. (2009, October 20). Government delays deal on EU watchdog. *Reuters*. Retrieved from http://uk.reuters.com/article/2009/10/20/uk-watchdogs-eu-idUKTRE59J1YL20091020

O'Grady, S. (2009, December 4). Britain gives in on European Bank supervision. *The Independent*. Retrieved from http://www.businessweek.com/globalbiz/content/dec2009/gb2009124_598167.htm

Parker, G., Tait, N., & Hall, B. (2009, March 19). Britain heads for EU rift over regulation. *Financial Times*. Retrieved from http://www.ft.com/intl/cms/s/0/060a0be6-14d2-11de-8cd1-0000779fd2ac.html#axzz2cdQ5uC5x

Pew Research Center. (2012, May 29). *European unity on the rocks*. Retrieved from https://www.pewresearch.org/wp-content/uploads/sites/2/2012/05/Pew-Global-Attitudes-Project-European-Crisis-Report-FINAL-FOR-PRINT-May-29-2012.pdf

Schäuble, W. (2012a, September 6). *Verursacher von Krisen müssen Kosten tragen*. Retrieved from https://archiv.bundesregierung.de/archiv-de/-verursacher-von-krisen-muessen-kosten-tragen%2D%2D134362

Schäuble, W. (2012b). *Ein neuer Ordnungsrahmen für die Finanzmärkte*. Frankfurter Allgemeine Zeitung. Retrieved from www.bundesregierung.de/Content/ArchivDE/Archiv17/Namensbeitrag/2012/11/2012-11-15-schaeuble-faz.html

Schäuble, W. (2012c, June 5). Für Europa gibt es keinen bequemen Weg. Interview mit Wolfgang Schäuble. *Handelsblatt*. Retrieved from https://www.handelsblatt.com/politik/deutschland/

schaeuble-im-gespraech-fuer-europa-gibt-es-keinen-bequemen-weg/6711698.html?ticket=ST-1781137-mM2pMfWxoLT0tApT1TLr-ap4

Schirm, S. A. (forthcoming). Refining domestic politics theories of IPE: A societal approach to governmental preferences. *Politics*.

Schirm, S. A. (2009). Ideas and interests in global financial governance: Comparing German and US preference formation. *Cambridge Review of International Affairs, 22*(3), 501–521.

Schirm, S. A. (2011). Varieties of strategies: Societal influences on British and German responses to the global economic crisis. *Journal of Contemporary European Studies, 19*(1), 47–62.

Schirm, S. A. (2013). Global politics are domestic politics: A societal approach to divergence in the G20. *Review of International Studies, 39*(3), 685–706.

Schirm, S. A. (2016). Domestic ideas, institutions or interests? Explaining governmental preferences towards global economic governance. *International Political Science Review, 37*(1), 66–80.

Schirm, S. A. (2018). Societal foundations of governmental preference formation in the Eurozone crisis. *European Politics and Society, 19*(1), 63–78.

Schulmeister, S., Schratzenstaller, M., & Picek, O. (2008). *A general financial transaction tax. Motives, revenues, feasibility and effects*. Vienna: Österreichisches Institut für Wirtschaftsforschung. Retrieved from https://www.wifo.ac.at/jart/prj3/wifo/resources/person_dokument/person_dokument.jart?publikationsid=31819&mime_type=application/pdf

Spiegel Online. (2012, January 9). Merkel will Finanzmarktsteuer light. *Spiegel Online*. Retrieved from https://www.spiegel.de/politik/ausland/treffen-mit-sarkozy-merkel-will-finanzmarktsteuer-light-a-807959.html

Spiegel Online. (2018, June 8). Germany has a special responsibility. *Spiegel Online*. Retrieved from https://www.spiegel.de/international/germany/interview-with-finance-minister-olaf-scholz-a-1211942.html

Steinbrück, P. (2008, September 29). We were all staring into the Abyss. *Spiegel Online*. Retrieved from http://www.spiegel.de/international/business/spiegel-interview-with-german-finance-minister-steinbrueck-we-were-all-staring-into-the-abyss-a-581201.html

Süddeutsche Zeitung. (2018, December 2). *Neuer Anlauf für Steuern auf Finanztransaktionen*. https://www.sueddeutsche.de/wirtschaft/finanztransaktionssteuer-eu-olaf-scholz-1.4235483

Survation. (2012). *Economy-election poll*. Retrieved from http://survation.com/wp-content/uploads/2012/12/Economy-Election-Tables.pdf

Tagesschau. (2013). *Zocker sollen die Zeche zahlen*. Retrieved from www.tagesschau.de/wirtschaft/finanztransaktionssteuer118.html

Taylor, S. (2009, March 4). UK welcomes de Larosière Report. *European Voice*. Retrieved from http://www.europeanvoice.com/article/2009/03/uk-welcomes-de-larosihre-report/64164.aspx

The Economist. (2009, July 2). Financial reform in the EU. Neither one thing nor the other. *The Economist*. Retrieved from http://www.economist.com/node/13944730

The Guardian. (2006, June 22). Gordon Brown's mansion house speech. *The Guardian*. Retrieved from http://www.theguardian.com/business/2006/jun/22/politics.economicpolicy

Van Loon, A. (2018). Domestic politics and national differences in restructuring EU financial supervision. *European Politics and Society, 19*(3), 247–263.

Waterfield, B. (2011, September 10). George Osborne rejects EU transaction tax. *The Telegraph*. Retrieved from https://www.telegraph.co.uk/finance/newsbysector/banksandfinance/8754834/George-Osborne-rejects-EU-transaction-tax.html

Weber, M. (2008, Spring). Banking and finance: What Europe's future financial marketplace will look like. *Europe's World*. Retrieved from http://www.europesworld.org/NewFrancais/Accueil/Article/tabid/190/ArticleType/articleview/ArticleID/20396/language/en-US/Default.aspx

World Values Survey. (2006). *World values survey wave 2005–2009, Online Analysis*. Retrieved from http://www.worldvaluessurvey.org/WVSOnline.jsp

Zimmermann, H. (2010). Varieties of global financial governance. British and German approaches to financial market regulation. In E. Helleiner, S. Pagliari, & H. Zimmermann (Eds.), *Global finance in crisis* (pp. 121–136). London: Routledge.

European Energy Governance: The Pursuit of a Common External Energy Policy and the Domestic Politics of EU Member States Preferences

Iryna Nesterenko

1 Introduction

Energy is one of the main drivers in the world's economic progress and development. Without energy, economic activities in modern societies would come to a stand. Most of the European Union (EU) member states do not possess sufficient domestic reserves of hydrocarbons and thus need to import them from other countries. This situation has many negative aspects: (1) high dependency on the supplying countries, (2) a need to cooperate with non-democratic or politically unstable regimes, (3) concerns about the security of supply, and (4) the possibility of third countries to use energy as a political weapon.

Since most of the EU member states find themselves in a similar fragile situation regarding their energy imports, it seems plausible that they would engage in closer cooperation to elaborate a common position towards suppliers; to increase the security in individual states and the EU. It is therefore puzzling why until now this cooperation did not occur to a meaningful degree. How can this lack of cooperation among the member states be explained? Which key factors play a role in shaping the preferences of member states towards their energy supplies? What impact does it have on the EU initiatives for a common external energy policy?

Nowadays, rapidly changing energy markets, geopolitics of supplying countries and transportation routes mean that even maintaining existing energy supplies will be a significant challenge. According to the prognosis, the demand for natural gas in the EU until 2035 is going to increase by 19% (BP 2017). This is due to the overall growth in energy demand of the member states and especially because of the energy transition and climate policy initiatives in many EU capitals. Natural gas is the most environmentally friendly fossil fuel. Reduction or even phaseout of coal and nuclear

I. Nesterenko (✉)
Political Science, University of Siegen, Siegen, Germany

energy in some member states, due to environmental and/or societal concerns, leaves these countries no other solution but to drastically increase the use of natural gas to guaranty their energy security and maintain the current level of economic development.

The need to establish a common external energy policy on the European level emerges therefore not only from the raising European energy needs, but as well from unquestionable and rapid changes in the international system. This is especially true considering a rising competition for the available resources and commodities. Alongside the emerging economies of China and India, many developing countries show a consistently increasing demand for fossil fuels. For the international system, it would mean rising multipolarity and interdependency on the one hand, and uncertainty on the other hand, due to the challenges of traditional structures. The gas markets, for example, are changing from the traditionally isolated regional type to the internationally interdependent. The situation will intensify further in light of the global transformations on the fossil fuels markets and the predicted growth of the energy consumption. This prognosis also points at the increasing import dependency of the EU on fossil energy sources. In 2014 over 80% of the natural gas imports to the EU originated from Russia, Norway and Algeria, which means a high dependency on a few partners (Eurostat 2016).

Considering these developments, the external energy policy of the EU became an increasingly important topic, and it looks like the issue will continue to gain in importance. Looking at the evidence presented above and the predictions for the next few decades, it is even more surprising—that until now no common European external energy policy was developed. That is despite the efforts of the European Council, the Commission, and despite the obvious necessity for the EU foreign policy and the adoption of the energy competence by EU through the Lisbon Treaty.

It appears that there is '[an] absence of a clear vision and policy towards external relations at the EU level' (Haghighi 2007: 5). Member states' cooperation regarding the external energy supply remains very low, and bilateral contracts are preferred over group action. Thus, the research question posed here is as follows: *What factors can explain that no common policy towards energy suppliers so far has emerged?*

In this work the liberal theory of national preference formation will be applied (Moravcsik 1993). Since this research only investigates the formation of preferences at domestic level, the second part of Liberal Intergovernmentalism (LI), namely intergovernmental bargains would not be used in this work.

The purpose of this chapter is to give a balanced overview of the developments in the field of external gas relations of member states with their non-European suppliers and assess the domestic stimuli behind the governmental preferences towards a common external energy policy. In the next section initiatives towards development of external energy policy in the EU will be shortly discussed. Section 3 provides justification of case study selection. Afterwards, theoretical framework of LI with the emphasis on national preference formation will be briefly introduced. Section 5 presents research question, hypotheses and operationalisation of this work. Then the aspect the EU energy relations with Russia and Algeria are being highlighted in order to illustrate current frameworks under which the cooperation is taking place. In

Sect. 7, the main body of the research is being conducted. It scrutinises the independent variables within the case studies in order to answer the research questions. The last section provides summary and conclusion of this work.

2   Evolution of the External Energy Policy

The political issue that once united Europe after World War II and gave start to the regional integration project in the 1950s is now one of the main discontent issues within the community. In February 2011, the first European summit devoted completely to energy issues took place in Brussels, where among others the external dimensions of energy politics played crucial role. The conclusion made at the end of the meeting of the heads of states and governments has not only a fundamental impact on the development of the Single European Energy Market but also serves as a cornerstone for the elaboration of external energy policy of the EU. It underlines explicitly: 'Safe, secure, sustainable and affordable energy contributing to European competitiveness remains a priority for Europe. Action at the EU level can and must bring added value to that objective. Over the years, a lot of work has been carried out on the main strands of an EU energy policy, including the setting of ambitious energy and climate change objectives and the adoption of comprehensive legislation supporting these objectives. Today's meeting of the European Council underlined the EU's commitment to these goals through a number of operational conclusions' (European Council 2011: 1). Regarding the European external energy policy, they declared, 'There is a need for better coordination of EU and Member States' activities with a view to ensuring consistency and coherence in the EU's external relations with key producer, transit, and consumer countries' (European Council 2011: 4).

In the conclusion on the energy summit in May 2013 the Council stated, 'given the increasing interlinking of internal and external energy markets, Member States will enhance their cooperation in support of the external dimension of EU energy policy' (European Council 2013: 4). Thus, the external dimension of the EU energy policy was underlined. Important to mention however is that the provision with primary energy carriers and the relationship with the producer and transit countries lies exclusively in the responsibility of the member states. In addition, the design of the energy mixes (the proportional percentage of the primary energy sources, e.g. oil and gas, that are used for the production of secondary energy, e.g. electricity) is the jurisdiction of the member states. The distribution of these competences was not affected by the Lisbon Treaty, member states still have last word on these issues. In the face of the security policy implications, the security of energy supply seen as a core area of the national sovereignty: '[. . .] many Member States had jealously guarded their sovereignty over energy policy, declaring it a sensitive national issue' (Geden et al. 2006: 9). In 2012, the European Parliament and the Council passed the 'Decision on establishing an information exchange mechanism with regard to intergovernmental agreements between Member States and third countries in the field of energy'. In 2017 this legislation was substituted by the new and improved version.

'Energy prices and geopolitics have been interconnected since the beginning of the twentieth century, but expanded globalization, increased industrialization, and booming fossil fuel supplies have made this relationship increasingly brittle' (Royal 2016). The kind of today's link between countries and companies engaged in the energy production, transportation and distribution was hard to imagine two decades ago.

In 2011 after official consultation among the member states on external energy policy, sectoral association 'The European Union of the Natural Gas Industry' (Eurogas) released its official position paper regarding this issue. In this statement Eurogas and its members acknowledge the importance of stable and reliable relations with main gas suppliers and articulated readiness to share their broad expertise with European legislators. However, Eurogas also underlines that it sees no need in additional legislative framework, since the EU already has all necessary mechanisms to provide sustainable dialogue with suppliers. It also emphasises that during the last 40 years private European gas companies have established trustworthy bilateral relations with exporting countries, and thus to continue this bilateral cooperation pattern is the best way to provide energy security in the EU. Eurogas stresses that the EU financial contribution to expensive infrastructure projects, such as new pipelines, would provide vital support to the industry (Eurogas 2011). In sum, sectoral association of private gas industry only conditionally support the EU involvement in their relations with suppliers. It sees the EU's role in providing better political dialogue, financially supporting new infrastructure projects and helping exporting countries to achieve, e.g. higher energy efficiency or reduce level of the CO_2 emissions.

3   Focusing on the Member States' Level of Analysis

The actorness of the EU in the context of energy security is often being discussed through the prism of EU–Russia relations. The reason for this is the high dependency on Russian supplies and the occurred disruption of these supplies in the last years as well as the current geopolitical tension due to the Russia–Ukraine conflict. However, national levels which are crucial for energy relations often remain on the margins of research although traditionally, member states of the EU are the central actors in the formation of energy policy regarding fossil fuels.

In the 1970 book *Energy and the Economy of Nations*, author makes the observation that, 'the co-ordination of the [European] Community's energy policy is one of the major preoccupations of the European Commission, although the conflict of interests among the six Member States has so far prevented, despite 10 years of assiduous preparation, any tangible or meaningful progress' (Jensen 1970: 14). Almost half a century later energy policy is still very high on the European agenda and the enlarged EU is still struggling to find a compromise in many areas of the energy policy due to the diverse interest of the member states. In this light, it appears plausible for this research to concentrate on the EU member states level. Even the introduction of the energy chapter in the Lisbon Treaty did not bring changes to this situation, because external energy issues remained in the power of the member states. In addition, the decision about the national energy mix continues to be a core competence of the national governments. Thus, they determine how much and which kind of fossil fuels are to be imported from the third countries. That is why, to understand the current developments in the energy policy area on the European level better, it seems plausible to analyse the energy policies of the member states.

The unit of analysis in this research are the following EU member states: Germany, Poland, France and Spain. These were selected to provide a range of different types of relationship with energy suppliers. In addition, all these countries have a different energy dependency on their suppliers and have a different historical legacy. Moreover, these countries are important actors when it comes to development of new energy policies and strategies on the European level. Germany is the biggest energy consumer in the EU and the outrider in many policy areas of energy. Over the years Germany had developed strong strategic partnership relations with Russia in the energy field, as well as in, e.g. trade and cultural cooperation. Poland is a regional power in Eastern Europe among the post-soviet countries. Poland's energy dependency from Russian gas is much lower compared to other Eastern and Baltic member states. However, the Polish government is leading the coalition that represents the concerns of these states regarding the quest of energy security and cooperation with Russia. France is the long-term ally of Germany on the European arena. Nonetheless, France has its own strategy regarding its energy security and in comparison, it has no one-sided dependency on supplies of natural gas. Spain, even though strongly dependent on Algeria as a main gas supplier, puts a lot of effort in diversifying routes and suppliers. Spain has largest LNG regasification infrastructure in the EU and thus can in future afford more flexibility regarding its routes of supply.

This selection of case studies provides a relatively representative cross-country mixture. However, it is not perfectly representative due to the significant differences in the energy sectors and energy dependency between the 28 EU countries.

4 Liberal Intergovernmentalism with a Touch of Geopolitics

By applying the LI and by comparing the variables which influence the position of the member states towards their suppliers, this research will present a way of comprehending domestic preference formation in the European external energy domain in the case of natural gas. Hence, it intends to provide a better understanding of domestic and European processes in the energy area.

Andrew Moravcsik developed LI which consists of a liberal theory of national preference formation and an intergovernmentalist account of strategic bargaining between states. This theory is based on two basic assumptions: States are the main actors and they act rationally. Due to the interest of this research's focus only the first part of the theory, an explanation of domestic preference formation process will be applied.

Moravcsik formulates an interest-based theory of LI, by using liberal character-istics to the formation of national preferences focusing on the impact of the eco-nomic interest groups on the domestic politics. 'European integration has been not a preordained movement towards federal union but a series of pragmatic bargains among national governments based on concrete national interests, relative power, and carefully calculated transfers of sovereignty' (Moravcsik 1998: 472). Thus, national interests are in the centre of any integration progress. Furthermore, Moravcsik argues that national preferences are largely shaped by domestic economic factors and trade and jointed through interest groups. Moravcsik states that 'the most influential groups are those, which find themselves in the situation of benefiting or losing greatly, depending on the outcome of the policy. The influence of societal groups and their interests differ and depend on the ultimate costs and benefits of future foreign policy in specific issue-areas. The determinant of domestic groups, that shape their interests and influence are domestic as well as international' (Moravcsik 1993: 483). Therefore, the decision of member states to cooperate in external energy policy depends on the ability of the domestic economic interest groups to engage in favourable cooperation with suppliers in the energy policy domain (supply contracts, infrastructure projects). If the benefits of interest groups in existing bilateral arrangements are higher than possible gain from common European strategy, such interest groups would not support common European approach. Moreover, if member states' domestic energy markets are well established and their energy mix is sufficiently diversified, the motivation to reach common agreement would be less strong.

In his theory Moravcsik does not dismiss the importance of the geopolitical factors; however, he emphasises that economic concerns have a priority during the process of preference formation. Geopolitical interests, according to Moravcsik, can be conceived as the armed or ideological intervention in a state's sovereignty (Moravcsik 1998: 6). In such sensitive policy area as energy, which together with the defence policy constitutes the second pillar of state's security concept, good relations to the supplier is a fundamental element. The resent debates on the Nord Stream 2 pipeline and US liquified natural gas (LNG) supplies have a clear geopo-litical argument. Although not part of the original LI, the geopolitical context should be included to analyse the policy field of energy. This concept should provide a better understanding of the state's relations with their suppliers.

In sum, LI provides a clear structure to analyse the national preference formation process, before the resulting interests are pursued during interstate bargaining rounds at the EU level. As the author says, 'National interests are, therefore, neither invariant nor unimportant, but emerge through domestic political conflict as societal groups compete for political influence, national and transnational coalitions form, and new policy alternatives are recognized by governments' (Moravcsik 1993: 481).

Table 1 Visualisation of the two independent variables used in analysis

Independent variable	Definition	Indicators (what to analyze)
Geopolitical context	The overall geopolitical experience of the country with its energy supplier	• Geopolitical tensions • Unresolved issue from the past • Countries ability to perceive supplier as a trustful and reliable partner
Power of the interest groups	Role of the interest groups in the domestic gas sector	• Preferences of the interest groups • Abilities of the interest groups to negotiate favourable contracts with the supplier in the bilateral way

Source: Author's own elaboration

5   Research Questions, Hypotheses and Operationalisation

The variables examined for each case include: (a) impact of the geopolitical legacy on the member state relations with its supplier; (b) analysis of the selected domestic interest groups and their preferences. Table 1 provides a better visualisation of the two independent variables.

Dependent variable in this case is the position of the member state governments regarding common European approach towards non-European gas suppliers.

The hypotheses thus are elaborated upon these independent variables, which presumably have an impact on the domestic formation of preferences of the EU member states under scrutiny. The following questions and hypotheses will determine the course of the analysis:

Member states, which in the past have had a negative unresolved geopolitical experience with their suppliers, tend to classify these suppliers as unreliable business partners. In this case, geopolitical concerns would play an important role in building states preferences.

RQ 1: *What role does the geopolitical/historical legacy of EU member states with their supplier play in the forming government preferences towards closer European cooperation in energy policy?*

H 1: *If a member state has a negative unresolved geopolitical legacy with a supplier, then it tries to minimise cooperation with this supplier and looks for alternatives. In this case, such an EU member state will show interest in common EU strategy in order to secure its energy supplies.*

National interest groups, which already have a good relationship with their supplier tend to keep the existing arrangements and would not support common European policy.

RQ 2: *Which factors play role in shaping the preferences of the member states?*

H 2: *If the domestic interest groups can achieve their goals without their government's cooperation with other EU member states, then they would prefer to continue a bilateral relationship with the suppliers.*

The main part of the research will concentrate on the period from 2005 until the present. During this time, major attempts to develop an external energy policy took place. It also correlates with the two main gas supply interruptions during the Russian–Ukrainian gas disputes, which had an enormous impact on the overall idea about the creation of the external energy policy. Signing of the cooperation agreement between Germany and Russia in 2005 to construct the Nord Stream pipeline was another relevant development that intensified the talks among the member states about a need of a common external energy policy towards suppliers. The time is also sufficiently long enough to trace the developments in this process and makes sure that they reflect actual situation in the EU. However, the parts of the study concerning the overall historical background of EU policymaking in the energy sector as well as the geopolitical relations between suppliers and consumers are not restricted in time. Furthermore, it appears sensible not to include all energy suppliers in this analysis, but to set an emphasis on Russia and Algeria. Russia is the biggest and Algeria is the third biggest supplier of the natural gas to the EU. Since both countries are non-EU states, with weak rule of law and unstable democratic system, they present potential risk to energy security of importing EU member states, and thus to the whole EU. Considering the EU's high dependency and vulnerability in the natural gas sector, the study concentrates on this specific energy carrier. This investigation will not include descriptions of the EU actorness in energy policy domain nor characterisation of the EU as global energy actor.

Each case study follows an identical structure which is based on providing background information on the energy dependency of selected member states, as well as their cooperation with Russia and/or Algeria on major infrastructure projects; afterwards follows an examination of independent variables that might impact external energy policy preferences. An analysis of these data should enable to determine general preferences of member states regarding European integration in natural gas policy area.

For the purpose of data collection primary and secondary sources are being used. As Moravcsik notices, the democratic states are responsive to their electorates, as the goal of elected politicians is to remain in office. Therefore, it is necessary to look at the statements of interest groups and sectoral associations, as well as statements of elected governmental politicians and heads of states for correlation purposes. Lobby groups and sectoral association are motivated to lobby the government to act in line with their demands. By taking these lobby activities into account, governments are responsive and hence often reflect these demands in their positions.

6 Overview of the EU Energy Relations with Russia and Algeria

This section provides an overview of legal and diplomatic frameworks of the EU with the main gas suppliers—Russia and Algeria. It is necessary to apprehend the evolution and the level of the EU involvement in these relations to be able to analyse the future possible development. Russia and Algeria have a long history of the energy relations with the EU. These relations had taken place mainly in bilateral setting between exporting and importing companies. From 1969, Western European countries, such as Italy and West Germany, had been receiving first gas imports from the USSR (Katzman 1988). Equally, Algeria has been a long-term partner of the EU. In the 1960s, first gas pipelines to Spain, France and Italy were built. This was followed by two more gas routes at the end of 1980s. Only in the last 20 years active attempts to create legal and diplomatic frameworks at the EU level with these two suppliers had been undertaken.

After the collapse of the Soviet Union the EU tried to provide a legal framework for energy cooperation with Russia. As a result, in 1994 The Energy Charta Treaty was signed. This framework was intended to provide protection of foreign invest-ments, dispute settlement mechanism and non-discriminatory trade in energy prod-ucts (Energy Charter 2019). Even though Russia signed this treaty, it promptly afterword refused to ratify it due to the concerns regarding the conditions of transit arrangements and third-party access to the pipelines. In order to insure stable condi-tions for cooperation and reliable energy exports and imports in 2010, the EU–Russia Energy Dialogue had been established. Areas of cooperation such as technological transfer, transportation networks, security of short- and long-term energy supplies are parts of this dialogue. As the response to Russia's military involvement in Ukraine, this dialogue had been officially suspended since 2014, and only occasional issue-specific meetings had been held (EEAS 2017). In 2011, under the umbrella of EU–Russia Energy Dialogue the roadmap of cooperation until 2050 had been signed. In this document mutual interdependence between the EU and Russia had been emphasised and advantages of future partnership in sectoral issues, such as gas, oil and electricity had been presented. Although designed as a common European guideline for future cooperation, this document accentuates the primacy of national interests in the relations with Russia (European Commission 2013).

In case of Algeria legal cooperation frameworks are less advanced than in the case of Russia. In 2005, the EU–Mediterranean Partnership Agreement entered into force creating a new basis for dialogue and supporting the stability in the North African region. The partners agreed on the priorities in supply security, energy industry competitiveness and environmental protection. The EU was concerned when in 2006 the Algerian government reversed a tentative liberalisation of the energy sector. Thus, a new step was made in 2007 by Greece and Italy to support the foundation of the Euro–Mediterranean Energy Community. In the same year, at the Euro–Mediterranean Energy meeting the two parts signed the '2008–2013 Priority Action Plan for Euro–Mediterranean cooperation in the field of energy'. This emphasised the importance of harmonisation of the energy market, the promotion of sustainable development and the development of initiative of common interest (EU Neighborhood Info Centre 2012). Despite these positive developments, southern EU member states still expressed a certain degree of frustration. The Spanish government voiced concern that it saw a relatively limited priority given to energy security issue within the EU–Mediterranean policy. Subsequently, 'The Strategic Partnership on Energy' was launched in 2015, insuring better cooperation in areas of natural gas, renewable energies and energy efficiency (European Commission 2019).

In sum, the EU had been actively establishing area-specific partnerships with Russia and Algeria to provide better cooperation possibilities for general energy matters and in particular in area of natural gas. However, these frameworks do not substitute bilateral relations between member states and importing countries, but rather give the EU an opportunity to be involved in political dialogue.

7 Member States' Relations with Russia and Algeria

The following sections scrutinise two independent variables—geopolitical context and preferences of national interest groups and looks closely at the relations of four states with their suppliers.

7.1 Germany

7.1.1 Geopolitical Context

Germany and Russia share a long and complex history. The periods of wars and conflicts left a mark on the relations between these two states. In the twentieth century, the two World Wars and the Cold War shaped the attitude of the countries towards each other. During the Cold War, the Soviet Union pursued different policies towards two German Republics given that the German Democratic Republic was a part of the Eastern Block. The 1970s were characterised by dialogue and acceleratory economic cooperation. By the 1980s, 'the post-war period of West Germany-Soviet antagonism was over, the West Germany and the USSR began to return to more historical patterns of cooperation' (Stent 1990: 38). With the collapse of the Soviet Union the period of reconciliation began. From the beginning of 1990s, Germany's relations with Russia can be characterised as a strategic partnership. Even the weakening of democratic rule, suppression of freedom of the press and human rights under President Putin seem not to influence much the relations between two countries. Germany and Russia still 'attach great significance to their close political and economic ties' (Roth 2009). First with the invasion of Crimea and Russia's military support of the conflict in the Eastern Ukraine some tension had been brought into Germany–Russia relations. Yet, in 2019 at the Munich Security Conference Chancellor Merkel emphasised, referring to countries' energy relations, 'If we got Russian gas already in the Cold War ... and the old German Federal Republic introduced Russian gas on a large scale—then I don't know why times today should be so much worse that we cannot say: Russia remains a partner' (Rettman 2019).

7.1.2   Energy Dependency

Germany is one of the most important players in European energy policy and the biggest energy consumer. Certain domestic policies, like the phaseout of nuclear power until 2022 and recently also coal phaseout until 2038 would increase Germany's import needs. Despite current energy transition and strong support of the renewable energies, Germany is heavily dependent on fossil fuels imports. It imports 88% of gas and 98% of oil to cover energy demands (Federal Ministry of Economics and Technology 2012).

Natural gas imports come to Germany via pipeline from Russia—35%, Norway—34% and the Netherlands—29%. According to information released by Gazprom in 2018, the exports to Germany increased by over 12% compared to 2017 (Keating 2018). Since Germany has relatively good diversified gas pipeline routes and in the last years engaged in new pipeline infrastructure projects with Russia it made a strategic decision not to invest in the construction of the large-scale LNG regasification terminal.

7.1.3   Infrastructure Projects

Among the EU member states Germany has one of the longest and closest energy relationships with Russia. The Germany–Russia energy relationship in the area of natural gas includes much more than simple gas imports. Cooperation takes place in gas production, deliveries and transmission as well as gas storage. Since 2005, Russia and Germany have signed several agreements concerning gas deliveries and infrastructure projects. The most important are the two Nord Stream pipelines. The company operating the pipeline, Nord Stream AG, is owned by Gazprom—51%, two German firms BASF/Wintershall—15.5%, E.ON Ruhrgas—15.5%, the Dutch firm Gasunie—9%, and the French ENGIE company—9% (Nord Stream 2019). The Nord Stream projects caused some controversies back in 2005. Former German Chancellor Gerhard Schröder worked very hard to secure the Nord Stream deal. Before leaving the office, he promised a €1 billion loan guarantee from the German government. It is interesting to mention that after Schröder ended his political career, he was named Chairman of the Nord Stream Shareholder's Committee. It is not surprising that current Chancellor Merkel criticised Schröder for mixing roles when he started working for the pipeline consortium after approving the project as Chancellor. However, she did not change Germany's approach towards this infrastructure project. Germany is convinced that due to the establishment of this direct connection, the EU should have no grounds to be worried about the security of supply. If any disputes between Russia and transit countries would occur, the Nord Stream pipeline would guarantee stable gas flows (Whist 2008).

7.1.4   Interest Groups

Germany and Russia do not only have a government-to-government relationship, but they are also involved in coordination and market penetration at the firm level. In the gas sector, companies are the main actors that negotiate deals with each other. For example, the Berlin-based Gazprom Germania, which is fully controlled by Gazprom, is involved in trading Russian and Central Asian gas in Germany and across Eastern and Western Europe (Gazprom Germania 2016). Gazprom Germania holds a 10.52% share of Verbundnetz Gas (VNG). VNG is active in natural gas exploration and production, trading, transport and storage (Verbundnetz Gas 2016). VNG also operates inside Germany and across Europe.

Moreover, since 2018 some small-scale LNG projects are being conducted in the port of Rostock together with the Novatek, Russia's biggest independent gas company and Belgian subsidiary Fluxy (Novatek 2018). This opens new area of cooperation between the countries. In addition, if Germany would decide to expand its LNG potential, Russia might dominate this market in Germany overriding the USA, which for a long time is trying to convince German government of buying US liquified gas.

In the German energy industry, the reliance on strategic partnerships has a long tradition and usually dominates over the competitive market arrangements. Among others Nord Stream and Nord Stream 2 projects are good examples which show the impact of the strategic international partnership on the energy industry. On one hand, due to the energy transition the domestic power and influence of nuclear and coal energy companies have slightly decreased. On the other hand, companies what are active on the gas market gained more power.

Germany, as one of the six founding European Coal and Steel Community (ECSC) countries, had shown a strong support for European integration. However, this general support was not automatically transferred into the energy policy area (Ipek and Williams 2010). Germany has troubles 'speaking with one voice' in the external dimension of the energy issues.

7.2   Poland

7.2.1   Geopolitical Context

Poland and Russia have a long, complex and troubled past. Russia has a long history of intervention in Poland that led to repeated partitions of Poland until the Polish state ceased to exist (Roszkowski 2007: 11). After World War II, Poland remained under communist control until 1989. 'Poland's position between Russia and Germany had been for years a source of worry to Poland, as the experiences from before the wars and in the immediate aftermath of World War II showed that those powers were bilaterally making decisions about the future of Poland' (Kaminska 2007: 2). Because of Poland's historical and geopolitical tensions, the fear for territorial integrity has been one of the main concerns of Polish government. However, political contacts between Poland and Russia continued after the Soviet Union collapsed. Since Poland's energy infrastructure, built mainly during the

Soviet Union, had been highly connected to Russia, it was not possible for security reasons to terminate political and economic relations.

The cooperation between the two countries worsened in 2005 when the right-wing party Law and Justice (PiS) came to power (Roth 2009: 8). Moreover, due to construction of Nord Stream pipeline which omits Poland and Baltic states, then Polish Foreign Minister Radoslaw Sikorski was concerned about decisions made behind Poland's back and compared the deal to Molotov–Ribbentrop Pact of 1939 (Beunderman 2006). This development was very disappointing for Poland because it hoped to cooperate with Russia to build a second pipeline for Yamal–Europe.

After the annexation of Crimea and Russian support of the separatist in Eastern Ukraine Poland took a position opposing Russian aggression. In this context, Poland underlines the importance of NATO troops on its territory for defence purposes. For Eastern EU member states, this meant that the security of their gas supplies was in danger. In this context, the governments of the Visegrad Group voiced their dissatisfaction of German–Russian negotiations about construction of the Nord Stream 2 pipeline. In 2018, Polish Minister of Foreign Affair Jacek Czaputowicz said that this project is a bad political deal since it provides Russia with additional financial means, which are being used to modernise the army and conduct aggressive military actions in Ukraine, Georgia and Syria (Wirtualny Nowy Przemysl 2018). Thus, Poland perceives Russia as geopolitical aggressor in the region and unreliable partner in energy relations.

7.2.2 Energy Dependency

Poland is almost entirely dependent on Russia for its supply of natural gas. However, gas plays a smaller role in Poland's energy mix than other fuels. Indeed, coal is Poland's most abundant natural resource and primary fuel source. Poland is the EU's biggest producer and exporter of coal, which dominates Poland's energy mix (IEA 2016b: 8). Poland uses coal for electricity generation while its second most common fuel source, oil, is used primarily in transportation and industrial applications. About 90% of Poland's gas imports come from Russia and about 10% from Germany, making Poland almost completely dependent on Russian gas imports to meet domestic demand (IEA 2016b: 10). Despite Poland's relatively low overall energy dependence, its reliance on coal makes it more difficult for the country to control CO_2 emissions and to meet EU targets (IEA 2016b: 12). That is why Poland is looking to diversify the sources of electricity generation.

7.2.3 Infrastructure Projects

As was mentioned before Poland was engaged in gas infrastructure project with Russia, the Yamal–Europe gas pipeline which became operational in 1999 (Yamal-Europe 2016). Until the first line of the Nord Stream pipeline was constructed Yamal–Europe was the only pipeline delivering gas to Western Europe not though the territory of Ukraine. This was strategically important for both Europe and Russia. Since then no major infrastructure project between Poland and Russia had been conducted.

To diversify its gas supply routes Poland needed to find new trading partners. Although it was not an easy task Poland seems to have found solution to the problem by building and expanding the LNG regasification terminal in Świnoujście. Long-term contract between Polish state-run company PGNiG and US company Cheniere on LNG deliveries had been signed in 2018 (Reuters 2018).

7.2.4   Interest Groups

Poland has several state-controlled energy companies, including gas monopoly PGNiG. Gas supply security has been one of the most important policy issues, regardless the fact that only 12.7% of Poland's energy mix has been captured by natural gas (IEA 2016b: 5). Because natural gas market in Poland has a very small share the operating companies have difficulties reaching their goal. As was mentioned before although Poland and Russia successfully cooperated on the Yamal–Europe project, this did not lead to additional gas projects, e.g. Yamal–Europe 2, nor did it establish a strategic energy partnership between the two countries.

The influence of gas industry in Poland would most probably increase during the next decade, as Poland would be pressured from the EU to reduce its coal consumption. Thus, it can be expected that relations with Russia in this sector would improve.

7.3   *France*

7.3.1   Geopolitical Context

Franco–Algerian geopolitical relations bear a special character due to the French colonial reign over Algeria from 1830 until 1962. The independence of Algeria in 1962 endangered France's security of energy supplies, and thus President Charles de Gaulle foreign policy was concentrated on keeping good relations with the new republic. After de Gaulle left his post in 1969 there was no genuine political will for compromise. As a result, in 1971 the attempts to renegotiate favourable oil and gas contracts collapsed and 'Algeria became the first Middle East country to nationalise its energy resources' (Nuenlist et al. 2010: 243). However, in the 1970s, France refused the US proposition to organise the consumers cartel to rival the Organisation of Petrol Exporting Countries (OPEC), and prefered a bilateral relationship with Arab regimes, which led to the creation of Euro–Arab Dialogue (Youngs 2009: 50).

7.3.2   Energy Dependency

French energy dependency is much different compared to the other case studies analysed in this work. The main reason is France's heavy reliance on nuclear power. This makes France far less dependent on energy imports and contributes to France's diversification of energy sources. France is Europe's second largest economy and its hydrocarbon resources are as limited as in many other EU member states. This means that fossil fuel needs rely heavily on imports. Natural gas makes up only about 16% of France's total primary energy supply, which is low compared to most European countries due to the use of nuclear power for electricity generation, and because France has a lower population density than many other member states. Natural gas is imported via pipeline and as LNG, and France's biggest natural gas suppliers include Norway—34%, the Netherlands—17%, Russia—13%, and Algeria—13% (IEA 2016a: 57).

7.3.3   Infrastructure Projects

In 2000, Gaz de France and Algerian Sonatrach firmed up a co-operation agreement towards a common commercialisation of 1 bcm of LNG per year. Moreover, as a part of its strategy to boost export volumes towards Europe, Sonatrach has acquired interests in major pipeline projects due to links with Algeria to Spain—Medgas (Gas and Oil 2000). The French also admitted that the bilateral dimension continued to predominate in relations with Algeria. Paris signed a new energy treaty with Algeria in 2006. In this official deal France and Algeria agreed to firmer guarantees on Algeria gas supplies in the short term, in return for French nuclear energy cooperation in the long term. France remains not only one of the important trading partners for Algeria, but also the biggest aid donors. In 2005, France paid 255 million euros of aid to Algeria (Grigorjeva 2016).

7.3.4   Interest Groups

In France, business and commercial interests play a large role in energy policy preferences. Many of France's national champions are involved in strategic partnerships with Russia. Electricite de France (EDF) and Gas de France SUEZ (GDF SUEZ) are both involved in major pipeline projects and TOTAL SA has a stake in the Shtokman natural gas field. As was mentioned above French companies are part of both Nord Stream projects. In addition, France has a number of lobby organisations, such as French Association of Petroleum Industry (UFIP) and The Movement of Enterprise of France (MEDEF), that have an impact on energy policy at the highest level. Indeed, former French Energy Minister Delphine Batho blames the pro-nuclear and shale gas lobbies for her summer 2013 firing. Batho 'said she was a victim of pressure from economic interests who wanted to overturn a 2011 fracking ban and were opposed to her aim of cutting France's dependence on nuclear energy by developing renewable energy sources' (Energy Daily 2012).

Since France has good and stable geopolitical relations with both Russia and Algeria and especially because its gas sector does not disproportionally rely on one supplier, it appears that rather economic interest groups and not geopolitics play role in shaping state preferences.

7.4 Spain

7.4.1 Geopolitical Context

In the beginning of 1960 Spanish Government and Algerian representatives negotiated off-take quantities of natural gas (Pawera 1964: 134). This boosted energy relations between the countries and improved the economic outlook of the pipeline project from Algeria to Spain. However, this put Spain in a fragile position of being overdependent on gas imports from politically unstable regions in Northern and Sub-Saharan Africa. Thus, in the beginning of the 1990s '[. . .] Spain attempted with little success to raise awareness of the problems of the Union's southern flank, and [. . .] criticised Northern members for being over-preoccupied with Central-Eastern Europe at the expense of the Mediterranean. Spain's self-appointed task has been to convince EU partners that the Maghreb is a European problem' (Haghighi 2007: 167). As a later outcome of Spain's lobbying at the EU level the above-mentioned EU–Mediterranean Partnership Agreement was signed. However, Spain remains far behind France in terms of the volume of its trade and cooperation with Maghreb. In the last years the relations became more complicated due to migration issues. In the last 2 years new cooperation agreement between Spain and Russia on LNG deliveries had been signed (LNG World News 2018). A decade ago the possibility of this relation was not even considered to be possible, since Russia had been supplying its European customers through pipelines. However, new globalised gas markets bring change in the well-established European cooperation patterns.

7.4.2 Energy Dependency

Natural gas accounted for 20.8% of total primary energy supply and 17.2% of electricity generation in 2014. Spain relies on natural gas imports as production is negligible. In 2014, imports were 36.4 billion cubic metres (bcm), originating mostly from Algeria—57.9% of the total, Norway—11.5%, Qatar—8.6%, and Nigeria—7.8%. In total, Spain received gas from 11 countries (IEA 2015: 23). Spain imports pipeline gas and liquefied natural gas, the pipeline gas accounts for 53% of total imports in 2014. The share of LNG in total imports is declining due to the high prices of the LNG gas and due to the opening of the second import pipeline from Algeria. However, the overall share of the LNG imports is still high and helps

Spain to diversify its gas imports by country. As a result, of these strategies Spain has the most diversified import structure in Europe (IEA 2015: 75).

7.4.3   Infrastructure Projects

The Spanish gas grid is connected with Algeria, Morocco, Portugal and Algerian gas is imported via Morocco over the 12 bcm/year Maghreb–Europa pipeline and, since 2010, over the 8 bcm/year Medgaz pipeline. Both import pipelines have several billion cubic metres of annual spare capacity (IEA 2015: 80).

In the mid-2000s, Spain had a bilateral negotiation with Algeria for the construction of a new gas pipeline between the two countries. This provoked critical comments from EU officials that this threatened to exclude Morocco and France and undermine the essential logic of a regional Euromed energy market.

The Medgaz project from Algeria to Spain was first proposed by Spanish Petroleum company CEPSA and Sonatrach to secure gas supply to Spain. Rapidly, several partners entered the project, including the main Spanish utilities as well as Total, GDF and British Petroleum (BP). In fact, Medgaz also targets France and the European market. Promoted by importers, the investment decision was taken by the end of 2006 and the pipeline became operational in 2011.

7.4.4   Interest Groups

Spain has few established gas companies operating worldwide in LNG markets. Gas Natural Fenosa, one of the biggest LNG operators in the world, stroke a deal in 2013 with Yamal LNG to deliver gas from 2017 onwards. Spanish sectoral gas association Sedigas called it an important geostrategic development. The deliveries of Russia LNG should cover 10% of Spain's gas demand (Sedigas 2017: 4). In November 2016 CEPSA and Sonatrach signed contracts to extend a partnership for Rhourde El Krouf and Ourhoud fields for 25 years and 10 years respectively. The previous contract between the companies is due to expire in 2019. In addition, they signed a memorandum of understanding for further cooperation in Algeria and internationally (Ahmed 2016). It seems that for Spain both geopolitical and economic consideration play an important role.

8   Summary of Findings and Conclusion

In four case studies under scrutiny in this work only in case of Poland geopolitical concerns still seem to play dominant role in shaping national strategy. Poland perceives Russia as an unreliable partner after the planned project of Yamal 2 was cancelled. Also, Russian aggression in the immediate neighbourhood made Poland concerned about its own military security. Since natural gas consumption in Poland is relatively small compared to the other countries gas companies do not have adequate leverage to negotiate with Russia. Thus, Poland actively supports the EU initiatives to establish common external energy policy. In the past, Spain complained about the EU's disinterest in the energy security of its southern member states and underlined a need for the EU involvement and support in establishing a legal framework for cooperation with Maghreb states. After the EU signed the cooperation agreement with North African countries, Spain had been concentrating on the bilateral level of cooperation with its suppliers. Also, some Spanish companies developed to be important LNG players in the region and successfully engage in infrastructure projects without the help from the EU. Moreover, LNG supply contract with Russia shows that Spanish gas market is open for new developments. The cases of Germany and France clearly show that they perceive their main gas suppliers as strategic partners and therefore, there geopolitical tensions playing no role in the cooperation. German and French companies are involved in various gas supply and infrastructure projects with Russia and show no interest in common European approach. Therefore, the H1 regarding negative unresolved geopolitical experience with supplier had been confirmed in case of Poland, and H2 regarding the ability of domestic interest groups to achieve their goals in bilateral settings had been confirmed in cases of Germany, France and Spain.

To answer the main research question, both variables geopolitical context and power of interest groups have an impact of shaping the preferences of the member states towards their energy suppliers. Thus, the EU initiatives for a common external energy policy face diverging domestic interests of member states. It appears highly unlikely that a common external European gas policy would be established in the coming decade. Based on the findings of this work it is evident, that domestic level of analysis can provide valuable insides in process of governmental preference formation and European cooperation. Therefore, further research that examines other energy policy areas by applying domestic politic theories is required to estimate the variety of national preferences and to evaluate the prospects of further EU integration in energy sector.

References

Ahmed, H. O. (2016). Algeria's Sonatrach and Spain's Cepsa extended oil field contracts. *Reuters Africa*. Available from http://206.132.6.105/article/idAFL8N1DN5W9

Beunderman, M. (2006). Poland compares German-Russian pipeline to Nazi Soviet pact, May 2, 2006. Hg. v. *EU Observer*. Available from http://euobserver.com/foreign/21486

British Petroleum. (2017). *A global view of gas – in maps and charts*. Available from https://www.bp.com/en/global/corporate/news-and-insights/bp-magazine/global-view-of-gas-infographic.html

Energy Daily. (2012). *French Ex-Minister blames energy lobbies for sacking*. Available from http://www.energy-daily.com/reports/French_ex-minister_blames_energy_lobbies_for_sacking_999.html

Energy Charter. (2019). *Energy charter treaty*. Available from https://www.energycharter.org/process/energy-charter-treaty-1994/energy-charter-treaty/

EU Neighborhood Info Centre. (2012). *Euro-Mediterranean energy cooperation: Working together for secure and sustainable energy.* Available from http://www.enpi-info.eu/mainmed.php? id=286&id_type=3

Eurogas. (2011). *Eurogas response to public consultation on external energy policy.* Available from https://eurogas.org/media_centre/eurogas-response-to-public-consultation-on-external-energy-policy/

European Commission. (2013). *Roadmap EU-Russia energy cooperation until 2015.* Available from https://ec.europa.eu/energy/sites/ener/files/documents/2013_03_eu_russia_roadmap_2050_signed.pdf

European Commission. (2019). *EU Neighborhood-South.* Available from https://ec.europa.eu/energy/en/topics/international-cooperation/eu-cooperation-other-countries/neighborhood-south

European Council. (2011). *Conclusions,* EUCO 2/11, Brussels.

European Council. (2013). *Conclusions,* EUCO 75/13, Brussels.

European External Action Service. (2017). *The European Union and the Russian Federation.* Available from https://eeas.europa.eu/topics/energy-diplomacy/35939/european-union-and-rus sian-federation_en

Eurostat. (2016). *Energy production and imports.* Available from https://ec.europa.eu/eurostat/ statistics-explained/index.php/Energy_production_and_imports

Federal Ministry of Economics and Technology. (2012, April). *Germany's new energy policy, heading towards 2050 with secure, affordable and environmentally sound energy.* Available from http://www.bmwi.de/English/Redaktion/Pdf/germanys-new-energy-policy

Gas and Oil. (2000, 9 June). *Sonatrach and Gaz de France announce joint venture.*

Geden, O., Marcilis, C., & Maurer, A. (2006). *Perspectives for the European Union's external energy policy: Discourse, ideas and interests in Germany, the UK, Poland and France.* Hg. v. SWP-Working Paper FG1. Berlin. Available from https://www.swp-berlin.org/ fileadmin/contents/products/arbeitspapiere/External_KS_Energy_Policy__Dez_OG_.pdf

Gazprom Germania (2016). *Building the future.* Available from http://www.gazprom-germania.de/ en/company.html

Grigorjeva, J. (2016, 30 September). *Starting a new chapter in EU-Algeria energy relations.* Berlin: Jacques Delor Institut. Available from http://www.delorsinstitut.de/2015/wp-content/uploads/ 2016/09/20160930_EU-Algeria-Grigorjeva-2.pdf

Haghighi, S. S. (2007). *Energy security. The external legal relations of the European Union with major oil- and gas-supplying countries* (Modern studies in European law, no. 16). Oxford, Portland: Hart.

International Energy Agency. (2015). *Energy policies of IEA countries. Spain 2015.* Available from https://www.iea.org/publications/freepublications/publication/IDR_Spain2015.pdf

International Energy Agency. (2016a). *Energy policies of IEA countries. France 2016.* Available from https://www.iea.org/publications/freepublications/publication/Energy_Policies_of_IEA_ Countries_France_2016_Review.pdf

International Energy Agency. (2016b). *Energy policies of IEA countries. Poland 2016.* Available from https://www.iea.org/publications/freepublications/publication/Energy_Policies_of_IEA_ Countries_Poland_2016_Review.pdf

Ipek, P., & Williams, P. (2010). *Firms strategic preferences, national institutions and the European Union's internal energy market: A challenge to European integration.* European integration online papers, volume 14, paper 15. Available from http://eiop.or.at/eiop/index.php/eiop/article/ view/2010_015a, 17.

Jensen, W. G. (1970). *Energy and the economy of nations.* Henley-on-Thames Eng: G. T. Foulis.

Kaminska, J. (2007). New EU members and the CFSP: Europeanization of polish foreign policy. *Political Perspectives, 2,* 1–24.

Katzman, J. (1988). The Euro-Siberian gas pipeline row: A study in community development. *Millennium – Journal of International Studies, 17,* 25–41.

Keating, D. (2018). How dependent is Germany on Russian gas?. *Forbes*. Available from https://www.forbes.com/sites/davekeating/2018/07/19/how-dependent-is-germany-on-russian-gas/#ecaada63b489

LNG World News. (2018). *Gas Natural Fenosa receives first Yamal LNG cargo*. Available from https://www.lngworldnews.com/gas-natural-fenosa-receives-first-yamal-lng-cargo/

Moravcsik, A. (1993). Preferences and power in the European Community: A liberal intergovernmentalist approach. *Journal of Common Market Studies, 31*(4), 473–523.

Moravcsik, A. (1998). *The choice for Europe. Social purpose and state power from Messina to Maastricht* (Cornell studies in political economy). Ithaca, NY: Cornell University Press.

Nord Stream. (2019). *Who we are*. Available from https://www.nord-stream.com/about-us/

Novatek. (2018). *Novatek and Fluxy plan to build an LNG terminal in Rostock*. Available from http://www.novatek.ru/en/press/releases/archive/index.php?id_4=2739&mode_4=all&afrom_4=01.01.2018&ato_4=31.12.2018&from_4=7

Nuenlist, C., Locher, A., & Martin, G. (2010). *Globalizing de Gaulle: International perspective on French foreign policy, 1958–1969*. Lexington Books.

Pawera, J. C. (1964). *Algeria's infrastructure. An economic survey of transportation, communication, and energy sources*. New York: Frederik A. Praeger.

Rettman, A. (2019). Merkel defends Russia ties, ridicules Trump on cars. *Euobserver*. Available from https://euobserver.com/foreign/144190

Reuters. (2018). *Poland's PGNiG signs long-term LNG deal with Cheniere*. Available from https://www.reuters.com/article/usa-energy-pgnig/polands-pgnig-signs-long-term-lng-deal-with-cheniere-idUSL8N1XJ2GW

Roszkowski, W. (2007). *Historia Polski. 1914–2005*. Wyd. 11., rozsz. Warszawa: Wydawn. Naukowe PWN.

Roth, M. (2009). *Bilateral disputes between EU member states and Russia*. CEPS working documents. Hg. v. Center for European Policy Studies. Available from http://www.ceps.eu/book/bilateral-disputes-between-eu-member-states-and-russia

Royal, T. (2016). The future of geopolitics and energy markets. *Geopolitical Monitor, 15*(05), 2016. Available from https://www.geopoliticalmonitor.com/the-future-of-geopolitics-and-energy-markets/

Sedigas. (2017). *Annual report*. Available from https://www.sedigas.es/pagina.php?p=11

Stent, A. (1990). *Russia and Germany reborn: Unification, the Soviet collapse and the new Europe*. Princeton: Princeton University Press.

Verbundnetz Gas. (2016). *VNG Group*. Available from http://www.vng.de/VNG-

Whist, B. S. (2008). *Nord stream: Not just a pipeline. An analysis of political debates in the Baltic Sea region regarding the planned gas pipeline from Russia to Germany*. FNI Report 15/2008, Fridjtof Nansens Institut.

Wirtualny Nowy Przemysl. (2018). *Niemcy nie odpuszczają w sprawie gazociągu Nord Stream 2*. Available from https://gazownictwo.wnp.pl/niemcy-nie-odpuszczaja-w-sprawie-gazociagu-nord-stream-2,319711_1_0_0.html

Yamal-Europe. (2016). *Gazprom export*. Available from http://www.gazpromexport.ru/en/projects/4/

Youngs, R. (2009). *Energy security. Europe's new foreign policy challenge*. (Routledge advances in European politics, p. 53). London, New York: Routledge.

The Functionality and Dysfunctionality of Global Trade Governance: The European Union Perspective

Anna Wróbel

1 Introduction

The World Trade Organization (WTO) is currently at a crossroads in the fulfilment of its fundamental functions due to the expanding crisis. It is up to the members of the organisation whether the current crisis will lead to the marginalisation of the organisation or whether it will be possible to gradually restore credibility and trust in the WTO as a mechanism for global trade governance. The challenges facing the WTO are not only about restoring the functionality of the organisation as a negotiating forum. The WTO's dysfunctionality is also manifested in relation to its other functions. In particular, the dispute settlement mechanism requires urgent action. In addition, the administration of multilateral trade rules, in particular the notification system for trade policy measures applied by members, also raises concerns.

The aim of the study is to analyse the actions taken by the European Union in order to counteract marginalisation of the organisation and restore effective operation of its basic functions. The study is divided into two parts. In the first part, the genesis of actions for WTO reform is indicated. In the second part, the EU proposals are discussed.

This chapter is part of the 'Global Economic Governance—Actors, Areas of Influence, Interactions' research project (OPUS, 2016/23/B/HS5/00118) funded by the National Science Centre, Poland.

A. Wróbel (✉)
University of Warsaw, Warsaw, Poland
e-mail: awrobel@uw.edu.pl

© Springer Nature Switzerland AG 2020
M. Rewizorski et al. (eds.), *The Future of Global Economic Governance*,
https://doi.org/10.1007/978-3-030-35336-0_11

2 Analytical Approach

The analytical approach of the study is based on a definition of a multilateral trading system based on Krasner's definition of an international regime, according to which it is defined as "sets of implicit or explicit principles, norms, rules, and decision-making procedures around which expectations converge in a given area of international relations" (Krasner 1983: 2). In this study, a multilateral trading system will therefore be treated as a kind of international regime, a set of implicit or explicit principles, norms, rules and decision-making procedures for international trade on which there is a converging expectation. Institutionally, the World Trade Organization is identified as a multilateral trading system. Due to the functions and the role of the WTO in the global economy, constituting one of the three pillars of the global economic order apart from the International Monetary Fund and the World Bank, this organisation may also be considered as the main element of global trade governance architecture (Wróbel 2016: 76). For this reason, the terms multilateral trading system, global trade governance and global trading system will be used as synonyms in this chapter.

In the chapter, the classification of functions of the multilateral trade system based on the classification formulated by Bernard M. Hoekman and Michael M. Kostecki is also used (2003: 25–36 and 51). The WTO has four main functions. First, it acts as a code of conduct for trade policy. Indeed, the WTO oversees a number of specific legal obligations governing the trade policies of its member states. Four annexes are attached to the WTO Agreement, including agreements setting out the principles that should guide WTO member states in their respective areas of international trade. Two further functions of the organisation, administrating the dispute settlement mechanism and providing multilateral surveillance of trade policies, contribute to the effective enforcement of these commitments. A multilateral dispute settlement mechanism has been established to ensure compliance with WTO rules. Any disputes arising in relation to WTO-administered trade agreements are subject to the Dispute Settlement Body (DSB), which sets up panels, oversees the implementation of panel recommendations, and authorises retaliatory measures if a member fails to comply with the panel's recommendations (Hoekman and Kostecki 2003: 74–78). The trade policies of WTO members are analysed not only in the context of trade disputes but also in the framework of the Trade Policy Review Mechanism (TPRM), which is designed to systematically examine the trade practices of member countries in order to improve their discipline in complying with WTO rules and to demonstrate the impact of these practices on the global trading system. The fourth function of the WTO, whose effective implementation is undoubtedly the greatest challenge for both the organisation itself and its members, is the forum for negotiations, which seeks to ensure progress on trade liberalisation through successive rounds of trade negotiations, where trade commitments of the participants in the system are exchanged (Wróbel 2016: 77–78).

The study focuses mainly on analysing the effectiveness of global trade governance in terms of two of the above functions: the negotiating forum and the trade dispute settlement mechanism and the WTO reform proposals put forward by the European Union in this respect. These proposals respond to the challenges for the multilateral trading system described in the first part of the chapter in the form of: the deadlock in Doha Development Round, the possibility of losing the effectiveness of the dispute settlement mechanism as a result of vacancies in the appellate body and the rise of preferential trade agreements.

3   Challenges to Global Trade Governance

3.1   Deadlock in Multilateral Trade Negotiations

The failure of the 11th WTO Ministerial Conference, which took place in Buenos Aires in December 2017, is proof of the deepening crisis in the organisation's negotiating function and certainly dispelled all hopes of concluding the Doha Round negotiations in the short term. After a period of increased dynamics in trade negotiations, related to Roberto Azevêdo becoming Director General of the WTO in September 2013 and the breaking of the impasse in trade negotiations during the two consecutive ministerial conferences held after the election, the progress of the organisation's work slowed down again. Compared to the ministerial conferences in Bali (3–7 December 2013) and Nairobi (15–19 December 2015), the meeting in Buenos Aires (10–13 December 2017) did not result in the adoption of a package of commitments.[1] Even in those areas which appeared to be the most promising in terms of their ability to achieve concrete negotiated results (e.g. public stockholding for food security in developing countries, fisheries subsidies and domestic support for services) before the conference, during the WTO discussions in Geneva, no significant results were achieved (Wróblewski and Stecz 2018: 418). The member states have not been able to reach a consensus on these issues. The meeting resulted in several relatively general ministerial decisions concerning the continuation of work and the launch of negotiation procedures for subsidies to fisheries (WTO 2017a), e-commerce (WTO 2017i), small economies (WTO 2017j), and TRIPS Non-Violation and Situation Complaints (WTO 2017h). In addition, some member states signed four declarations concerning the continuation of work in the area of domestic regulations on services (WTO 2017c), e-commerce (WTO 2017b), investment facilitation for development (WTO 2017d) and a support programme for micro-, small- and medium-sized enterprises (WTO 2017e, f). These contain only general support for conducting work in the areas indicated and are treated as a manifestation of political support for conducting talks. The commitment of many members to the multilateral trading system and its rules, as declared at the meeting, did not translate into concrete results. When summarising

---

[1]This was the first WTO Ministerial Conference to be held in South America. It was attended by some 4500 participants.

the proceedings of the XI Ministerial Conference, deep disappointment with this was expressed by the Director General Roberto Azevêdo (WTO 2017g).

It is difficult to identify one main reason for the dysfunctionality of the World Trade Organization as a forum for effective trade negotiations. The current crisis in the multilateral trading system has been caused by several factors, partly interlinked, such as the evolution of the multilateral trading system in terms of its subjective and material scope, the change in the balance of power in the global trading system, and the organisation of negotiations.

Initiated by the signing of the General Agreement on Tariffs and Trade (GATT) in 1947, the evolution of the multilateral trading system has involved three processes: a gradual increase in the number of members of the system, a change in its scope and an institutionalisation process culminating in the establishment of the WTO. The number of GATT/WTO participants has increased from 23 in 1947 to 164 today. As with other international organisations, the significant number of members and the way decisions are made does not facilitate agreement among members. An additional difficulty is the gradual expansion of the scope of the global trading system. The GATT Uruguay Round, in particular, was a breakthrough in this respect. It extended the scope of the multilateral trading system to three new areas: trade in services, trade aspects of intellectual property rights and trade aspects of investment (See Feketekuty 1998: 79–100; Hoekman 1993: 1528–1539). Even more ambitious is the Doha Declaration of the Ministerial Conference, which sets out the framework for the current round of negotiations. The multilateral negotiating agenda of the Doha Round included the following topics: (1) implementation of existing agreements; (2) agriculture; (3) Non-Agricultural Market Access (NAMA); (4) services; (5) protection of intellectual property (geographical indications, TRIPS, health rules); (6) Singapore themes (investment, competition policy, transparency in government procurement, trade facilitation); (7) WTO rules (relating to anti-dumping, subsidies, regional trade agreements, trade dispute settlement); (8) environmental protection; (9) internet trade; (10) small countries' problems; (11) technical cooperation; (12) least developed countries' problems; (13) special and different treatment of developing countries; (14) trade, debt and financial relations, and (15) the relationship between trade and technology flows.

The problem with the lack of efficiency in trade negotiations in the current round seems to be not only the consequence of the increase in the number of members and the extension of the scope of the GATT/WTO. A greater difficulty is the shift in the balance of power in the multilateral trading system due to the growing importance of developing countries in the global economy. It increases the capacity of this group of countries to influence the functioning of the multilateral trading system. Developing countries have consolidated their negotiating priorities more than in previous negotiation rounds, which, together with this greater economic strength of their economies, makes it difficult for developed economies to push through their vision of international trade liberalisation. The need to take greater account of the interests of developing countries in trade negotiations is a major structural change in global trade governance. Reaching an agreement between north and south at the WTO is also hindered by the specific situation in which the economic interests of the USA and the

European Union intersect with the political interests of Brazil, India and China. The last three countries are not only seeking favourable market access conditions, but are also seeking political prestige and international recognition as "economic powers" (Wróbel 2014: 102). Contrary to the initial period of formulating the rules of the multilateral trading system, today there is no sufficiently strong hegemon to impose on other countries a solution that would suit his interests. After the Second World War, the USA largely 'tailor-made' the rules of the trading system. It is now no longer in a position to impose on other WTO members solutions that meet US economic needs. In the face of the steadily growing strength of emerging markets and in a duet with the European Union, this seems impossible.

A major obstacle to the conclusion of the Doha Round negotiations is the very formula of the Doha Round, according to which "nothing is agreed until everything is agreed" (the single undertaking principle) (Wolfe 2009: 835–858). As a result of the single undertaking principle, although a convergence of views between the participants in the negotiations has been achieved on a number of important issues, a lack of agreement on one issue precludes the implementation of an agreement on the agreed issues. One of the most important areas of the Doha Round negotiations, which blocks the positive conclusion of negotiations and the entry into force of less controversial commitments, is the agricultural sector. It is also a sector that perfectly illustrates the north–south dispute that has already been mentioned (See Clapp 2006: 563–577; Martin and Anderson 2006: 1211–1218).

The WTO Ministerial Conference held in Bali on 3–7 December 2013 was supposed to be an attempt to break the crisis of the Doha Round negotiations and at the same time an impulse to increase the dynamics of the negotiations and thus facilitate their conclusion. The importance of this meeting for overcoming the crisis in WTO negotiations should first of all be kept in mind in the departure from the absolute observance of the single undertaking principle. During the preparations for the ninth Ministerial Conference, it was proposed to change the approach in negotiations to a more selective one. It was decided to focus on the most pragmatic and realistic negotiation issues selected from the broad agenda of the Doha mandate, on which there was a good chance of reaching a compromise, and thus the adoption of the so-called Bali Package (WTO 2013a, b, c, d, e, f, g, h, i, j). Such a solution should certainly be considered a success of the Bali Conference (Hajdukiewicz 2015: 41).

Efforts to break the deadlock in agricultural negotiations continued within the framework of the next WTO ministerial conference. The outcome of the tenth WTO Ministerial Conference, which took place in the capital of Kenya, Nairobi, on 15–19 December 2015, is the so-called Nairobi package, which includes six ministerial decisions on agriculture (WTO 2015b, e, f), cotton (2015a) and issues related to the special and different treatment of the least developed countries (WTO 2015c, d). Four of these relate to agricultural trade (WTO 2015a, b, e, f).

As mentioned earlier, the Buenos Aires Ministerial Conference also failed to contribute to the WTO's recovery from the crisis in trade negotiations. It reiterated the need for action to improve the efficiency of the WTO as a negotiating forum. It is currently difficult to assess whether the continued work in the areas covered by the decisions and declarations of the Buenos Aires Ministerial Conference, as announced, will produce concrete results by the next WTO Ministerial Conference, scheduled for 2020 (WTO 2018e).[2]

The lack of progress in the Doha Round negotiations is a barrier to adapting the multilateral rules of international trade to the new challenges currently facing the global economy. Since 1995, i.e. since the creation of the WTO, WTO members have not been able to update the Uruguay Round regulations due to the above-mentioned problems. In particular, the WTO is currently unable to cope with the increased role of state-owned enterprises, the challenges posed by the specificity of digital trade or forced technology transfers. To address some of these new trade issues following the deadlock in multilateral trade negotiations, members have turned to bilateral free trade agreements or larger regional or plurilateral agreements—such as the Comprehensive and Progressive Agreement for Trans-Pacific Partnership (CPTPP)[3] or the Regional Comprehensive Economic Partnership (RCEP).[4]

According to WTO data, as of 14 May 2019, the number of preferential trade agreements (PTAs) in force is 312, of which 240 are bilateral and 72 plurilateral. A particular intensification of activities of WTO members concerning the conclusion of PTAs has been observed since 2006. This results from the suspension of the Doha Round negotiations in June 2006. Despite a later return to multilateral negotiations, this trend continued, deepening the crisis of the WTO as a negotiating forum. Obtaining greater market access for the main trading partners under PTAs and easier opportunities for reaching compromises with fewer participants in the negotiations have reduced the interest of many WTO members in multilateral negotiations. It therefore seems that today PTAs are gradually becoming an alternative to multilateral trade negotiations, thus contributing to a change in the system of world trade governance and its progressive disintegration.

When considering the role of PTAs in the global trading system, it should be noted that they are not only an instrument to facilitate access to foreign markets, but can also be a tool to create new rules in international trade. Agreements of this type are more and more often referred to as "WTO plus" or "WTO extra" (See Marceau 2009: 124–128; Ya Qin 2003: 483–522). Such formulations indicate that, in addition to deepening the free trade commitments developed within the World Trade Organization, PTAs may also create new disciplines not yet included in agreements developed within this forum.

---

[2]On 26 July 2018, the General Council of the WTO decided that the XII WTO Ministerial Conference will be held in Astana in 2020. It will be the first ministerial meeting of the WTO in Central Asia.

[3]Parties to the agreement: Australia, Brunei Darussalam, Canada, Chile, Japan, Malaysia, Mexico, New Zealand, Peru, Singapore and Vietnam.

[4]RCEP negotiations were launched by ten ASEAN member states (Brunei Darussalam, Cambodia, Indonesia, Lao PDR, Malaysia, Myanmar, the Philippines, Singapore, Thailand and Vietnam) and six ASEAN FTA partners (Australia, People's Republic of China, India, Japan, the Republic of Korea, and New Zealand).

3.2   Implications of US Trade Policy for the Multilateral Trading System

The new challenge for the multilateral trading system today is the change in US trade policy following Donald Trump's appointment as President of the USA. Even during the election campaign, the WTO was criticised by the candidate for its ineffectiveness in relation to unfair trading practices. Not only was the achievement of multilateral trade liberalisation undermined, but also regional and bilateral agreements. One of the first decisions taken by Donald Trump after his inauguration was to withdraw the USA from the Trans-Pacific Partnership (TPP). The new administration then proceeded to implement further electoral promises. Under the slogan "Trade Deals Working for All Americans", the process of renegotiating the North American Free Trade Agreement (NAFTA) began. In line with the announcement "to use every tool at the federal government's disposal to end trade abuses" (The Economist 2017: 57), the use of protectionist policy instruments in relation to trading partners has been stepped up.[5] A particularly striking example of this policy is the introduction of tariffs on steel and aluminium in March 2018 for reasons of national security. In this case, in order to protect a specific sector of the economy, it was decided to use a justification, which should be used only in particularly exceptional situations. It is, therefore, no surprise that the US trading partners have reacted by retaliating in response. The concern about the introduction of duties on steel and aluminium is well reflected in the words of the Canadian WTO delegate who, at the General Council on 7 March 2018, said "the United States is taking the risk of opening a Pandora's box" (WTO: *Chiny na czele grupy. . .*). In this way, US policy creates the risk of trade wars.

The metaphor of "opening Pandora's box" may also refer to other actions taken by the USA in its current trade policy. In particular, it describes well the blocking by the USA of the nomination of members to the WTO Appellate Body (AB). If this practice continues, the Appellate Body will not have enough members to consider cases. In December 2019, when the terms of two more members expire, the WTO dispute settlement system will cease to function effectively. The Appellate Body will not be able to make decisions due to the lack of a sufficient number of eligible members. Thus, the organisation will be deprived of an effective dispute settlement mechanism. As a result, the possibilities for monitoring the commitments made so far will be limited.

Concerns about US trade policy are expressed by many WTO members, not just those already affected by more protectionist measures. During the review of US trade policy at the end of 2018 (17 and 19 December 2018), virtually all delegations that took the floor, underlining the significant contribution of the USA to the establishment of the multilateral trading system, starting with the signing of the

---

[5]US trade policy is currently based on four pillars: (1) Defending national sovereignty over trade policy; (2) Restrictive strengthening of US trade legislation; (3) Using all means to open foreign markets; and (4) Negotiating new and better trade agreements.

General Agreement on Tariffs and Trade in 1947 through successive trade negotiation rounds, expressed deep concern at the current US trade policy and position
within the organisation. In particular, attention was drawn to the increased use of
anti-dumping and countervailing measures compared to the previous period under
review, the threat of new safeguard measures for security reasons and the blocking
by the USA of the election of Appellate Body judges (AB) and the lack of interest of
other members in the WTO's reform efforts. The natural reaction of WTO members
to the economic nationalism of the USA was to use the instruments created by the
world trade system, i.e. the dispute settlement mechanism and the trade policy
review mechanism. Already on 7 March 2018, during the meeting of the General
Council of the WTO, China together with a group of 18 other countries opposed to
the US tariffs on steel and aluminium called on President Donald Trump to abandon
this project. Subsequently, at a meeting of the Dispute Settlement Body (DSB) on
18 December 2018, China requested the establishment of a panel to rule on US
tariffs on imports of Chinese goods under Section 301 of the 1974 Trade Act (WTO
2018h). Following a confirmatory Chinese request, the Dispute Settlement Body
established a panel on 28 January 2019 on this issue (WTO 2019).

4 Revitalising Global Trade Governance: The European Union Perspective

In the context of the deepening crisis in the multilateral trading system, some WTO
members have taken initiatives to restore its effectiveness not only in the area of
trade negotiations, but also with regard to monitoring and dispute settlement mechanisms. In September 2018, the European Commission published a concept paper
that contained ideas for developing concrete proposals for reforming the World
Trade Organization. This document follows the decision of the European Council
of 28–29 June 2018 which gave the Commission a mandate to continue its efforts to
modernise the WTO in order to make it more relevant, effective and responsive to
the challenges of today's world economy (Rada Europejska 2018). The concept
presented on 20 September 2018 in Geneva during the meeting on WTO reform
convened by Canada covers three main areas: (1) rule-making, (2) regular work and
transparency, and (3) dispute settlement (European Commission 2018).

The modernisation of the WTO's regulatory framework was seen as a central
element of the reform of the organisation. Reform in this area should firstly update
WTO rules and integrate key issues for world trade into the multilateral trade regime
as it develops. Secondly, the WTO rule-making process itself and the model/
organisation of the negotiation process should be modernised, creating the conditions for such an update of the rules. In practice, this means that some of the WTO
members interested in finding solutions to individual issues can take action on their
own. Such agreements, covering some or all of the WTO members negotiated under
the auspices of the WTO, would be an integral part of the multilateral trading system.

Future WTO legislative action should aim to restore balance and a level playing field through rules concerning the use of subsidies in industry and the activities of state-owned enterprises (European Commission 2018). The organisation's attention should also focus on e-commerce regulation. The WTO should also be more closely involved in achieving Sustainable Development Goals (SDGs) and developing a more flexible approach to the application of the rules adopted by members according to their level of economic development (new rules for the application of special and differential treatment in future agreements).

Enhancing the efficiency of the trade negotiation process through procedural measures is also an important objective of WTO reform. The EU has indicated in its proposal the need for more flexibility in this regard. In line with the promoted concept of flexible multilateralism, WTO members interested in resolving a specific issue that is not yet ready for full multilateral consensus should be able to regulate it through plurilateral negotiations. The benefits of this solution would be available to all other members under the applicable Most Favoured Nation (MFN) clause. At the same time, the EU stresses the need for continued efforts to strengthen the WTO's multilateral negotiating, involving all WTO members, by building the political commitment of WTO members, strengthening the role of the WTO Secretariat in trade negotiations and the implementation and monitoring of the commitments entered into. The issue of more frequent ministerial conferences and more intensive processes at the level of senior officials is also being considered (European Commission 2018).

In addition to restoring the functionality of the WTO trade negotiations, the EU's proposals relate to the regular work of the main bodies and committees of the organisation. Long-term modernisation objectives in this area include: ensuring transparency of the trade policy measures of members; improving the notification system; resolving specific trade issues before referral to the Dispute Settlement Body; and gradually adapting to current WTO legal challenges.

In view of the real threat of a loss of functionality of the dispute settlement mechanism related to the activities of the USA, the EU proposals broadly refer to this area of activity of the organisation. If the USA continues to block the nominations of judges to the Appellate Body, the WTO dispute settlement system will cease to work by December 2019 at the latest. With these next vacancies, there will be less than three members of the Appellate Body, the minimum number required to consider an appeal. In this situation, a party to a dispute may try to block the adoption of panel rulings by appealing against them. When considering the reasons for US policy in this area, one should pay attention to the previously mentioned, controversial unilateral actions by the USA to introduce more restrictive trade policy tools for reasons of national security. It, therefore, appears that the USA is taking a pragmatic approach in an attempt to block possible future negative trade dispute settlements related to its current trade policy.

In order to implement the WTO modernisation agenda, the EU has started cooperation with other member countries of the organisation, including, inter alia, the USA and Japan (in the framework of trialogues); China (in the framework of the special working group set up at the last EU–China summit); and other partners (including the G20 summits). This has led to concrete proposals for the WTO. At the Council for Trade in Goods (12–13 November 2018), the EU, together with Argentina, Costa Rica, Japan, the USA and Taiwan, tabled a proposal for Procedures to Enhance Transparency and Strengthen Notification Requirements under WTO Agreements (WTO 2018f, g). This document is based on proposals first presented by the USA at the 11th Ministerial Conference in December 2017.

The European Union submitted further proposals for WTO reform to the General Council on 12 December 2018 in the form of two communications on the Dispute Settlement Body. The first one was tabled with China, Canada, India, Norway, New Zealand, Switzerland, Australia, Korea, Iceland, Singapore, Mexico, Costa Rica, Montenegro and New Zealand (WTO 2018a, b). The second contains proposals formulated by the EU, China, India and Montenegro (WTO 2018c, d). The purpose of the proposed amendments is to strengthen the effectiveness, independence and impartiality of the Appellate Body, inter alia, as a result of the adoption of new regulations concerning outgoing AB members, which clearly specify when they may continue to perform their functions until the end of the ongoing appeal proceedings, the establishment of one longer term of office for Appellate Body members (from 6 to 8 years), increasing the number of its members from seven to nine, involved full time, launching the automatic selection procedure when the position is vacant. The proposals also relate to the duration of the appeal proceedings,[6] the scope of interpretation of the rules under consideration[7] and the introduction of annual meetings of WTO members and the Appellate Body.

In addition to the European Union, other WTO members are also taking steps to reform the organisation. Canada is particularly active in this area. Not only did Canada present its proposal for WTO modernisation on 21 September 2018, but it also initiated a process of plurilateral cooperation in this area in the form of the Ottawa Group on WTO Reform (Ottawa Group on WTO Reform).[8] The beginning of this cooperation was a ministerial meeting with representatives of 13 members of the organisation, which took place in Ottawa on 24–25 October 2018. It resulted in a joint declaration expressing support for a rule-based multilateral trading system and underlining the essential role that the WTO plays in facilitating and protecting trade. At the same time, it expressed deep concern about the observed trends in international trade, notably the increase in protectionism, which has a negative impact on the WTO and threatens the multilateral trading system as a whole (Ottawa Group 2018). The European Union participates in the work of the Ottawa Group.

---

[6]The appeal proceedings should be concluded within 90 days unless the parties agree otherwise.

[7]The legal issues at stake do not include the interpretation of national legislation.

[8]The Ottawa Group is composed of Australia, Brazil, Canada, Chile, the European Union, Japan, Kenya, Korea, Mexico, New Zealand, Norway, Singapore and Switzerland. The group is chaired by Jim Carr, Canadian Minister for International Trade Diversification.

5 Conclusions

Currently, the World Trade Organization is facing a number of old and new challenges. These include increasing protectionism and the threat of trade wars associated with this policy. WTO members are not only concerned about the more restrictive trade policy measures introduced by one of the strongest economies in the world, but also about the actions of the USA aimed at weakening the effectiveness of the WTO dispute settlement system, which, alongside the trade policy review mechanism, is the basis for monitoring the adopted world trade rules. In the absence of significant progress in trade negotiations, the blocking of the dispute settlement system leads to the marginalisation of the World Trade Organization. The WTO will then lose its functionality in two of its most important areas of activity.

It is, therefore, to be welcomed that some members of the organisation, including the European Union, started in 2018 to work towards the modernisation of the multilateral trade system in order to boost negotiations, ensure the effectiveness of the dispute settlement mechanism and ensure transparency and monitoring of the trade policies of members of the organisation. Actions should also be taken in the WTO framework to alleviate existing tensions between members, in addition to bilateral discussions that are taking place in connection with the introduction of, or plans to introduce, more unilateral restrictive market protection measures. Recent efforts to reform the special and differential treatment regime may also be an important element in alleviating tensions in bilateral trade relations between members. It seems that many things are right in the statements by Dennis Shea, the United States' WTO Ambassador, who has repeatedly raised doubts about the use of this instrument by China, the world's largest exporter of goods. As part of the modernisation of the multilateral trading system, it is therefore necessary to address the definition of the distinction between developing and developed countries and the scope and differentiation of preferences within the SDT[9] system, making it more flexible.

The plurilateral negotiations initiated at the last ministerial conference in Buenos Aires and the decision of Davos to start negotiations on e-commerce are good symptoms of countries' efforts to maintain the efficiency of global trade governance. A test of WTO members' commitment to intensifying trade negotiations will be meeting the 2019 deadline for developing rules on subsidies in fisheries. The intensification of WTO work in 2019 will also be related to the 12th Ministerial Conference planned for June 2020, which, for the first time, will take place in Central Asia. In addition, efforts to reform the WTO are to be assessed at the next G20 summit in June 2019 in Osaka. It is to be hoped that these meetings will be an opportunity to update the existing rules of international trade in order to respond to the needs of a world economy. The experience of the Doha Round so far has shown that this process is impossible on the basis of the single undertaking principle. We should, therefore, expect further work and proposals from WTO members to develop

---

[9]SDT—special and differential treatment.

an alternative approach to cooperation and regulation within the organisation in such a way that takes into account the increasingly diverse needs of members, resulting, inter alia, from differences in the level of economic development. This may result in the development of solutions enabling differentiated participation in negotiations depending on the ability of members to accept new or deeper liberalisation commitments.

It seems that, in the present conditions, rapid changes to the rules of the WTO's functioning and, even more so, the adoption of new rules for international trade are not possible. Despite clear evidence that trade is a factor in economic growth and development, rules and institutions aimed at reducing restrictions on international trade are increasingly fragile, as evidenced by the deepening crisis in the WTO. Among the reasons for this are structural changes in the global economy which, combined with technological change, have given rise to growing concerns that the benefits of trade are not shared fairly and that the existing rules do not reflect a balance of rights and obligations for WTO members. Increasing differences between WTO members constitute, and will continue to constitute, a significant obstacle to further multilateral trade liberalisation. The growing economic nationalism of the current hegemony and international trade rule maker is an extremely serious problem, even a threat to the future of the WTO. The increasing protectionism of the USA, resulting in counter-replies from the economies affected by such policies, poses a serious challenge to global trade governance. Blocking the WTO dispute settlement system will deprive other countries of an important tool to influence US trade policy. It, therefore, seems that the unwillingness of the USA to fill vacancies in the Appellate Body is a deliberate action of this superpower in connection with its current trade policy.

Paradoxically, when assessing the current crisis of the Appellate Body and other US measures in trade policy, one can find some potentially positive sides to this situation. The blocking by the USA of the election of AB members forced other members of the organisation to reflect more deeply on the functioning of the dispute settlement system and the possibilities of improving its effectiveness and eliminating the defects identified so far. If agreement can be reached among the members of the organisation to introduce at least some of the changes proposed by the EU and Canada, it may improve the functioning of the dispute settlement system in the future. However, a condition for this is a change in the approach of the USA. If the USA's position leads to the loss of the Appellate Body, the system will lose its credibility, which will be very difficult, if not impossible, to rebuild.

In addition to the reform proposals put forward, while searching for the positive aspects of the current WTO crisis related to undermining the rules created by the current hegemony, it is worth emphasising that this forced the actions of other members interested in maintaining a functioning multilateral trading system. Examples are the actions of the European Union described in this chapter which, by linking the benefits of trade with the issue of a functioning multilateral trading system, seek to prevent the marginalisation of the WTO.

While rethinking the priorities for the WTO in the near future, it is, therefore, essential to emphasise the need for urgent action to restore the dispute settlement function and improve the monitoring function in order to restore confidence in rules-based trade and to give impetus to new and further negotiations. Subsequently, work should focus on developing more effective functioning of the bodies of the organisation and the dispute settlement system as well as pluri- and multilateral activities to develop new international trade rules in line with the changing structure of the world economy. In order to be successful, WTO reform will have to cover all its functions. However, as WTO decisions are based on consensus, the chances of a thorough revision seem limited. Therefore, WTO reform should cover broader institutional issues and members should re-examine some of the organisation's rules, including the decision-making system. The other way is to restore confidence in and act on the substance of multilateralism. The ability to compromise is an essential condition for the effectiveness of the multilateral trading system.

References

Clapp, J. (2006). WTO agriculture negotiations: Implications for the global south. *Third World Quarterly, 27*(4), 563–577.

European Commission (2018) *Concept paper, WTO modernization, introduction to future EU proposals*. Retrieved January 10, 2019, from http://trade.ec.europa.eu/doclib/docs/2018/septem ber/tradoc_157331.pdf

Feketekuty, G. (1998). Trade in services – Bringing services into the multilateral trading system. In J. Bhagwati & M. Hirsch (Eds.), *The Uruguay round and beyond* (pp. 79–100). Essays in Honour of Artur Dunkel: Heidelberg: Springer.

Hajdukiewicz, A. (2015). Znaczenie "Pakietu z Bali" dla procesu liberalizacji handlu w ramach Rundy Doha WTO. In S. Wydymus & M. Maciejewski (Eds.), *Liberalizacja i protekcjonizm we współczesnym handlu międzynarodowym* (pp. 41–56). Warszawa: CeDeWu.

Hoekman, B. M. (1993). New issues in the Uruguay round and beyond. *The Economic Journal, 103*(421), 1528–1539.

Hoekman, B. M., & Kostecki, M. M. (2003). *The political economy of the world trading system. The WTO and beyond*. New York: Oxford University Press.

Krasner, S. D. (1983). Structural causes and regime consequences: Regimes as intervening variables. In S. D. Krasner (Ed.), *International regimes* (pp. 1–21). Ithaca, New York: Cornell University Press.

Marceau, G. (2009). News from Geneva on RTAs and WTO-plus, WTO-more, and WTO-minus. *Proceedings of the Annual Meeting (American Society of International Law), 103*, 124–128.

Martin, W., & Anderson, K. (2006). The Doha agenda negotiations on agriculture: What could they deliver? *American Journal of Agricultural Economics, 88*(5), 1211–1218.

Ottawa Group. (2018, 25 October). *Joint Communiqué of the Ottawa ministerial on WTO reform*. Ottawa. Retrieved January 10, 2019, from https://www.canada.ca/en/global-affairs/news/2018/10/joint-communique-of-the-ottawa-ministerial-on-wto-reform.html

Rada Europejska. (2018). *Posiedzenie Rady Europejskiej (28 czerwca 2018 r.) – Konkluzje*. Retrieved January 10, 2019, from https://www.consilium.europa.eu/media/35952/28-euco-final-conclusions-pl.pdf

The Economist. (2017). Sino-American trade. *Rules of engagement*. Retrieved January 30, 2019, from https://www.economist.com/finance-and-economics/2017/01/28/america-china-and-the-risk-of-a-trade-war

Wolfe, R. (2009). The WTO single undertaking as negotiating technique and constitutive metaphor. *Journal of International Economic Law, 12*(4), 835–858.

Wróbel, A. (2014). Funkcjonalność i dysfunkcjonalność wielostronnego systemu handlowego WTO. *Zeszyty Naukowe Uniwersytetu Szczecińskiego. Współczesne Problemy Ekonomiczne. Globalizacja. Liberalizacja. Etyka, 8*, 97–107.

Wróbel, A. (2016). Ewolucja system zarządzania handlem światowym. In M. Rewizorski (Ed.), *Globalne zarządzanie i jego aktorzy. W poszukiwaniu rozwiązań dla zmieniającego się świata* (pp. 76–96). Warszawa: Dom Wydawniczy Elipsa.

Wróblewski, M., & Stecz, K. (2018). Wyniki XI Konferencji Ministerialnej WTO – aktualne problemy, tendencje i wyzwania dla multilateralnego systemu handlu. *Prace Naukowe Uniwersytetu Ekonomicznego we Wrocławiu, 523*, 400–415.

WTO. (2013a). *Cotton, ministerial decision.* WT/MIN(13)/41.

WTO. (2013b). *Duty-free and quota-free market access for least developed countries, Ministerial Decision* WT/MIN(13)/44.

WTO. (2013c). *Export competition, ministerial declaration.* WT/MIN(13)/40.

WTO. (2013d). *General services, ministerial decision.* WT/MIN(13)/37.

WTO. (2013e). *Monitoring mechanism on special and differential treatment, ministerial decision.* WT/MIN(13)/45.

WTO. (2013f). *Operationalization of the waiver concerning preferential treatment to services and service suppliers of least developed countries, ministerial decision.* WT/MIN(13)/43.

WTO. (2013g). *Preferential rules of origin for least developed countries, ministerial decision.* WT/MIN(13)/42.

WTO. (2013h). *Public Stockholding for Food Security Purposes, Ministerial Decision* WT/MIN (13)/38.

WTO. (2013i). *Trade facilitation agreement.* WT/MIN(13)/36.

WTO. (2013j). *Understanding on tariff rate quota administration provisions of agricultural products, as defined in article 2 of the agreement on agriculture, ministerial decision.* WT/MIN(13)/39.

WTO. (2015a). *Cotton.* WT/MIN(15)/46 — WT/L/981.

WTO. (2015b). *Export competition.* WT/MIN(15)/45 — WT/L/980.

WTO. (2015c). *Implementation of preferential treatment in favour of services and service suppliers of least developed countries and increasing LDC participation in services trade.* WT/MIN(15)/ 48 — WT/L/982.

WTO. (2015d). *Preferential rules of origin for least developed countries.* WT/MIN(15)/47 — WT/L/917/Add.1.

WTO. (2015e). *Public stockholding for food security purposes.* WT/MIN(15)/44 — WT/L/979.

WTO. (2015f). *Special safeguard mechanism for developing country members.* WT/MIN(15)/43 — WT/L/978.

WTO. (2017a). *Fisheries subsidies, ministerial decision of 13 December 2017.* WT/MIN(17)/64, WT/L/1031.

WTO. (2017b). *Ministerial conference – eleventh session – Buenos Aires – 10 – 13 December 2017 – joint statement on electronic commerce.* WT/MIN(17)/60.

WTO. (2017c). *Ministerial conference – eleventh session – Buenos Aires, 10–13 December 2017 – joint ministerial statement on services domestic regulation* WT/MIN(17)/61.

WTO. (2017d). *Ministerial conference – eleventh session – Buenos Aires, 10–13 December 2017 – joint ministerial statement on investment facilitation for development.* WT/MIN(17)/59.

WTO. (2017e). *Ministerial conference – eleventh session - Buenos Aires, 10–13 December 2017 – joint ministerial statement – declaration on the establishment of a WTO informal Work Programme for MSMES.* WT/MIN(17)/58.

WTO. (2017f). *Ministerial conference – eleventh session – Buenos Aires, 10–13 December 2017 – joint ministerial statement – declaration on the establishment of a WTO informal Work Programme for MSMES – Revision.* WT/MIN(17)/58 Rev 1.

WTO. (2017g). *Ministerial conference - eleventh session - Buenos Aires, 10–13 December 2017 – Address by Mr Roberto Azevêdo – WTO Director-General – MC11 closing session – 13 December 2017.* WT/MIN(17)/74.

WTO. (2017h). *TRIPS non-violation and situation complaints, ministerial decision of 13 December 2017*. WT/MIN(17)/66, WT/L/1033.

WTO. (2017i). *Work programme on electronic commerce, ministerial decision of 13 December 2017*. WT/MIN(17)/65, WT/L/1032.

WTO. (2017j). *Work programme on small economies, ministerial decision of 13 December 2017*. WT/MIN(17)/6, WT/L/1030.

WTO. (2018a, 10, 12–13 December). *Communication from the European Union, China, Canada, India, Norway, New Zeland, Switzerland, Australia, Republic of Korea, Iceland, Singapore, Mexico and Costa Rica to the General Council, Revision, General Council*. WT/GC/W/752/Rev.1.

WTO. (2018b, 12–13 December). *Communication from the European Union, China, Canada, India, Norway, New Zeland, Switzerland, Australia, Republic of Korea, Iceland, Singapore, Mexico, Costa Rica and Montenegro to the General Council, Revision, General Council*. WT/GC/W/752/Rev.2.

WTO. (2018c, 12–13 December). *Communication from the European Union, China, India and Montenegro to the General Council, Revision, General Council*. WT/GC/W/753/Rev.1.

WTO. (2018d, 12–13 December) *Communication from the European Union, China, India to the General Council, General Council*. WT/GC/W/753.

WTO. (2018e, 26 July). *Minutes of the meeting, general council*. WT/GC/M/173.

WTO. (2018f, 1 November). *Procedures to enhance transparency and strengthen notification requirements under WTO agreements communication from Argentina, Costa Rica, the European Union, Japan, and the Unites States, General Council, Council for trade in goods*. JOB/GC/204, JOB/CTG/14.

WTO. (2018g, 8 November). *Procedures to enhance transparency and strengthen notification requirements under WTO agreements communication from Argentina, Costa Rica, the European Union, Japan, and the Unites States, General Council, Council for trade in goods*. JOB/GC/204/Add.1, JOB/CTG/14/Add.1.

WTO. (2018h, 7 December). *United states – tariff measures on certain goods from China, request for the establishment of a panel by China*. WT/DS543/7.

WTO. (2019). *DS543: United States — tariff measures on certain goods from China*. Retrieved January 30, 2019, from https://www.wto.org/english/tratop_e/dispu_e/cases_e/ds543_e.htm

WTO. (n.d.). *Chiny na czele grupy państw przeciwnych cłom w USA na stal i aluminium*. Retrieved January 10, 2019, from https://www.pb.pl/wto-chiny-na-czele-grupy-panstw-przeciwnych-clom-w-usa-na-stal-i-aluminium-907393

Ya Qin, J. (2003). 'Wto-plus' obligations and their implications for the world trade organization legal system – an appraisal of the China accession protocol. *Journal of World Trade, 37*(3), 483–522.

Printed in Great Britain
by Amazon

34613001R00110